joy
in the
mountains

by LOU AND ALICE WINOKUR

A remarkable guidebook on Where to Go and What to Do
in the Southern Appalachian Mountains
including The Blue Ridge Parkway and surrounding area.

With an Introduction by Dr. Cratis D. Williams,
Special Assistant to the Chancellor,
Appalachian State University, Boone, North Carolina.

Published by Lou and Alice Winokur
P.O. Box 2532, Boca Raton, Florida 33432

To our Dear Friend, ELEANOR GREEK,
without whose inspiring, encouraging, and loving support
this book would not have been written.

Contents

Mountain folklorist, folk performer, and recognized leading authority on Appalachian heritage, culture, literature, music, folkways, and speech.

Cratis Williams

introduction

Alice and Lou Winokur have put together in their *Guidebook: Joy in the Mountains* all of the best that is available to the tourist and the vacationer in the Appalachian wonderland sloping away from Mt. Mitchell into western North Carolina, eastern Tennessee, and southwestern Virginia.

An unspoiled land of forests, parks, small farms, tumbling streams, bright skies, and breath-taking panoramas of mountain ranges flowing away into blue distances, Southern Appalachia is the top of the land east of the Mississippi, the jeweled crown of the South.

It is the birthplace of rivers. From their bold headsprings at its crest bound lovely streams that tumble through gorges toward the east, the west, the north, the south, streams of living water that teem with aquatic life.

Winding their way through gaps, between majestic cliffs, down draws, and along the streams are ancient trails beaten by buffalo a thousand years ago, followed by Indian hunters before the white man arrived, blazed by the pioneer before the land was available for settlement.

6

Here and there are remnants of the primeval forest, and on every hand stretches of evergreen and hardwoods weave lush summers of cool green and flaunt autumnal holidays of vivid color preeminent in glory.

In early winter the snows come, blown in through wind gaps that mark the beds of rivers that were already old before man appeared on earth. High winds that scream among the groaning forests and howl along the eaves of the houses, temperatures that one moving northward could not feel again before reaching central Ontario, snows that blanket the landscape, tumble along the ridges, and roll in shifting drifts down the valleys and along the highways make a paradise for skiers from December to March.

Here in this magnificent land live the sturdy and hardy mountain folk whose ancestors braved wilds 200 years ago to establish themselves in the State of Franklin, the first independent "nation" of English-speaking folk organized west of the Atlantic Ocean. Much of the speech, manners, independence, pride, and hospitality of the ancestors remains, and they passed down to their children of today their skills in handcrafts, folk traditions, songs, dances, and social customs. These traditions, evident on every hand, are celebrated throughout the region in festivals, fairs, exhibits, and shows.

A land traversed by modern highways and threaded by excellent secondary roads that lead the visitor to many a hidden retreat, quaint village, ancient homestead, secluded summer place, or natural wonder far in psychological miles from the "madding crowd's ignoble strife," Southern Appalachia beckons to nearly one hundred million Americans who are within two days by automobile. Those who wish to experience the best of what appeals to them most will find in the Winokurs' *Guidebook: Joy in the Mountains* the help they need in planning their vacation to this tri-state mountain corner of North Carolina, Virginia and Tennessee.

Cratis Williams
Appalachian State University
Boone, North Carolina

Alice and Lou

preface

Lou and Alice enjoy the unlimited advantages of living in a university town during the school year and look forward to vacationing close to a college for the many activities open to the public. And that's why they decided one summer to locate near Appalachian State University in Boone, N.C.

Traveling on and off the beaten path throughout the United States, Europe, Canada, the Caribbean, and South America, they found that there aren't many places where man and nature have combined more effectively in providing the tourist with so many diversified attractions than within a two-hour drive of the Boone-Blowing Rock area. And therein hangs this tale.

At their holiday hide-a-way, they harmonized readily with their mountain sanctuary surroundings and proceeded to explore the sights and savor the beauty. After gathering information from innumerable sources, chatting with mountain folk, driving thousands of miles down country roads and around the mountains and valleys — they found themselves laden with exciting details for a fabulous venture! They are eager to share their research, their explorations, their discoveries, their joy, and exuberant enthusiasm. What better way than to publish a unique guidebook saving the traveler valuable time, countless footsteps, and needless frustration, as well as painting a "roadmap" in bold colors of their love affair with the tri-state mountain corner of North Carolina, Tennessee and Virginia.

The book acquaints the tourist from Timbuktu or a new resident of the area with the vast number of opportunities to relax, engage in sports or be a spectator, enjoy the unusual fairs and festivals, become aware of the rich heritage of historic homes and sites, and get to know the exceptional qualities of the Appalachian mountain people and their original handcrafts.

All of this and more are within the 55 chapters which list more than 1500 events, attractions, and activities ranging from "A" (Aerodynamics — hang gliding) to "Z" (Zircon — rockhounding), by far the most comprehensive directory ever published for this region of the Southern Appalachians.

Even the armchair adventurer can enjoy the vitality and free spirit expressed in *Joy in the Mountains.*

And now a word of advice for the trip planner: you are strongly urged to check with the sponsoring organization, local Chamber of Commerce, or the local newspaper to confirm date, time, and place of a happening since the authors are not responsible for changes. Events, dates, and information listed are the latest available at the time of publication. Annual Events are arranged by date in order of their occurrence.

In a compilation of this nature it is not possible to include an exhaustive listing of where to go and what to do. This guidebook, however, does present a very wide selection of mountain events and travel information. Those groups whose **annual** affairs were not included are invited to submit detailed information for possible consideration in subsequent editions.

The writers express grateful appreciation to:

— Staff members of local Chambers of Commerce and others who helped make this travel guide a reality;

— Jerry Reece, former Executive Director of the Boone Area Chamber of Commerce for his courteous cooperation in checking the Boone area activities and for his valuable suggestions;

— Appalachian State University administrative staff: Herbert W. Wey, Chancellor; Cratis D. Williams, Special Assistant to the Chancellor; James W. Jackson, Dean, College of Continuing Education; Alvis L. Corum, Dean of Learning Resources; Gerald M. Bolick, Director, Division of Community Services; and Leland L. Nicholls, Assistant Dean, Arts and Sciences, for their commendatory encouragement and beneficial ideas;

— Hugh Morton of Grandfather Mountain, noted photographer, for his eloquent photos of scenic wonders;

— Danielle Withrow, Director, Blue Ridge Creative Arts Council, for reviewing the cultural events listed for Ashe, Avery, and Watauga Counties;

— Valborg Crossland and Lorraine Sinkler, longtime friends, for enthusiastically encouraging the authors when they most needed it;

— And last, but by no means least, their sons and daughters-in-law, Marshall and Janice, Eliot and Irene, for wholeheartedly supporting this literary travel venture.

Lou and Alice Winokur, P.O. Box 2532, Boca Raton, Florida 33432

1 why the tri-state mountain corner of n.c.-tenn.-va.

If you'd like to take a vacation where you'll fall in love with this world and experience a variety of joyous, enriching pleasures....

If you'd like to get in touch with yourself, to recharge, look down on clouds and relax away from the hum-drum, everyday routine, watching Mother Nature unfold a brilliant extravaganza in color, no matter what the season....

If you'd like to drive leisurely over one of the world's unsurpassed scenic attractions, the billboard-free Blue Ridge Parkway of the Southern Appalachians where maximum speed is 45 miles per hour, feasting your eyes on carpets of wildflowers and waves of mountain ranges lying along the horizon like crinkled sheets....

If you'd like to be in the heart of some of our country's greatest natural treasures, the state and national parks and forests, of which you, as a taxpayer are a part owner, where you may backpack, hike, camp, swim, boat, and fish in over a thousand miles of stocked streams, rivers and lakes, enjoy ranger-

Hugh Morton

guided hikes, nature talks and movies as well as many other exciting programs (educating the kids while they think they're just having fun)....

If you'd like to golf on a department-store variety of some of the most challenging championship golf courses in the country, up among the clouds, flanked by mountain laurel, rhododendron and dense green woods, breathing clean, invigorating air (whether you're a duffer or seasoned pro)....

If you'd like to play all the tennis your heart desires, no matter what the weather (with pros if you prefer) at a wide choice of superb tennis court locations....

If you'd like to swim indoors in Olympic-size pools during cold weather, and outdoors at beautiful lakes in summer, or sail, waterski, canoe, ride the rapids, or motorboat....

If conservation hunting in champion timberlands for deer, grouse, 'coon, rabbit, squirrel, quail, bear and turkey, on millions of acres of Game Lands managed for the betterment of wildlife population, is your bag....

If you'd like to ski day or night to improve your style, or to learn how the easy way under expert guidance, on miles of varying slopes and trails, under the best skiing conditions south of New York State, at attractive ski-package rates including ski equipment and relaxing apres-ski entertainment....

If you're a roller skater, ice skater, figure skater, or just would like to learn how to skate, indoors or out-of-doors, winter or summer, in some of the finest facilities of the Southeast....

If you're taking a vacation with the kids and you'd like to have it pan out by "striking it rich" rockhounding in the internationally famous 225-square-mile Spruce Pine Mineral Kingdom for aquamarines, emeralds, garnets, and rubies in active mines, and participate in the Annual Spruce Pine Mineral and Gem Festival....

If you'd like the kids to visit the three-acre black bear environmental habitat atop 6,000-foot Grandfather Mountain, and, in addition, thrill to the hang-glider exhibitions, or be there for the annual two-day colorful gathering of the Scottish Clans and watch the pageantry of the Highland Games, hear the bagpipe bands while the kilts of the Scottish Dancers whirl....

If you'd like the kids to ride the 100-year-old narrow-guage steam locomotive, *Tweetsie*, and "live" through a Western movie with surprise attack by outlaws and then visit the nearby Country Fair for the kiddie rides on a ferris wheel, roller coaster and helicopter....

If you'd like to give the kids the time of their lives at the Land of Oz, reached by skylift gondola, at the top of Beech Mountain in Banner Elk, meeting Dorothy, shaking the Cowardly Lion's tail and following the Yellow Brick Trail....

If you're a rock, country music, gospel singin', folk singin', guitar pickin',

Blue Grass, bagpipe, jazz, fiddlers' convention, symphonic or chamber music follower, or folk dancin', square dancin', mountain cloggin', enthusiast....

If you'd like to picnic at the 600-acre rhododendron gardens on the heights of the incredible 6,285-foot Roan Mountain during the June Festival when clouds of deep purple, crimson and lavender Rhododendron Catawbiense are at their peak with giant, single flowers the size of a child's head....

If you'd enjoy antique, tobacco and livestock auctions, flea markets, numerous church, club, yard and garage sales where the unusual and rare antique is still available, or enjoy the mountain artisan or craftsman demonstrations and sale of weaving, pottery, candle-making, toy-making, and woodworking, or enjoy going to a good, ol' fashioned Country Fair....

If you're a history buff on historical sites, museums, dramas like *Horn in the West* with a professional cast of 75 depicting Dan'l Boone and other pioneers courageously opening up the West in their search for freedom....

If you'd like to take advantage of learning while vacationing, like taking a course just for fun from culinary cooking to automotive repairs, afternoon or evening in any one of seven colleges and eight technical institutes, and attending exciting sports events at nominal prices or for free at Appalachian State University in Boone or Eastern Tennessee State University at Johnson City, as well as cultural events such as guest artists and lecturers, plays and concerts....

Then here's where it's all together! Here, in the Southern Appalachians — where the warm, wonderful, resourceful mountain people are keeping alive the heritage of fiddlin', corn shuckin', housewarmin', churchgoin', quiltin', singin', dancin', wildcraftin', handicraftin', paintin', woodcarvin', picklin', preservin', jam-and-jelly makin', gatherin' the delicious, wild sourwood and locust honey, apple-cider pressin', and jes' plain friendly settin' on the porch a spell — is where you'll find plenty of breathing room, plenty of golden silence, plenty of activity for the energetic!

So, for starters, just settle down for a while in the Greater Boone-Blowing Rock region, in this tri-state mountain corner of western North Carolina, northeastern Tennessee, and southwestern Virginia, an area of natural wonders not duplicated by any other region in the world. You'll want to come back again and again!

And would you believe "all this and heav'n too" is within easy driving distance for half the population of the United States or overnight by car, bus, or train, yet still private and secluded, and it's just a few hours by plane from anywhere in the United States....

Hope you'uns aim to head for these parts RIGHT SOON!!

?????????????????

2   did you know that...

(within a two-hour drive of boone)

- The Blue Ridge Parkway is reputed to have the most scenic stretches of highway in the world.
- Like the Garden of Eden, Boone — 40 miles east of Damascus, Va. — is the beginning source for headwaters of four great rivers: Ohio (New River), Pee Dee (Yadkin), Santee (Johns-Catawba) and Tennessee (Watauga) and that they flow north, east, south and west.

  And the Lord God planted a garden eastward in Eden ... And a river went out of Eden to water the garden; and from thence it was parted and became into four heads...Gen. 2:8,10.

- Dan'l Boone, about 200 years ago, opened the Wilderness Trail to Cumberland Gap crossing the Blue Ridge Parkway (now Milepost 280).
- One of the few remaining Wagon Trains in the United States still rolls along from Wilkesboro to Jefferson.
- *Horn in the West* drama recreating the history of the pioneers' westward movement in their quest for freedom is one of the oldest outdoor plays presented summers continuously since 1951 and is the highest theater of its kind east of the Mississippi.
- Dan'l Boone camped in Boone near the site of the monument on the Appalachian State University campus.
- The four highest peaks in southern Appalachia: Mount Mitchell, Grandfather, Roan and Beech Mountains are in this area and Mount

13

Mitchell is the highest peak east of the Mississippi and the oldest state park in North Carolina (1915).

- The Blue Ridge Mountains are considered to be among the world's oldest (over one billion years), and were named so because of the soft blue haze shrouding them.
- Grandfather Mountain was so-named by the Indians because from afar it appears like the outline of an old man's face sky-gazing.
- The Linville Gorge is the wildest nature preserve in eastern America.
- The stalagmite and stalactite formations of Linville Caverns and Bristol, Tenn., Caverns have been developing for 400 to 600 million years.
- The average elevation of Watauga County is the highest of any other comparable area east of the Mississippi.
- The Union Grove, N.C., Old-Time Fiddlers and Blue Grass Convention, going strong since 1923, is the oldest Country Music stompin' gatherin' in the world.
- Mountain handcrafts are one of the predominant art forms of this area from which many mountaineers earn a livelihood.
- This tri-state mountain corner area is an All-Year-Variety-Vacationland with an unsurpassed combination of recreational facilities, special attractions, natural grandeur, historical sights and unique handcrafts.
- This region is the skiing capital of the Southeast.
- Within 50-miles of Boone-Blowing Rock there are about 50 golf courses.
- There's an 11-month trout fishing season on all public mountain trout streams closed only from March 1 to the first Saturday in April.
- North Wilkesboro has over a million apple trees. (Think Spring!)
- Wilkes County is one of the nation's leaders in egg and poultry production.
- Wilkes County is the world's leader in the manufacture of mirrors.
- The New River running through Ashe County, believed to be the oldest river in North America and the second oldest in the world, is the only remaining free-flowing river in the eastern U.S., and is the only river flowing east to west over the Appalachians; a 26.5-mile segment is now part of the National Wild and Scenic River System.
- There are few places where one can fish for such a wide variety of species as in this compact area.
- The only place in the world where snow falls upside down is at The Blowing Rock.
- Blowing Rock is one location of the Continental Divide where waters flow both east to the Atlantic Ocean and west to the Gulf of Mexico.
- "Spruce Pine Mineral Kingdom" (225-square-mile area) has a greater variety of gems and minerals than any other area of similar size in the world and produces more mica and feldspar than anywhere in the U.S.
- This "Gem Paradise" is open for digging to your heart's content for precious stones that are still plentiful.
- The only active emerald mine in North America is the Big Crabtree Emerald Mine, three miles north of Little Switzerland.

- There are more than 30 waterfalls to visit in this area.
- The phenomenon of the mysterious Brown Mountain Lights may be seen at dusk from Jonas Ridge and Wiseman's View at Linville Gorge.
- There are as many plant-life zones in a two-hour trip from higher to lower levels of the Blue Ridge Parkway as one would pass through in driving a thousand miles from Canada to Georgia.
- Throughout the vast continent of Europe there are fewer types of wildflowers than grow in the Blue Ridge Mountains.
- The enormous variety of flower species found in this location is similar to those that grow in China and Japan.
- Montezuma is the carnation capital of the Southeast.
- The world's largest display of Catawba Rhododendron is found on Roan Mountain.
- The wild flame azalea, mountain laurel and several species of rhododendron grow in wild, ecstatic profusion in the surrounding mountains.
- Avery County is known as the shrubbery capital of North Carolina.
- Ashe County exports more Fraser fir and white pine trees than any other county in North Carolina.
- One of the first monuments to peace, two poplars tied together, now known as the Treaty Tree, still stands near Lenoir symbolizing the agreement between the Cherokee and Catawba Indians to cease fighting.
- At Sycamore Shoals, Elizabethton, Tenn., in 1772, The Watauga Association, the first majority-rule system of American democratic government, was formed and the first permanent American settlement outside the original thirteen colonies was established.
- *Watauga* is the Indian word for *Whispering Waters.*
- More than 30 species of salamander are to be found here, the largest variety frequenting any similar size area in the world.
- In July, the oldest gathering of Scottish clans in the United States as well as the Highland Games are held on Grandfather Mountain.
- Lees-McRae College in Banner Elk, located at 3740 feet elevation, is the highest college campus east of the Mississippi.
- One of the oldest continuing Annual Horse Shows in the United States takes place at Blowing Rock in July.
- Two grist mills are still grinding out cornmeal and buckwheat flour, one in Meat Camp near Boone and one north of Abingdon, Va.
- The Mast General Store in Valle Crucis is nearly 100 years old and still very much alive selling merchandise from diapers to dynamite.
- Celo Community (1937), near Burnsville, is the oldest commune in America.
- Watauga is one of seven of the 100 counties in North Carolina having the largest number of towns between 100-200 years old.
- The Appalachian Center, Belk Library at ASU, has the most outstanding collection of coverlets and handmade spreads in the United States as well

as one of the world's largest collections of authentic recordings of mountain music and other Appalachia memorabilia.

- The *Clinchfield Special* is the oldest passenger-operating steam locomotive in the United States, regularly chugging through the beautiful Nolichucky Gorge and the Blue Ridge Mountains.
- The *Tweetsie* train actually ran between Boone and Johnson City, Tenn., on the *Tweetsie Railroad* for more than 50 years.
- The joyous mountain heritage is preserved in part through gospel singing, fiddlers' conventions, blue grass and country music, mountain clogging and square dancing.
- The Barter Theatre, Abingdon, Va., the second oldest theater building in the United States, is the first and only state-subsidized theater in the United States and the oldest and largest legitimate summer theater south of the Mason-Dixon Line and maintains the largest professional company in continuous residence outside of New York City.
- Tennessee operates seven Welcome Centers around the clock for weary and information-hungry drivers.
- Cranberries are still growing in the town of Cranberry.
- The only high-fired stoneware dinnerware plant in the United States, iron mountain, operates at Laurel Bloomery, Tenn.
- If you ever see and do everything included between the covers of this book, YOU will be more familiar with this picturesque corner of the globe than many of the natives.

3   **how to get here**

No matter which direction you're coming from, the Boone-Blowing Rock area is just an overnight drive from the great population centers of northern, midwestern and southeastern United States on convenient, easily accessible, good roads.

If you're driving from the Midwest, head for Bristol or Johnson City, Tenn. From Johnson City it's an hour and a half farther on US 321 to Boone and it's about the same distance from Bristol southeast on US 421.

If you're coming from the east, get on US 421 at Winston-Salem which is just 85 miles from Boone.

From the south, head for Asheville, 95 miles southwest of Boone, take I-40 east to Marion, then north on US 221 to Linville and on to Blowing Rock (a very winding road); or at the junction of US 221 and NC 105 at Linville, take NC 105 to Boone. If you have time for a more casual trip, don't forget to drive on the leisurely, peaceful Blue Ridge Parkway.

From the Palm Beach area of Florida, it's a 15-hour drive. If you plan to get

17

on the Blue Ridge Parkway, add another three or four hours to allow time to savor the picturesque rural landscapes. Take the Florida Sunshine Parkway north to I-75 into Georgia, by-pass Atlanta on I-285 to I-85, then northeast to Spartanburg, finally, north on US 221 to Blowing Rock; or at Linville, northwest on NC 105 to Boone.

New Yorkers and their neighbors have a 15-hour unstrenuous drive south on I-81 to US 58 to Damascus, Va., south on Tenn. 91 to Mountain City, then south on US 421 to Boone. If you're not pushed for time, you should certainly get on the Skyline Drive at Shenandoah National Park in northern Virginia leading onto the Blue Ridge Parkway. Of course, you'll be slowing down to 45 miles per hour on the Parkway (294 miles long) for spectacular, billboard-free, pollution-free, relaxed driving. You'll relish the special stopping-off places for picnicking, and the overlooks where you can gaze out on the glorious majesty of the towering peaks, always a reminder that man should rise higher than his earth consciousness. Man! It's the greatest!!!

Should you prefer to fly from the North, South, West or East, there's an airport at Hickory, just 40 scenic miles southeast of Blowing Rock on US 321. Piedmont Airlines has nine flights per day connecting with major airlines in other cities. At Hickory you may rent a car and start your tour by sightseeing in this well-known furniture center.

Flying in from the West or Southwest, there's also the Tri-City Airport of Bristol, Johnson City, and Kingsport, Tenn., and then a drive of 40 miles east to Boone.

There are several private airports for small planes. Beech Mountain Airport in Banner Elk (898-5261), 25 miles from Boone, has a 4600-foot paved runway. Flights between DeKalb Peachtree Airport, Atlanta and Banner Elk leave daily at 9:30 a.m. and 4:30 p.m. from Beech. Eppes Air Service provides for freight-on-board all flights.

The Boone-Blowing Rock Airport (264-8760), two miles southeast from Boone on US 321, with fuel service but unpaved, has an unlighted landing strip about 2500 feet long. And Spruce Pine Airport has a 3000-foot north-south hard surface runway at 2750 feet elevation. It is open to planes through Light Twin Engine Classificaton and has no facilities. (Unattended phone 765-9981. If no answer, 765-2349.)

Mountain Wilderness Airport, ten miles south of Burnsville, N.C., on NC 197, with field elevation 2890 feet, a 3000-foot turf runway, north-south landing strip, 100-octane fuel, large tie-down area, is attended through Light Twin Engine Classification. No repairs at field (682-3244).

For those who prefer letting someone else do the driving, two bus companies, Trailways and Greyhound, service Boone and Blowing Rock. The bus station is at 211 S.Depot St., Boone (264-2102). Like the mailman, no matter what the weather, you'll be delivered safely.

C'mon, grab your binoculars, camera, knapsack and sturdy hiking shoes AND GET ON DOWN HERE!

SPRING SUMMER FALL WINTER

4   when to come

To help you decide when to come where the livin's super and where four distinct, marvellous seasons of the year prevail, with settings made to order for a scenic calendar, here are the seasonal averages: the average summer temperature (June, July and August) is 67 degrees; winter's average (December, January and February) is 35 degrees; spring (March, April and May) averages 50 degrees; and fall (September, October and November) has a 52-degree average.

Mountain ranges to the west, north and south, in this kilometer-high country, protect the area from northern blizzards and southern heat waves. Yet, there are few spots like this in the world where New England and eastern Canadian vegetation grow side by side with semi-tropical vegetation. If you have a favorite season of year, come up here to experience it at its best. Boone and Blowing Rock, for example, are famous for cool, refreshing, clean summer air. Average temperatures are 10 to 12 degrees lower than the flatlands of North Carolina. No matter how warm it is anywhere else in the United States, even on the hottest days of the year, here the highest average temperature is in the 70's dropping off to the 50's or 60's during the night. The thermometer almost never reaches 90. And although the summer growing time is the wettest season, the sun shines more than half the daylight hours to the delight of the honeybees!

Winters, on the other hand, provide a sharp contrast, including dependable cold weather punctuated with dramatic snowfalls and lots of sunny days. Well-maintained ski slopes await winter sports buffs. This is truly the King of all seasons for crowds coming from the South, Midwest and Mideast. Freezing temperatures are practically a daily event, and yet, rarely are there lasting extremes of inclement weather. With *Joy in the Mountains* in hand, winter offers a very exciting and varied "menu" including day and night action on the ski slopes as well as all the university and college events listed.

On the other side of the coin, if you live far south or far north and have little opportunity to experience the magic of spring unfolding, disclosing, revealing its mysteries and treasures of growing things, the perfect choice for watching Mother Nature's pageant is the Spring Spectacular! Spring comes early with lots of warm, wafting, apple-blossom days and lingers long. The shiny trout and other varieties of fish in the cold mountain streams or whirling pools are fairly jumpin' for the fisherman whose fancy turns to thoughts of "catching the biggest one yet."

But if you've never seen the huge tapestry of mountain woodland leaf coloring, or experienced the visual excitement of varied hues from soft, muted tones of yellow and orange to vivid purple and flaming crimson, you haven't lived! The mountainsides are truly awesome, draped against a lush background of evergreens. This superb extravaganza of autumn fire and brilliance is one of the dramas of life — changing outer forms while the inner remains birthless, ageless, deathless. As you enjoy the color spectrum and masses of rich hillside colors during Indian Summer Days, from the comfortable, well-banked, winding road of the Blue Ridge Parkway, or other mountain heights, take time to relax and rejoice. The incessant rhythm of life confronts you at every turn, inviting you to be still, be very still and know "God's in His Heav'n and all's right with the world."

Dressing up for the Fall Fashion Show starts with berries, sumac and other small plants turning bright red, followed by dogwoods, gums and sourwoods in hints of red and copper. Then come the maples, elms, ashes and tulip poplars in yellow to crimson with the final crescendo thundering in the silence — kaleidoscopic hues and tones of yellow-orange buckeye, hickory and sassafras "mitten" leaves turning orange. By mid-October the climax and finale of the fall garb wind up with the oaks adding their cadenza of red.

Since leaf coloring moves from high altitudes where it's colder earlier, down the mountain slopes to low altitudes, the earlier the season, the higher up you go for the show. For your visual delight, here's a color log to aid in your recognition of the autumn leaf transition:

Light yellow: striped maple, willow
Yellow: ash, poplar redbud
Golden yellow: poplar
Bright yellow: birch, mountain ash, sugar maple
Orange yellow: birch, hickory, tuliptree
Clear yellow: beech
Golden orange: American beech
Orange to scarlet: sassafras, mountain maple
Orange scarlet: sugar maple

Yellow to brown: hickory
Dark purple: mountain ash, white ash
Crimson to wine red: red maple
Red: black cherry, sugar maple
Brilliant red: sumac
Scarlet: dogwood, sourwood
Burgundy: black gum
Dark red to russett: red oak

And now for a typical year's average weather week by week. But no matter what the weather, there are always the all-year sports of tennis, swimming, ice and roller skating, and for those brimming with vitality, "tripping the light fantastic." No matter when you come — it might help to know that most of the time it's not too hot, it's not too cold, it's jes' right!

WEATHER GUIDE

Week End.	Av.Temp. High	Av.Temp. Low	Inches Rain	Inches Snow	No. of Dry Days	Week End.	Av.Temp. High	Av.Temp. Low	Inches Rain	Inches Snow	No. of Dry Days
Jan. 6	49	28	.27	0	4	July 7	75	59	2.80		2
13	51	30	2.30	1	6	14	71	61	.13		6
20	41	23	.19	0	6	21	75	60	.49		3
27	48	28	.39	0	5	28	73	60	.12		3
Feb. 3	56	36	.41	0	3	Aug. 4	73	66	1.01		5
10	40	21	1.47	7	3	11	69	59	1.54		1
17	50	32	.69	0	5	18	72	58	.65		5
24	54	33	2.02	0	4	25	73	57	.26		6
Mar. 3	41	24	.44	3	5	Sept. 1	75	62	.11		5
10	46	21	.52	6	4	8	65	58	3.85		2
17	49	35	3.46	1	1	15	70	56	1.44		3
24	58	40	1.57		3	22	65	56	.34		5
31	55	38	2.10		5	29	67	44	.14		6
Apr. 7	54	27	.09		6	Oct. 6	63	32	0		7
14	58	36	.19		5	13	67	43	0		7
21	59	40	.14		5	20	57	34	0		7
28	71	45	.74		4	27	66	38	0		7
May 5	66	53	.91		3	Nov. 3	72	45	0		7
12	66	48	1.02		3	10	60	34	.05		6
19	69	57	2.84		1	17	49	26	1.12	3	2
26	70	55	2.80		2	24	53	32	1.03	0	4
June 2	72	55	3.80		2	Dec. 1	40	24	2.67	14	5
9	72	54	.57		5	8	35	22	.66	2	4
16	75	57	1.35		5	15	44	27	.74	1	6
23	77	58	.23		5	22	40	24	1.36	5	2
30	77	60	.78		5	29	51	36	1.25	0	6

5   information please

Have you any idea of the wide range of services some local Chambers of Commerce offer you as visitor, tourist or local resident? Supposing you arrive in town for a vacation and haven't the foggiest notion of where to stay or eat, your best bet is to make it down to the Chamber of Commerce office before 5:00 p.m. for a listing of motels, hotels, campsites, restaurants and a street map, plus detailed verbal information as to just how to get where you're going. Or even better, write for this information before leaving home.

As you look about the Chamber office you'll find a stacked literature rack of attractions and events, as well as brochures on places to visit outside the area covered in this book. Facts and statistics about a community, available on request, may include listings of businesses, city offices, schools, libraries, churches, hospitals, real estate offices, clubs and organizations and information on all phases of the community from routine to extraordinary, and are provided courteously and promptly.

There's usually an abundance of research material available ranging from setting up a permanent or vacation home to establishing a business or even finding employment.

From the point of view of you, the tourist, the Chamber works to promote the highest standards of business ethics even acting at times as an intermediary should you encounter a difference of opinion in a business transaction.

So-o-o-o visit the friendly individuals at the Chamber, get acquainted with all they have to offer and if they are unable to answer questions, they should know who can. And by all means check with them on dates and hours of scheduled activities covered in this book, or name of sponsoring organization.

At the end of this chapter is a listing of Chambers of Commerce in this four-season vacation land, within a two-hour drive of Boone and Blowing Rock, serving about 100 towns and cities.

And if you really want to feel warmth and hospitality after leaving your home state, or feel like a V.I.P. with the red carpet rolled out for you, do stop at the state information centers. You'll be received cordially by the "Welcome Center" which is ready to furnish you with free information on routes to reach your destination speedily or for "getting lost" off the beaten path. All of these information centers are easily accessible on major highways; some even have picnic areas and playgrounds, and offer a cool drink of fruit punch. You may find answers to questions you didn't know you had.

Here's a listing of the locations of state information centers in North Carolina, Tennessee and Virginia:

NORTH CAROLINA STATE INFORMATION CENTERS

I-40 10.5 miles southwest of Tennessee line.

I-85 2 miles south of Virginia line.

I-85 2 miles north of South Carolina line.

I-95 ½ mile south of Virginia line.

TENNESSEE WELCOME CENTERS (open 'round the clock!)

I-81 near Bristol.

I-24 and I-75 near Chattanooga.

I-55 near Memphis.

I-65 near Ardmore.

I-65 near Mitchellville.

I-75 near Jellico.

VIRGINIA STATE HIGHWAY TRAVEL INFORMATION STATIONS

VA 13 Accomack County, ¾ mile south of Maryland line.

I-64 Alleghany County, 2½ miles east of West Virginia line.

I-66 Prince William County, ¼ mile west of Bull Run.

I-81 Frederick County, 4 miles south of West Virginia line.

I-81 Washington County, north of Virginia-Tennessee state line.

I-85 Mecklenburg County, north of Virginia-North Carolina state line.

I-95 Greensville County, north of Virginia-North Carolina state line.

I-95 Spotsylvania County, 1¾ miles south of Route 17.

NORTH CAROLINA CHAMBERS OF COMMERCE

ALLEGHANY COUNTY — Alleghany County C. of C., (Roaring Gap, Sparta) Sparta, N.C. 28675. (919) 372-4252.

ASHE COUNTY — Ashe County C. of C., (Jefferson, W. Jefferson) P.O. Box 31, W. Jefferson, N. C. 28694. 246-9550.

AVERY COUNTY — Avery County C. of C., (Banner Elk, Crossnore, Linville, Newland, Grandfather Mt.) Deerfield Bldg., P.O. Box 775, Banner Elk, N.C. 28604. 898-5888.

BURKE COUNTY — Burke County C. of C., (Morganton, Valdese) 216 Collett St., P.O. Box 751, Morganton, N. C. 28655. 437-3021.

CALDWELL COUNTY — Lenoir-Caldwell County C. of C., P. O. Box 510, Lenoir, N. C. 28645. 754-6181.

CATAWBA COUNTY — Catawba County C. of C., (Catawba, Clairemont, Conover, Hickory, Maiden, Newton) P.O. Box 1828, Hickory, N.C. 28601. 328-6111.

McDOWELL COUNTY — McDowell County C. of C., (Marion, Old Fort) 20 N. Logan St., City Hall Bldg., P.O. Box 230, Marion, N.C. 28752. 652-4240.

MITCHELL COUNTY — MITCHELL COUNTY C. of C., (Bakersville, Little Switzerland, Penland, Spruce Pine) Oak Ave., Spruce Pine, N. C. 28777. 765-9180.

WATAUGA COUNTY — Boone Area C. of C., (Boone, Watauga County) Blowing Rock Road, Boone, N. C. 28607. 264-2225.

WATAUGA COUNTY — Blowing Rock C. of C. Inc., Main St., Blowing Rock, N. C. 28605. 295-7951.

WILKES COUNTY — Wilkes C. of C., Inc., (Wilkesboro, N. Wilkesboro) P.O. Box 727, 412 8th St., N. Wilkesboro, N. C. 28659. (919) 838-8662.

YANCEY COUNTY — Yancey County C. of C., (Burnsville, Micaville, Celo, Pensacola, Bald Creek, Cane River, Mt. Mitchell State Park) Burnsville, N.C. 28714. 682-2312.

TENNESSEE CHAMBERS OF COMMERCE

CARTER COUNTY — Carter County C. of C., W. Elk Ave., P.O. Box 190, Elizabethton, Tenn. 37643. (615) 543-2122.

UNICOI COUNTY — Unicoi County C. of C., P.O. Box 703, Erwin, Tennessee, 37650. (615) 743-3000.

WASHINGTON COUNTY — Johnson City Area C. of C., (Bristol, Johnson City, Jonesboro) 339 E. Main St., P.O. Box 180, Johnson City, Tenn. 37601. (615) 926-2141.

WASHINGTON COUNTY — Greater Bristol Area C. of C., P.O. Box 1039, 510 Cumberland St., Bristol, Tenn. 24201. (703) 669-2141.

VIRGINIA CHAMBERS OF COMMERCE

GRAYSON & CARROLL COUNTIES — Galax-Carroll-Grayson C. of C. (Galax, Independence) P.O. Box 1006, 405 N. Main St., Galax, Va. 24333. (703) 236-2184.

SMYTH COUNTY — C. of C. of Marion, Inc., Center Bldg., P.O. Box 602, Marion, Va. 24354. (703) 793-3161.

WASHINGTON COUNTY — Washington County C. of C. (Abingdon, Damascus, Emory) 127 W. Main St., Abingdon, Va. 24210 (703) 628-3966.

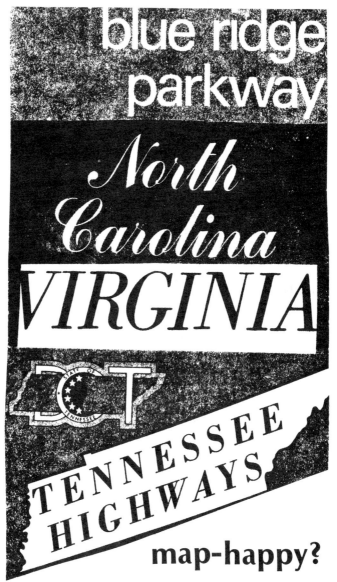

6   **map-happy?**

For a successful vacation trip a traveler's "best friends" are a few good maps. Especially good ones to use for getting here are the free official highway maps published by the North Carolina Department of Transportation, Travel & Promotion Division, Department of Natural and Economic Resources, Raleigh, N.C. 27611, the Virginia State Travel Service, 6 North South St., Richmond, Va. 23219, and the Tennessee Department of Transportation, 106 Highway Bldg., Nashville, Tenn. 37219. All are available also at the State Welcome Centers and local Chambers of Commerce.

After acquiring these three basics, you'll want to get individual city, town or county maps of places mentioned in this guide book when you visit the local Chambers of Commerce. Add to these the useful *Cone-Price Parks Roads and Trails Map* available at both Cone Memorial Park and Julian Price Memorial Park on the Blue Ridge Parkway, showing all the paved and gravel roads, 25 miles of carriage, horseback riding and hiking trails, fishing lakes, campgrounds and mountain elevations.

For finding the off-the-beaten-path roads, the *Back Roads Map of the Blue Ridge* is indispensable, particularly for the adventurous. It includes county roads which have numbered signposts and are state maintained. The map details Boone, Blowing Rock, Blue Ridge Parkway, Jefferson, Lenoir, Linville, Spruce Pine, Mountain City and Lake Watauga, Tenn., plus camping sites and hiking trails. Most Chambers of Commerce sell it at a small charge.

Be sure to pick up the excellent, handy, accordion-pleated *Blue Ridge Parkway* map at any Chamber for general information about the Parkway, use of Visitor Areas and special places to stop at indicated Mileposts.

For the intrepid hiker and mountain climber, there's the *100 Favorite Trails* map of the Great Smokies and Carolina Blue Ridge, compiled by the Carolina Mountain Club of Asheville and The Smoky Mountains Hiking Club, Knoxville, Tenn. This highly detailed map includes trail descriptions of 15 sections of the 2,000-mile Maine-to-Georgia Appalachian Trail, plus 5,000 campsites both publicly and privately operated. A folded, pocket-size edition is for sale from The Stephens Press, Inc., Box 5655, Asheville, N.C. 28803.

If you just happen to be a map collector who loves camping, hiking, boating, swimming, fishing, hunting, and/or horseback riding, write for the following free, superb national and state recreational area maps:

North Carolina

Forest Supervisor, Pisgah National Forest, National Forests of North Carolina, P.O. Box 2750, Asheville, N.C. 28802.

Appalachian Trail, Pisgah National Forest, same as above.

North Carolina State Parks, P.O. Box 27687, Raleigh, N.C. 27611.

Tennessee

Forest Supervisor, Cherokee National Forest, U.S. Forest Service, P.O. Box 400, Cleveland, Tenn. 37311.

Appalachian Trail, same as above.

Tennessee State Parks, Tennessee Department of Conservation, 2611 West End Ave., Nashville, Tenn. 37203.

Information Office, TVA Recreation Areas Map, Knoxville, Tenn. 37902.

Upper Holston Lakes Map, same as above.

Virginia

Forest Supervisor, Jefferson National Forest, 3517 Brandon Ave., Roanoke, Va. 24015.

Appalachian Trail, same as above.

Mount Rogers National Recreation Area, Mount Rogers Citizens Development Corp., Box 100, Abingdon, Va. 24210.

Hungry Mother State Park, Division of Parks, 1201 State Office Bldg., Capitol Square, Richmond, Va. 23219.

And specifically for hunting and fishing in North Carolina, write for the latest *Hunting and Fishing Maps for North Carolina Game Lands* issued by the Wildlife Resources Commission, Game Division, Raleigh, N.C., which contain maps showing the general size and location of all the Game Lands (2 million acres) in the state.

AND THAT'S NOT ALL! For even more detailed information for persevering hikers and backpackers, where the most obscure trails are spelled out, the following maps should be very useful: *U.S. Series of Topographic Maps* available from U.S. Geological Survey as well as dealers in backpacking and hiking equipment, with or without a green forest overprint. *The Johnson City, Tenn. Topographic Map* details many of the trails in the areas covered in this book. The scale is four miles per inch. *Tennessee Valley Authority and U.S. Geological Survey Topographic Maps* with or without green tint are available from TVA, 815 Pound Building, Chattanooga 37401 or 102-A Union Building, Knoxville, Tenn. 37902. *U.S. Geological Survey Maps* are also available from 1109 N. Highland Ave., Arlington, Va. 22201 or Army Map Service, San Antonio, Texas 78234, scale 2,000 feet per inch.

Now, if you don't find your way around without guesswork or frustrations, don't blame us! And, if you get lost in the woods, give us a call!!! Happy Traveling.

EXTRA!

7   the happy media

Good news! Thanks to the altitude of the Greater Boone-Blowing Rock area, excellent quality programs are broadcast and received both over AM and FM radio stations. Timely commentary, ample national and local news and sports coverage, outstanding cultural offerings, local activities and a unique public service — *Swap Shop* — are aired daily.

Station WATA, Boone, 1450 on the AM dial, starting at 8:30 a.m., Monday through Friday, features a Bulletin Board program summarizing the daily calendar of events and other announcements. From 10:15 to 10:30 a.m. over this station, you can buy, sell, swap or give away items via the *Swap Shop* as well as hear about exciting rummage or yard sales. Old-fashioned items like a pot-bellied stove, a wringer-type washing machine, surrey with a fringe on top — or sheep, bulls, horses, a bumper crop of transparent apples, strawberries, raspberries, cucumbers, squash or even a pet skunk if you happen to fancy one — are all fodder for the *Swap Shop* mill. It's just about the most popular air time around. And for musical entertainment, there's plenty of country, rock, easy listenin' and other varieties as well as plays, throughout the 5:00 to 1:00 a.m. day. The stock market report hasn't been overlooked — it's on each day at 6:05 p.m.

If you long for classical music, theater, lectures, discussions, seminars, educational programs of all kinds, Afro-Americana, unlimited jazz, music of yesteryear, masterworks, showtime tunes, here's where it's at. WETS, 89.5 FM, a national public radio station, emanating out of Eastern Tennessee State University in Johnson City; WFOD-FM at 88.5, Wake Forest University, Winston-Salem, as well as the other FM stations listed below will provide loads of fine listening.

Television programs are plentiful — in addition to the major network shows, there are public broadcasting stations for a great variety of cultural and consumer interest features as well as fine children's programs. And — there's cable TV!

In addition to information-packed "hometown" newspapers, big city newspapers are available at Carolina Pharmacy in Boone and Storie's Soda Shop in Blowing Rock.

As you can very well see, you're never far from anywhere thanks to the *happy media* which holds this world together, even when you're up here away from home....

RADIO STATIONS

ABINGDON, VA. — WBBI. 1230AM, 92.7FM.
BOONE, N.C. — WATA. 1450AM.
BRISTOL, VA. — WFHG. 980AM.
BRISTOL, VA. — WOPI. 1490AM, 96.9FM
BRISTOL, VA. — WZAP. 690AM
BRISTOL, VA. — WKYE. 1500AM.
BURNSVILLE, N.C. — WKYK. 1540AM.
ELIZABETHTON, TENN. — WBEJ. 1240AM.
ERWIN, TENN. — WEMB. 1420AM
GALAX, VA. — WBOB. 1360AM, 98.1FM.
HICKORY, N.C. — WHKY. 1290AM, 102.9FM
HICKORY, N.C. — WIRC. 630AM.
HICKORY, N.C. — WSPF. 1000AM.
HICKORY, N.C. — WXRC. 95.7FM.
JOHNSON CITY, TENN. — WETB. 790AM.
JOHNSON CITY, TENN. — WJCW. 910AM.
JOHNSON CITY, TENN. — WETS. 89.5FM.

JONESBORO, TENN. — WJSO. 1590AM.
JONESBORO, TENN. — WQUT. 101.5FM.
LENOIR, N.C. — WJRI. 1340AM.
LENOIR, N.C. — WKGX. 1080AM.
MARION, N.C. — WBRM. 1250AM.
MARION, VA. — WMEV. 1010AM, 93.9FM.
MARION, VA. — WOLD. 1330AM, 102.3FM
MORGANTON, N.C. — WMNC. 1430AM, 92.1FM
MOUNTAIN CITY, TENN. — WMCT. 1390AM.
N. WILKESBORO-WILKESBORO, N.C. — WKBC. 810AM, 97.3FM
N. WILKESBORO-WILKESBORO, N.C. — WWWC. 1240AM.
SPARTA, N.C. — WCOK. l060AM.
SPRUCE PINE, N.C. — WTOE. 1470AM.
VALDESE, N.C. — WSVM. 1490AM.

LOCAL NEWSPAPERS

(Included for each paper are county served and day(s) published. If no area code, use 704.)

ABINGDON, VA. — *Journal-Virginian.* Washington. Thurs. (703) 628-2962.
ABINGDON, VA. — Washington County *News.* Washington. Thurs. (703) 628-7101.
BAKERSVILLE, N.C. — Mitchell *Ledger.* Mitchell. Thurs. 688-3613.
BLOWING ROCK, N.C. — *Blowing Rocket.* Watauga-Caldwell. Fri. 295-7522.
BOONE, N.C. — Watauga *Democrat.* Watauga. Mon. & Thurs. 264-3612.
BRISTOL, VA. — Bristol *Herald-Courier.* Washington. Daily. (703) 669-2181.
BRISTOL, VA. — Bristol *Virginia-Tennesseean.* Sullivan. Daily exc. Sun. (615) 669-2181.
BURNSVILLE, N.C. — Yancey *Journal.* Yancey. Thurs. 682-2120.
ELIZABETHTON, TENN. — Elizabethton *Star.* Carter. Daily exc. Sat. & Sun. (615) 542-4151.
ERWIN, TENN. — Erwin *Record.* Unicoi. Wed. (615) 743-4112.
GALAX, VA. — The Galax *Gazette.* Carroll-Grayson. Tues. & Thurs. (703) 236-5178.
GRANITE FALLS, N.C. — Granite Falls *Press.* Caldwell. Thurs. 396-1124.
HICKORY, N.C. — Hickory *Daily Record.* Catawba. Daily exc. Sun. 874-2551.
JOHNSON CITY, TENN. — Johnson City *Press-Chronicle.* Washington. Daily. (615) 929-3111.
JONESBORO, TENN. — *Herald and Tribune.* Washington. Wed. (615) 753-3136.
LENOIR, N.C. — Lenoir *News-Topic.* Caldwell. Daily exc. Sun. 758-7381.
MARION, N.C. — McDowell *News.* McDowell. Mon., Wed., Fri. 653-3313.
MARION, VA. — Smyth County *News.* Smyth. Tues. & Thurs. (703) 783-5121.
MORGANTON, N.C. — *News-Herald.* Burke. Daily exc. Sat. & Sun. 437-2161.
MOUNTAIN CITY, TENN. — The *Tomahawk.* Johnson. Wed. (615) 727-6121.
NEWLAND, N.C. — Avery *Journal.* Avery. Thurs. 733-2448.
NEWTON, N.C. — *Observer-News Enterprise.* Catawba. Daily exc. Sat. & Sun. 464-0221.
N. WILKESBORO, N.C. — The *Journal-Patriot.* Wilkes. Mon. & Thurs. (919) 838-4117.
SPARTA, N.C. — Alleghany *News.* Alleghany. Thurs. (919) 372-8231.
SPRUCE PINE, N.C. — Tri-County *News.* Mitchell. Thurs. 765-2071.
VALDESE, N.C. — Valdese *News.* Burke. Wed. (919) 874-9111.
W. JEFFERSON, N.C. — *Skyland Post.* Ashe. Wed. (919) 246-4121.
YADKINVILLE, N.C. — Yadkin *Ripple.* Yadkin. Thurs. (919) 279-2341.

8 at home away from home

If you've come to this area from another region or from a foreign land not knowing a single person, you can easily meet a kindred spirit by getting in touch with any club or organization you prefer be it civic, professional, volunteer, or one you've never heard of before. You name it — it's probably here.

Meeting folks with whom you have a common interest will quickly make you feel at home and may widen your circle of friends. Anyway, it's a marvellous opportunity to make the most of your vacation, for people in these mountain communities are friendly, warm, hospitable, honest, courageous, devoted to their land, loyal to family, keep their word, and, their natural dignity is reflected in genuine simplicity.

Worthwhile community and homespun fun projects go on all year and visitors are welcome as participants or spectators. Are you a gardener? There are no less than eleven garden clubs in the Boone-Blowing Rock area to visit and perhaps learn something new. Would you like to know about hang gliding, Blue Grass Music or the Boone Mountain Melody Chapter of Sweet Adelines? Have you a yen to learn about the Appalachian heritage? Are you a retiree? A bridge player? Would you like to join a craftsman's association? Do you own a Corvette? Races are held periodically and there's an active club in Boone. There's even a Christmas Tree Growers Association!

Just glance at this listing of Watauga County clubs and organizations, primarily in Boone, and call the local Chamber of Commerce for the phone number of the current club president and "break the ice." Other counties have similar listings. You'll find there's "no stranger within the gates" in these mountain towns no matter which county you're visiting. The first step is up to you!

CLUBS AND ORGANIZATIONS

Civic Clubs — American Legion; ASU Junior Jaycees; Blowing Rock Jaycees; Circle K Club; Civitan; Civitan, Foscoe; Community Newcomers; Environmental Commission; Jaycees; Junior Civitan; Junior Jaycees; Kiwanis; Kiwanis, Banner Elk; Lions; Optimist; REACT (CB); RSVP (Retired Senior Volunteer Persons); Rotary, Blowing Rock; Rotary; Royal Order of Moose; Ruritan, Blowing Rock; Ruritan, Cove Creek; VFW Post 7031; Watauga County Amateur Radio Club.

Coin Club — Watauga Coin Club.

Community Clubs — Beaver Dam; Blowing Rock; Cove Creek; Deep Gap; Foscoe; Matney; Meat Camp; Valle Crucis.

Discussion Groups — Great Decisions Discussion Group

Education Clubs — Education Club.

Extension Homemakers — Appalachian; Beaver Dam Club; Beaver Dam Crafters; Bethel; Boone; Brushy Fork; Cove Creek; Creative; Foscoe; Good Neighbors; Green Valley; Sunrise Sunset; Trio Club.

Garden Clubs — Appalachian; Blowing Rock; Blue Ridge; Colonial; Council; Cove Creek Elementary School Junior; Dogwood; Gardenerettes; Mountaineer; Rhododendron; Soil Turners Junior.

Handcraft Associations — Blue Ridge Hearthside Crafts; HANDS Craftsmen's Association; Southern Highland Handicraft Guild.

Music Clubs — Boone Barbershoppers (SPEBSQSA); Boone Mountain Melody Chapter of Sweet Adelines; N.C. Bluegrass Association, Lenoir.

Nature Clubs — Audubon Society of Grandfather Mountain; Sierra Club.

Other Social Clubs — American Association of Retired Persons; Duplicate Bridge; Parents Without Partners.

Sports Clubs — Appalachian Corvette Club; Mountain Gliders Hang Gliders Club, Johnson City, Tenn. (615) 928-8605; The Order of the Raven; Watauga Gun Club; Watauga Junior Horse Club.

Women's Clubs — American Assn. of University Women; American Legion Auxiliary; Appalachian Women's Club; Business and Professional Women's Club; Cove Creek Worthwhile Women's Club; Daughters of the American Revolution; Friday Afternoon Club; Jaycettes; League of Women Voters; Pioneer Ladies Civitan Club of Boone; Worthwhile Women's Club: Arts, Education, Homelife, Public Affairs.

Youth Clubs — Blue Ridge Beagle Club; Boy Scouts; Girl Scouts; 4-H Clubs.

9 mountain vittles

Mountain folk are always ready for a celebration or for an ol'-fashioned good time with plenty of tasty vittles and a foot-stompin', hand-clappin', banjo-strummin', shoe-cloggin' shindig. With a "Y'all have a good time, now, y'hear," everyone is welcome at public social suppers be it a pig roast, ox roast, bear hunter's dinner, country ham supper with oodles of ham biscuits, fish fry, barbecue picnic, or an Italian spaghetti dinner, with an abundance of homemade rolls, breads and desserts.

Just look between the covers of *Joy in the Mountains* for annual fairs and festivals or friendly monthly get-togethers or social functions. Watch the newspapers and listen to the local radio announcements for other mountain feasts from country kitchens. Oftentimes they include entertainment, an auction, contest, and door prizes.

Now is a great time to "break bread" with a mountaineer and meet a friend.

(Phone sponsor or C. of C. to confirm information. If no area code is shown, use 704.)

YEAR-ROUND

FERGUSON, N.C. — Wilkes County Ferguson Ruritan Club Chick-n-ques. Famous throughout county.

SPRUCE PINE, N.C. — Barbecue Supper. Second Saturday. Grassy Creek Firehouse, 3 miles south on NC 26. 5:00 — 8:00 p.m. 763-9277.

ANNUAL EVENTS

APRIL

BOONE, N.C. — Dinner — Foreign Language Week. Third week. Wesley Foundation, ASU. Sponsor: Spanish Honor Society. 7:00 p.m. 262-3095.

BOONE, N.C. — German Buffet —   **Foreign Language Week.** Third week Center for Continuing Education, ASU. Sponsor: ASU Language Clubs. 262-3095.

MAY

BANNER ELK, N. C. — Mountain Homecoming Spring Festival Pig Roast (See Ch. 54). First Saturday. Lees-McRae College. Sponsor: Banner Elk Area Resort Association.

ELIZABETHTON, TENN. — Carter County Wild Flower Tour Buffet-style Dinner (Since 1959). Second Friday. American Legion Memorial Building. Reservations required. Sponsor: Carter County Chamber of Commerce. (615) 543-2122 or 542-4200.

GALAX, VA. — Volunteer Fire Department Auxiliary Dinner. Sponsor: Volunteer Fire Department.

JUNE

BOONE, N.C. — CB Dinner Dance (since 1976). 264-9260.

JULY

JONESBORO, TENN. — "Jonesborough Days" Spaghetti Supper. July 3 (Independence Day Celebration). Davy Crockett High School Cafeteria. Sponsor: Jonesboro Civic Trust. P.O. Box 180, Jonesboro, Tenn. 37659. 5:00 — 8:30 p.m.

BANNER ELK, N.C. — Roasting of the Hog. Independence Day Celebration (since 1973). Beech Tree Village, Beech Mountain. Sponsor: Beech Mountain Volunteer Fire Department. Roast: 5:00 — 8:00 p.m. Square Dancing: 8:00 — Midnight.

MARION, VA. — Ice Cream supper. Second Saturday. Bear Creek Lutheran Church.

NEWTON, N.C. — Catawba County Historical Association and Museum Picnic. Fourth Wednesday.

BANNER ELK, N.C. — Flea Market Shrimparoo. Last Saturday. Fire Department Building. Sponsor: Grandfather Home Alumni Association.

MID-JULY TO MID-AUGUST

VALDESE, N.C. — Waldensian Spaghetti Supper. American Legion Home, one block from Amphitheatre. Saturdays before play begins. 5:00 — 8:00 p.m.

AUGUST

BURNSVILLE, N.C. — Mount Mitchell Crafts Fair Barbecue (See Ch. 29) First Saturday. Town Square. Sponsor: Yancey County Chamber of Commerce.

NEWLAND, N.C. — Avery County Rescue Squad Ham Supper. Second Saturday. Avery High School Cafeteria. 5:00 — 8:00 p.m.

BLOUNTVILLE, TENN. — Chuck Wagon Supper Country Hoe Down (See Ch. 54). Third Friday. Sponsor: Sullivan County Bicentennial Committee. 5:30 p.m.

NEWLAND, N.C. — Shriners Ox Roast (since 1973). Third or fourth Saturday. Avery High School Cafeteria. Sponsor: Avery Shriners. 5:00 — 9:00 p.m.

BOONE, N.C. — Meet the Mountaineers Barbecue. Late in month. ASU Varsity Gym. 6:00 p.m. 262-2038.

SEPTEMBER

BANNER ELK, N.C. — Labor Day Pig Roast. Sunday before Labor Day. Viewhaus Restaurant, Beech Village, Beech Mountain. Also dancing and live music. Sponsor: Beech Mountain Volunteer Fire Dept. 4:00 — 7 p.m.

ROAN MOUNTAIN, TENN. — Roan Mountain Naturalists Rally Dinner (See Ch. 32). First Friday. Roan Mountain Elementary School. Sponsor: Roan Mountain Citizens Club.

OCTOBER

MARION, N.C. — Bear Hunter's Dinner (since 1932). First Saturday. Lake Tahoma Grill, US 70W. 724-4421.

BLOWING ROCK, N.C. — Blowing Rock Rescue Squad Supper. Second Saturday. Elementary School Cafeteria. 295-3504.

COMERS ROCK, VA. — Elk Creek Valley Wildlife Banquet. Second Saturday. Comers Rock Clubhouse.

BANNER ELK, N.C. — Homecoming Picnic. Third Saturday. Lees-McRae College, Tate Lawn. Also parade and football game. Noon.

BOONE, N.C. — Homecoming Buffet Picnic. Fourth Saturday. ASU, Conrad Stadium, under circus tent. 11:30 a.m.

BOONE, N.C. — Watauga County Farm-City Week Banquet. Fourth Thursday. National Guard Armory. Community Songfest. SCD Farmer of the Year Award. Sponsor: Chamber of Commerce. 6:30 p.m.

BOONE, N.C. — Watauga County REACT 2890 Dinner (CB's). Last Saturday. National Guard Armory. Entertainment, Male Beauty Contest. 6:00 — 10:00 p.m.

DECEMBER

MILLIGAN COLLEGE, TENN. — Madrigal Dinner Festival (See Ch. 53). First week. Milligan College.

Hugh Morton

10 mountain speshuls

It's no longer a secret that the Southern Appalachians are flowing over with special attractions — things to do and places to visit unlike any other.

For example, there's always some mystery attached to caverns and caves and each one is completely unique. And it's this very mystery and challenge that appeal to speleologists, the experts who explore caves and caverns. When you visit the caverns listed here, you'll find you've crossed a "threshold" as you observe how the force of the pent-up water has worn away the earth, forming tunnels. It's another world where drop by drop the falling water becomes the interior designer fashioning colonnaded halls as the stalagmites (from floor) and stalactites (from ceiling) meet. As this water seeps over some obstruction and leaves mineral deposits of travertine, the resulting sculpture may resemble a striking, arrested waterfall or some delicate rock tracery. You're allowed to take pictures in these caverns — there are very beautiful colors to be captured, revealed under the artificial light.

The listing below should start you off on exploring adventures, such as visiting an Agricultural Experiment Station, viewing in awe the intriguing Brown Mountain Lights, spending a terrific day at Grandfather Mountain, Land of Oz on Beech Mountain, Country Fair and Tweetsie Railroad, Hillbilly World, standing on The Blowing Rock, or figuring out the puzzling natural phenomena at Mystery Hill.

All are experiences to write home about. And if you're one who enjoys recording events for posterity, take along your movie equipment; and shutterbugs, take your cameras, too, you'll be glad you did!

(Phone sponsor or C. of C. to confirm information. If no area code is shown, use 704.)

YEAR-ROUND OR SEASONAL

BLUE RIDGE PARKWAY — The Brown Mountain Lights Phenomenon. (Milepost 310). Best seen from Lost Cove, Cliff's View, Wiseman's View, Jonas Ridge. The lights appear like large stars traveling erratically along the mountain, popping and fading. More abundant when the atmosphere is very clear and humidity low, shortly after dark. In winter, lights increase in number shortly before dawn — intriguing!

BRISTOL, TENN. — Bristol Caverns. A majestic, fantastic, awesome experience into another world. Stalagmites and stalactites narrower than straws and wider than tree trunks, together with impressive, massive columns in cavernous "rooms." Underground River reflects astonishing formations. Guided tours. The largest in the Smoky Mountain Region. Picnicking. Seven days a week, 8:00 a.m. — 8:00 p.m. summer; 8:00 a.m. — 6:00 p.m. winter. Closed for church worship Sunday mornings. (615) 764-4656.

LAUREL SPRINGS, N.C. — Upper Mountain Experiment Station. 13 mi. SW of Sparta on NC 88. Research is conducted on crops and animals. Visitors welcome. (919) 982-2501.

LINVILLE, N.C. — Linville Caverns. An inside-the-mountain adventure (Humpback Mountain). Underground stone wonders carved out of the hard earth core: Natural Bridge, Frozen Waterfall, Franciscan Monk and others. Trout swim in underground stream. Picnicking in wooded areas, fireplace grills and firewood. Gift Shop features minerals and unusual stones as well as native handcrafts. Seven days a week. Guides. 7:00 a.m. to dark. Always comfortable temperature. 756-4171.

OLD FORT, N.C. — Andrews Geyser. A 200-foot "Old Faithful" west of Old Fort. Right on old US 70W approximately three miles, then right turn on Mill Creek Road for about three miles to Geyser on left. To complete round trip continue in same direction which comes out to Ridgecrest on I-40. Geyser, surrounded by a park with picnic tables, presents an impressive show.

MARCH

LINVILLE, N.C. — Grandfather Mountain. US 221. Elevation 6000 feet. Spectacular, hairpin-curving road to top of 5000-acre recreation area. Over one billion years old; some of the oldest rock formations in the world. Visitor Center at summit includes convention hall, gift and souvenir shop, snack bar, mineral and flower exhibits, rainbow, brook and brown trout aquarium, U.S. Weather Bureau Station. Mile-high Swinging Bridge for views up to 100 miles. Split Rock, natural geologic wonder. Bear family in three-acre environmental habitat. Marvellous hiking areas. (See Ch. 12.) Woodsy picnic areas at lovely overlooks.

Calendar through November 15. Daily 8 a.m. - 7 p.m.

May 1-25 — Blooming of Lady Slipper, Vaseyi and Trillium.

May, first Sat. and Sun. — Hang Gliding Championship.

May 24-June 20 — Blooming of Laurel, Flame Azalea and Red Rhododendron.

June, last Sunday — "Singing on the Mountain".

June-November — Hang gliding exhibitions.

July, second weekend — Highland Games and Gathering of Scottish Clans (See Ch. 54.)

July 1-15 — Blooming of White Rhododendron.

August, third weekend — Camera Clinic.

September, fourth weekend — Thursday thru Sunday. Masters of Hang Gliding.

October 5-25 — Pageant of autumn foliage. Best views of Grandfather are from Foscoe, Boone and Blowing Rock, revealing the black, bare rock forming the profile of a venerable man's face, either from left to right or right to left. 733-2800.

APRIL
BLOWING ROCK, N.C. — The Blowing Rock. Oldest North Carolina attraction. Vast breathtaking panorama (overlooking John's River Gorge). Many legends exist about this overhanging shelf but it's true that light objects thrown off The Rock are returned by the strong prevailing up-current winds, even causing snow to fall upside down. Observation tower, gardens, gazebos and Visitor's Center make for a worthwhile visit. Children under six free. Open through October. 295-3615.

BLOWING ROCK, N.C. — Mystery Hill. Museum of natural phenomena in rustic, pioneer, mountain atmosphere. For lovers of mystifying facts, like reversing the law of gravity. Visitors are encouraged to experiment. Open through October.

MAY
BLOWING ROCK, N.C. — Country Fair. At meadow adjacent to *Tweetsie* Railroad. Kiddie rides, Ferris wheel, small roller coaster, merry-go-round, helicopter rides, miniature golf, working craftsmen, livery stables. 3 p.m. to 11 p.m. Open through October. 264-7234.

JUNE
BANNER ELK, N.C. — Land of Oz theme park. Top of Beech Mountain, one mile high. Movie comes alive; stroll Yellow Brick Road and meet Dorothy, Cowardly Lion, Scarecrow and Tinman. Ride 4000 feet high on a gondola and take a thrilling flight in a colorful, giant balloon with a 360-degree panoramic view of unsurpassed mountain scenery. Nature trails. At Beech Tree Village main lift entrance of Oz, relax on the village green or watch craftsmen leather crafting, woodworking, glass-blowing. Picnicking. Loads to do — spend the whole day! Open through Labor Day. 295-2231.

BLOWING ROCK, N.C. — Tweetsie Railroad theme park (also nighttime entertainment). Three-mile ride on antique coaches; full-size steam locomotives originally pulled freight and passenger cars between Boone and Johnson City, Tenn. on the East Tennessee & Western North Carolina Railroad. A replica of an 1890 western town, *Tweetsie* Palace "saloon," trip to Gold Mine in the Sky by chair lift and to Mice Mine No. 9. Also Deer Park, a petting zoo of deer and goats. Working craftsmen. Seven days a week up to Labor Day, after that on a reduced schedule through Nov. 264-8630 or 906l.

HAMPTON, TENN. — Hillbilly World. 10,000 acres of fun, relaxation, 30 rides and shows, over 100 wild animals, scenic 7-mile train ride; camping, picnicking, swimming, fishing. Open through October. (615) 725-2051.

Hugh Morton

11   the great outdoors

Whether you're vacationing here, studying here, thinking of moving here, considering retiring here, or simply passing through. . .and you enjoy the simple pleasures of outdoor living, a continual changing background of fantastic 3-D scenic, season-changing colors, an opportunity to examine and observe an amazing variety of wildflowers, plants, butterflies, birds, mushrooms, salamanders and other creatures, — and recreation activities appeal to you. . . this is the chapter that will give you some direction for experiencing surprising mountain-top adventures. What's more, a number of the recreation facilities and activities listed are open all year in some areas of the Blue Ridge Parkway, national and state forests and parks, Tennessee Valley Authority (TVA) Lakes and along the Appalachian Trail. Many of these recreational areas offer waterskiing, boating, canoeing, fishing, swimming, camping, conservation hunting, horseback riding, and the classic beauty of waterfalls. All of them offer hiking, picnicking, hunting with a camera, geological wonders, and the freedom of just resting! For a release from tension, for getting in harmony with yourself and others, nature is just what the doctor ordered — a clockface without hands, a suspension in space, — the quietness, glory and grandeur of the Absolute, a oneness with what was here, is here now, and forever will be here. As the popular songhit so aptly puts it,

"The rhythm of life is a powerful beat,
With a tingle in your fingers and a tingle in your feet."

A good place to sample a nature experience upon one of the most unique, scenic drives in the world *sans* billboards, telephone poles, pollution, noise and commercial vehicles is the *Blue Ridge Parkway,* 469 toll-free miles of captivating scenery. No ordinary road, it lies along a major migration route for birds — 100 different species have been counted during early spring. The Parkway is an outdoor classroom for the mountain culture, of weathered cabins and barns, cattle and sheep roaming the grassy slopes and meadows, split rail fences, and typical mountain farms. Frequent overlooks and wayside exhibits help to explain it all: the people, the mountains, the forests, the flowers, plants and wildlife. Picnic spots appear often and many include self-guided trails. The unspoken message is, "Come, enjoy, we love ya!" From June through Labor Day, Visitor Centers are welcoming places well stocked with information about their special areas, handcraft demonstrations and sales, as well as exhibits from running a water-powered gristmill to making sorghum molasses.

For another kind of wide-eyed, mind-expanding experience, the three national forests: Cherokee in Tennessee, Jefferson in Virginia, and Pisgah in North Carolina, totaling almost two million acres (isn't that staggering?) with mile-high mountains, flashing cataracting waterfalls, towering forests, rushing, meandering streams and rivers offer an effective antidote to the doldrums. For family togetherness, you can't beat camping out under the stars, listening to the sounds of Mother Nature, the murmured whispering of trees, the nocturnal symphony of the insects and frogs and other critters, each one sounding off his own note. . . echoing and reechoing. . . Add to this the guided hikes, the delightful, informal naturalist day programs as well as sing-a-longs around the evening campfire. And considering the abundant opportunities and facilities for sportspeople, that boggle the mind, there's no disputing the fact that America's parks are one of its prized natural resources!!

If you're a seasoned, hardy backpacking hiker and are eager to try the Appalachian Trail, there are 250 miles in this territory of the highest, most rugged hiking of the whole Appalachian Trail. It's well marked with white paint blazes and as you wend your way you can look up and sing:

> "I will lift up mine eyes unto the mountains,
> From whence shall my help come?
> My help cometh from Jehovah,
> Who made heaven and earth."
> Psalm 121

Chapter 12 lists the entrance points to this area.

In Ole Virginny there's a state park with a very strange name, **Hungry Mother State Park,** which includes Hungry Mother Lake and Hungry Mother Creek. In case you're wondering, the unusual name stems from the legend of the mother, Molly Marley, who while fleeing an Indian raiders' base with her young child, succumbed after living on berries for days. The youngster, unable to rouse his mother, wandered away and finally reached some people; all he could say was "Hungry — Mother!" That ends the sad part of the tale. The best part is what awaits you here at the 2180-acre, all-year camping-hiking-fishing-horseback-riding-picnicking recreation area. There is an abundance of opportunity for exploring on your own. (Boat rentals, concession stands, swimming beach and bathhouse are open from Memorial Day to Labor Day.)

If you have a preference for Swiss Alpine scenery, or have never been to Switzerland, there's no better place to come than to the **Mount Rogers National Recreation Area** of the **Jefferson National Forest,** stretched across southwest Virginia. There's a strong resemblance to Switzerland — pastoral "symphonies" of peaceful well-rounded green meadows dotted with placid cattle and sheep quietly grazing. Mount Rogers, 5729 feet, the highest point in the state with a commanding view of the 154,000-acre Swiss Alpine setting, offers five campgrounds with a variety of facilities for overnight stays or day outings. For a scenic drive, Whitetop Mountain, Virginia's second highest peak with a northern hardwood forest, looks out on a superb three-state view. A campfire theater features varied naturalist programs all summer. This area also has a Chapel of the Hills, Feathercamp Tower, two fish hatcheries, and a horse livery.

Grayson Highlands State Park, reached from US 58 near Volney, is the latest development of the **Jefferson National Forest.** During the heavy fall deer-hunting season special hunter access roads and special hunter camps are open — how about that?!! If you get a Mount Rogers Recreation Area Map, there are some outstanding scenic drives outlined.

For a change of pace — a wild rugged challenge — you may like to enter the primitive **Linville Gorge Wilderness,** 7600 acres in Pisgah National Forest (entry by permit only), one of the few truly "nature in the raw" experiences. Unusual and strange rock formations, precipices, craggy slopes, steep cliffs and inclines with sheer drops of more than 600 feet, fissures resulting both from centuries of weathering and the carving of the Linville River all hold a "cliff-hanging" fascination for the viewer. Just to be a name-dropper, there's Hawksbill Peak, Sitting Bear, Table Rock — resembling a great, giant fortress — and the Chimneys — jutting spires and overhanging cliff shelves — all overlooking the 12-mile chasm of "gorgeous" Gorge!!! Surrounded by the Linville mountains on the east side and Jonas Ridge on the west side, the river cascades from the mountain top forming the Upper Falls, then over a smooth 12-foot rock shelf creating the Lower Falls, and finally, a 90-foot drop into deep pools. All this is a more than 2000-foot swift, spectacular descent of river over massive boulders and other huge rocky obstructions, an awesome sight that will hold you motionless, transfixed, unable to look away! This is a forest of evergreens, 30-foot high rhododendron bushes, and rare plant and vine species found nowhere else in eastern United States, some growing right out of rock. For hikers and backpackers of the rock-climbing variety, there is a wide assortment of climbs (see Chapter 13) for the beginner, intermediate and advanced. There's excellent trout fishing, of course, and bear hunting is allowed in season.

Along the North Carolina-Tennessee line, 10 miles south of Roan Mountain, Tenn., on Tennessee 143 and 13 miles north of Bakersville, N.C., on NC 261, lie perhaps two of the greatest attractions of the **Pisgah National Forest, N.C.** and **Cherokee National Forest, Tenn.**: one, the incredible **Roan,** 6286-foot-high-mountain and two, its 20,000-acre **Roan Mountain State Park.** If you've never seen a complete rainbow, this is the place to catch this rare sight. The rhododendron specimens on this mountain are to be found nowhere else in the world. It's about an hour and a half drive to the 600 acres of the "world's largest Rhododendron Gardens" on the Roan Bald, which attract visitors from around the world. Mounds and banks of crimson, lavender and deep purple of the Catawbiense Rhododendron are perfect subjects for an extraordinary, brilliant extravaganza "painting," so bring along your camera. Twin-Springs Recreation Area is about six miles from the Gardens on Tenn. 143. The enormous variety of wildflowers, like manna sprinkling the rich green of the grass, is probably unmatched anywhere. The skillful landscape architecture maintains an aesthetically pleasing relationship of firs and other trees, natural grasses and wildflowers. (See Chapters 32 and 33.)

Another oddity to be seen is the large number of tiny hummingbirds gathering around springs and sheltered hollows. Rockhounds will delight in prospecting for epidote, unakite, feldspar, quartzite, and other mineral specimens. A wealth of ferns, lichens, clubmosses and mushrooms will enchant naturalists. And, in addition to all the sports activities for hikers, campers, and fishermen, there are now winter sports.

Do you know where the Great Lakes of the South are? Answer: Tennessee — a state that has it all together at the favorite recreation attractions created by the Tennessee Valley Authority, the **TVA Lakes.** Excitement as well as relaxing pleasures are yours at these man-made lakes which run from wide open stretches of lowland lakes and rugged, winding shorelines to rising forested mountain slopes. State and local governments have developed these public recreation areas for water skiing, canoeing, sailing, yachting, paddleboating, and motor-boating. There are opportunities to enter sailboat regattas, speedboat races, and many other boating activities of interest locally, regionally and even nationally. Boat docks and launching ramps are numerous in this fisherman's Garden of Eden: early fall and spring are best for largemouth, smallmouth, white and spotted bass, walleye, sauger, crappie, sunfish, trout, searun striped bass and muskellunge. Hunting, swimming, hiking around the lakes and "in the mountain greenery where God painted the scenery," camping and lodge-overnight facilities, and loads of history await you here.

Listed below is just a mere sampling of the fabulous recreational facilities in this area that should lead you to explore on your own and to do your own thing.

ABINGDON, VA. — Spring Creek Dock, South Holston Lake. Route 5. Gas, food, fishing.

ABINGDON, VA. — Washington County Park, South Holston Lake. Route 1. Launching ramp, fishing, swimming, tent and trailer camping.

ABINGDON, VA. — Wheeler's Dock, South Holston Lake. Route 1. Launching ramp, gas, food, lodging, fishing, swimming, trailer camping. (703) 628-2850

ABINGDON, VA. — Wolf Creek Boat Dock, South Holston Lake, Route 1. Launching ramp, gas, food, fishing.

BAKERSVILLE, N.C. — Roan Mountain. 600-acre "world's largest rhododendron gardens."

BLOWING ROCK, N.C. — Municipal Park, Main St. Tennis, horseshoes, summer supervised programs, swings, slides, picnicking, grills, porch chairs facing Main Street to relax in while "people watching."

BLUE RIDGE PARKWAY, N.C. — Doughton Park. (Milepost 241.1) 6000 acres. Bluff Mountain (central highpoint) and surrounding area are covered with meadows of clover and red-top; famous view of Basin Cove. Hiking trails, fishing, camping, trailer sites, forest type picnic grounds, "heath garden" of mountain laurel, rhododendron, leucothoe, blueberry, huckleberry and menziesia. Naturalist walks and talks, as well as food and souvenir shop, lodging, car service. Moonshine Still Exhibit and Caudill Cabin Exhibit.

BLUE RIDGE PARKWAY, N.C. — E. B. Jeffress Park. (Milepost 272) 600 acres. 3570-foot elevation. Hiking trails — one leads to Falls Creek Cascades, unusually beautiful, self-guiding tour. Oak and hickory forest with lush growth of rhododendron and mountain laurel. Picnicking, water fountain, rest rooms.

BLUE RIDGE PARKWAY, N.C. — Cone Memorial Park. (Milepost 294.1) 3517 acres, 25 miles of hiking trails, bridle paths and carriage roads passing through forests of yellow poplar, huge hemlocks and a wider variety of trees and shrubs than any other recreation area on the Parkway. Parkway Craft Center houses Pioneer Museum, craft demonstrations. Naturalist programs. Bass Lake fishing, 22 acres. Trout Lake fishing, 16 acres. Horse-drawn carriage rides. 295-7938.

BLUE RIDGE PARKWAY, N.C. — Price Memorial Park. (Milepost 297.1) 47-acre trout-stocked, man-made lake. Camping, picnicking, hiking, naturalist programs in outdoor amphitheatre. Rowboating and canoeing (canoe rentals). A wonderful resting place. 963-5911.

BLUE RIDGE PARKWAY, N.C. — Linville Falls Recreation Area. (Milepost 316.4) 440 acres. Upper and Lower Falls, magnificent cascades of spiraling falls. An abundance of rare species of plant life by the river banks. Camping, picnicking, hiking, fishing and naturalist programs in amphitheatre.

BLUE RIDGE PARKWAY, N.C. — Crabtree Meadows Recreation Area. (Milepost 339.5) 253 acres. Flowering crab blooms each May followed by lush carpets of wildflowers. Crabtree Falls is greatest attraction, reached by path from picnic grounds. Hiking, naturalist programs, amphitheatre, trailer camp, camp grounds, food, gift shop, coffee shop and service station.

BLUE RIDGE PARKWAY, N.C. — View of Black Mountain Range. (Milepost 342.2)

6000-foot average elevation. Called "Black" because of dark green Fraser fir and red spruce covering slopes. Highest mountain range in East; forms hook. Canadian type climate. State highway from Parkway to summit. From here you see the eastern arm which is the highest.

BLUE RIDGE PARKWAY, N.C. — Mount Mitchell State Park.(Milepost 349.9)(Closed in winter). 1224 acres, 6684-foot peak. Climate, plants, animals similar to Canada. Observation tower, restaurant, lodge. Picnicking, hiking, camping, naturalist programs, natural history museum, craft shop. 675-4611.

BLUE RIDGE PARKWAY, N.C. — Craggy Mountain Scenic Area. (Milepost 363-369.6) 850 acres. Carter Creek Falls. Spectacular wildflower variety area, especially beautiful in May and June. Blackberry blossoms in June, easy pickin' no barbs. Abundant purple Catawba Rhododendron. Lovely hiking trails with pale green lichens and mosses looking like tiny trees. Picnicking, drinking fountains, rest rooms.

BLUE RIDGE PARKWAY, N.C. — Graybeard Mountain View. (Milepost 363.6) Peak is 5365 feet. First or last closeup view of Blue Ridge. 200-year-old forest of yellow birch, yellow buckeye, and beech of stunted growth known as Peach Orchard. Lovely overlook.

BLUE RIDGE PARKWAY, N.C. — Craggy Dome View. (Milepost 364.1) Masses of rhododendron covered slopes in full bloom mid-June.

BLUE RIDGE PARKWAY, N.C. — Pinnacle Gap View. (Milepost 364.6) Visitor Center contains exhibits on natural heath gardens, mountain "balds" and wildflowers. Self-guiding nature trails and rather rough hikes up the Pinnacle.

BLUE RIDGE PARKWAY, N.C. — Bee Tree Gap. (Milepost 367.7) 4769-foot elevation. Entrance to Craggy Gardens Picnic Grounds at Bee Tree Creek.

BLUFF CITY, TENN. — Underwood Park. Camping, swimming, picnicking.

BOONE, N.C. — Seven Devils. Lake memberships available. Boating, fishing, swimming, sailing.

BOONE, N.C. — The Daniel Boone Park. 30 acres (opposite *Horn in the West* grounds). Bicycle and hiking trails, flowering shrubs and trees, children's wading pool.

BOONE, N.C. — Watauga County Parks and Recreation Commission, 609 E. King Street. Well-rounded year-round program: hobby classes, ballet, tap dancing, clogging, Karate, baton, golf and tennis clinics, swimming at the Swimming Pool Complex with children's tot lot, four tennis courts and softball court. Summer: Cove Creek, Mabel, Parkway Schools and Boone Playground (latter next to *Horn in the West* has picnic area), have well-supervised programs concentrating on a variety of themes such as hobbies and talents of each child, arts and crafts, games, puppet shows, movies, dog shows, children's plays and talent shows. Individual and team sports winding up with a big bang at the annual tournament at end of July. Winners of local tournaments meet at Optimist Park for the Field Day in Aug. when awards are made. 264-9511,8522.

BOONE, N.C. — Views from the Top. Strenuous hiking, rough terrain. **Rich Mountain,** 4700-foot elevation, firetower. **Howard's Knob,** 4420-foot elevation (via Cherry St.). North side to Grandfather, Table Rock, Hawksbill, "Snake" and "Baldy" peaks; east is

Bushy Mountain. This is the best view of Boone Valley and surroundings. **Tater Hill Park,** 5372 feet, east of Rich Mountain. View to Boone, Vilas, and Cove Creek across to scenic triangle of Grandfather, Beech and Roan as well as Blowing Rock and Linville. (Access Howard's Creek Rd. off NC 194).

BRISTOL, TENN. — Friendship Dock. South Holston Lake. Route 4. Launching ramp, gas, food, lodging, camping, fishing, swimming.

BRISTOL, TENN. — Jacobs Creek Recreation Area. 12 miles southeast, 2 miles northeast on Forest Service Road 32. Cherokee National Forest. Eastern shore South Holston Lake. Launching ramp, camping, fishing, hiking, picnicking.

BRISTOL, TENN. — Lakeview Boat Dock. South Holston Lake. Route 4. Launching ramp, gas, food, lodging, fishing.

BRISTOL, TENN. — Laurel Yacht Club. South Holston Lake. Route 4. Launching ramp, gas, food, lodging, fishing.

BRISTOL, TENN. — Little Oak Mountain Recreation Area. S. Holston Lake. Route 4.

BRISTOL, TENN. — Painter Creek Boat Dock. South Holston Lake. Route 4. Launching ramp, gas, food, lodging, fishing.

BRISTOL, TENN. — Steele Creek Park. 3 miles west of business district. 1200 acres. Wilderness area. Swim and golf memberships, 9-hole championship course. Boating, paddle boats. Picnicking. One-half mile train ride, lodge rentals, naturalist programs.

BRISTOL, TENN. — Sullivan County Park. South Holston Lake. Route 4. Launching ramp, camping, fishing.

BUSICK, N.C. — Black Mountain. NC 30, 10 miles northwest of Marion. Pisgah National Forest. 47 camping units. Fishing-hiker's paradise. 5.5-mile trail to summit of Mount Mitchell. Waterfalls, naturalist programs, amphitheatre.

BUSICK, N.C. — Carolina Hemlock Campground. 4 miles north on NC 80. Pisgah National Forest. Camping, fishing, hiking, picnicking, swimming, rockhounding in old mica mines.

BUTLER, TENN. — Gregg's Dock. Watauga Lake (Watauga River). Route 1. Launching ramp, gas, food, lodging, fishing.

BUTLER, TENN. — Hank's Boat Dock. Watauga Lake (Watauga River). Route 2. Launching ramp, gas, food, lodging, fishing.

BUTLER, TENN. — Midway Dock. Watauga Lake (Watauga River). Route 1. Launching ramp, gas, food, camping, fishing.

BUTLER, TENN. — Sink Mountain Recreation Area. Watauga Lake. Tenn. 67.

BUTLER, TENN. — Walt's Boat Dock. Watauga Lake. Tenn. 67. Launching ramp, gas, food, lodging, fishing, tent and trailer camping.

DAMASCUS, VA. — Backbone Rock Recreation Area. Cherokee National Forest. Unusual geological formation. Camping, fishing, hiking, picnicking, hunting.

DAMASCUS, VA. — Backbone Rock Wayside Park. Natural stone bridge. Easy short hike up stone steps crossing Backbone Rock, descending to wayside picnic area by babbling brook.

DAMASCUS, VA. — Bear Tree Campground. 6 miles northeast on US 58, left on Forest Service Road 837. Mt. Rogers National Recreation Area. 200 family units. Beaver ponds, fishing and lots of wonderful hiking paths.

DAMASCUS, VA. — White Top Mountain. 5344-foot elevation. East on US 58 approximately 14 miles, left on Va. 600. Virginia's second highest peak; longest car road to a mountain summit. Spectacular views of North Carolina, Virginia and Tennessee. Camping, picnicking, hiking, horseback riding.

EDGEMONT, N.C. — Mortimer Recreation Area. Forest Service Road 464. Pisgah National Forest. Camping, fishing, hiking, picnicking, swimming.

ELIZABETHTON, TENN. — Low Gap Recreation Area. 5 miles north on Tenn. 91, left on Forest Service Road 202. Cherokee National Forest. Camping, hiking, picnicking.

ERWIN, TENN. — Limestone Cove Recreation Area. Tenn. 107. Cherokee National Forest. Camping, hiking, hunting, picnicking.

ERWIN, TENN. — Rock Creek Recreation Area. Approximately 4 miles east of US 19W on Forest Service Road 30. Cherokee National Forest. Boating, camping, car tours, hiking, nature talks, picnicking.

GALAX, VA. — Grayson Highlands State Park. Mount Rogers National Recreation Area. Camping, hiking, picnicking, summer crafts center, authentic mountain cabin.

GALAX, VA. — Public Park. 18 acres. Five lighted tennis courts, baseball and football stadium with seating for 1500.

HAMPTON, TENN. — Carden's Bluff Campground. Watauga Lake. Boat dock, tent and trailer camping, fishing, hiking, nature talks, swimming.

HAMPTON, TENN. — Dennis Cove Recreation Area. 8 miles southeast on Forest Service Road 50. Cherokee National Forest. Camping, fishing, hiking, picnicking, swimming.

HAMPTON, TENN. — Doe River Gorge Recreation Area. 2 miles southeast on Tenn. 19E. Cherokee National Forest. Camping, fishing, hiking, hunting, swimming.

HAMPTON, TENN. — Fish Springs Dock. Watauga Lake. Route 2. Launching ramp, fishing, hiking, tent and trailer camping.

HAMPTON, TENN. — Lakeshore Dock. Watauga Lake. Route 2. Launching ramp, gas, food, lodging, hiking, swimming.

HAMPTON, TENN. — Lake View Park. Cherokee National Forest. 3 miles east of Hampton. Camping, fishing, hiking, hunting, swimming.

HAMPTON, TENN. — Shook Branch Recreation Area. Watauga Lake. US 321.

HAMPTON, TENN. — Watauga Point Recreation Area. Watauga Lake. Route 2. Fishing, hiking, picnicking, swimming.

HICKORY, N.C. — Lake Hickory. West on N.C. 18. Fishing, sailing, swimming, motorboating.

HICKORY, N.C. — Lake Rhodhiss. North on NC 127. Fishing, sailing, swimming, motorboating.

HICKORY, N.C. — Recreation Department, 1515 12th St. Drive, NW. A diversified recreation program for adults and children at seven parks throughout the city. Picnic, playground and ballfield facilities, basketball. Spray, wading and swimming pools, tennis courts and recreation buildings. 322-7046.

JEFFERSON, N.C. — Mount Jefferson State Park. 4900-foot elevation. Panoramic views of tri-state mountain corner, Grandfather and Pilot Mountains. Hiking, picnicking.

JOHNSON CITY, TENN. — Knob's Creek Dock. Boone Lake. Route 4. Launching ramp, gas, food, lodging, fishing, hiking.

JONESBORO, TENN. — Boone Yacht Club. Boone Lake. Route 4. Launching ramp, gas, food, fishing.

JONESBORO, TENN. — Boone's Creek Marina. Boone Lake. Route 4. Launching ramp, gas, food, fishing, hiking.

JONESBORO, TENN. — Jay's Boat Dock. Boone Lake. Route 4. Launching ramp, gas, food, fishing, hiking.

JONESBORO, TENN. — Rockingham Boat Dock. Boone Lake. Route 4. Launching ramp, gas, food, lodging, fishing.

LINVILLE, N.C. — Grandfather Mountain. 6000-foot elevation. (See Ch. 10)

LINVILLE, N.C. — Linville Gorge Wilderness. 7600 acres. Twelve-mile long gash of solid rock, one of America's unspoiled, scenic, rugged, primitive gorges. Rare plant species blooming together and combination of four native rhododendron species. Eastern rim of gorge may be viewed from a point accessible by car. Wiseman's view on western rim is breathtaking. Also, mysterious Brown Mountain lights may be seen from here. Backpacking, trout and bass fishing, hiking on challenging trails, hunting for bear, deer, raccoon, ruffed grouse, squirrel. Picnicking. Permit required for entry. 652-4841.

MARION, VA. — Hungry Mother State Park. 3 miles north on VA. 16, Exit 16 from I-81. 3270-foot elevation. 2180 acres. Nature Center at base of Molly's Knob. Sandy beaches along six-mile shoreline of 108-acre lake with bass and crappie fishing. 12 miles of hiking trails. Paddle boat, camping, swimming, boating. Furnished cabins for six with electricity, fireplaces. Nature study with naturalists. Horseback riding. Evening programs. Open all year. Swimming beach, bathhouse, restaurant, boat rentals and concession stands open from Memorial Day to Labor Day. (703) 783-3422.

MARION, VA. — Mount Rogers National Recreation Area of Jefferson National Forest. Mount Rogers 5729-foot elevation.

MORGANTON, N.C. — Optimist Park. 13 miles north of NC 181. On Steel Creek. Fishing, picnicking, swimming.

MORGANTON, N.C. — Canal Bridge Access Area. West on NC 126. Lake James, south side. Boating, fishing.

MORGANTON, N.C. — Mimosa Boat Dock. Lake James, south side. Boating, fishing.

MORGANTON, N.C. — White Creek Access Area. Lake James, north end. Boating, fishing.

N. WILKESBORO, N.C. — W. Kerr Scott Reservoir. (1470 acres, 55-mile shoreline.)

Bandits Roost Park. Launching ramp, swimming, tent and trailer camping, picnicking.
Bandits Roost Public Service Area. Lanching ramp, restaurant, snack bar, marina.
Boomer Road Park. Launching ramp, swimming, picnicking.
Damsite Park. Launching ramp, picnicking.
Goshen Road Access. Launching ramp.
Marley's Ford Access. Launching ramp, picnicking.
Smitheys Creek Park. Launching ramp, swimming, tent and trailer camping, picnicking
Tailwater Access Area. Fishing pier.
Warrior Creek Park. Launching ramp, swimming, tent and trailer camping, picnicking.

PINEY FLATS, TENN. — Davis' Dock. Boone Lake. Route 2. Launching ramp, gas, food, fishing.

PINEY FLATS, TENN. — Sportsman's Dock. Boone Lake. Route 1. Launching ramp, gas, food, fishing.

PINEY FLATS, TENN. — Tri-Cities Boat Dock. Boone Lake. Route 1. Launching ramp, gas, food, fishing.

ROAN MOUNTAIN, TENN. — Roan Mountain State Park. 1492 acres. Tenn. 143 Camping, hiking, picnicking, swimming, skiing.

ROARING GAP, N.C. — Stone Mountain State Park. 2109 acres. 5 miles west on US 21. Has 600-foot granite mass with 3-mile circumference at base. Hiking, great rockclimbing, nature study. Undeveloped. (919) 957-8185.

SUGAR GROVE, VA. — Raccoon Branch Campground, 3 miles south on Va. 16, I-81, Exit 16. Mount Rogers National Recreation Area, Jefferson National Forest. Camping year-round. Virginia Highlands Horse Trail — longest horse trail in the state. Trout fishing. Two-mile trail to Dickey Knob with scenic view of Rye Valley.

TROUTDALE, VA. — Grindstone Campground. 6 miles west on Va. 603. At foot of Mount Rogers. Late spring through fall. 108 family units, hot showers. Campfire theater. Trail to summit. Trout fishing. Nearest to Fairwoods Craft Center and livery stable. Craft Center open daily 9 a.m. — 6 p.m.

TROUTDALE, VA. — Hurricane Campground. Mount Rogers National Recreation Area. Late spring through fall. 34 family units in basin of deep valley. Showers. Campfire theater. Hiking.

VOLNEY, VA. — Grayson Highlands State Park. West on U.S. 58. Jefferson National Forest. Fishing, hiking, nature talks, picnicking.

12

these boots

were made

for walkin'

When the urge to take a hike comes over you, do you lie down until the feeling goes away? If you do, you're bound to realize, while in the supine position, that you may be missing out on some of the most exhilarating adventures in life — which incidentally, are free!

True, you may not be bear-lunged, or goat-footed, or agile-bodied, and true, even a short jaunt may seem to be nothing short of a major expedition up Mt. McKinley. But when you're on a hiking trail surrounded by the great out-of-doors, attentive to woodland messages, rest assured your awareness of nature will be heightened. It will seem as though the clock stood still — no beginning or ending to time — as though you're living in eternity embraced by the cathedral hush of the forest. There's freedom to wholly participate in the wonder of a blade of grass, to watch the dew turn into glistening rough gems, to feel the differences among leaves — every leaf has a structure and beauty of its own — to nuzzle a flower for a fragrant whiff, to watch a crawling bug. There'll be time to listen to a birdcall or admire a butterfly cavorting merrily, to gaze at a cloud, or simply to look up at the expanse of azure sky and to soak in the gentle sounds and tempo of nature from an imaginatively placed tree stump. The challenge of a homespun nature walk and the grandeur of these highlands should relieve you of tiredness, irritability and boredom and raise your spirits heavenward. If you're up early, you'll appreciate the morning come over the mountain peaks, slowly descending into the valley dispelling mists from streams and rivers. It will be an unfoldment — a basking in inner freedom, feeling the pulse of solitude...

And now for a sample listing of hikes — additional ones are mentioned in Ch. 11 — which gives you a wide choice from the very easy to the more strenuous treks. And for the really experienced, hardy hiker, there's also a number of entrance points to the famous Maine-to-Georgia Appalachian Trail, steeped in early American history. The Appalachian Mountain Club has conveniently constructed campsites about 15 miles apart to provide accommodations for the weary traveler. Incidentally, you'll find the most enjoyable gait — not too fast nor too slow — is a three-mile-an-hour steady, rhythmical stride. And by placing one foot *directly* in front of the other, oddly enough, you'll cover more ground, save steps, and be less tired.

In any event, it's good advice to take at least a five-minute rest period each hour of hiking, especially if you're breathing hard. If you're hiking for more than a day, start moving the next day even if your muscles seem stiff and you'll soon be in shape again.

Watch it! You're going to wind up feeling you have more bounce to the ounce.

HIKING TRAILS

BLUE RIDGE PARKWAY MILEPOSTS

217.5 — Cumberland Knob Recreation Area. Casual hiker trails, longer one at Gulley Creek.

238.5 — Cedar Ridge. Long and strenuous, about 4 miles.

241 — Bluff Ridge. Long, somewhat strenuous, approximately 5 miles.

241 — Fodder Stack Mountain Trail. One mile hike, at times steep.

243.4 — Alligator Back Trail. To top of Bluff Mountain, not strenuous, great views!

243.5 — Grassy Gap Fire Road. Easy, short route to Cove Creek.

244.7 — Flat Rock Ridge Trail. Long, about 5 miles. Other Doughton Park trails around camp ground, lodge and dining room plus inviting walks through grasslands with many rewarding views.

260.6 — Jumpin'-Off Rocks. Short round trip trail through woodlands.

272 — E. B. Jeffress Park. Self-guiding, casual nature trail to Cascades, a 30-minute round trip to beautiful waterfalls returning through an evergreen maze of rhododendron and mountain laurel. Also **Tompkins Knob,** south one-half mile to Jesse Brown Cabins; easy walk on floor of pine needles to former site of Cool Spring Baptist Church.

294 — Moses H. Cone Memorial Park
Flat Top Mountain Road. Through fields and forests, easy to moderate 2.25 miles; half-way up is family cemetery, magnificient view. **Rich Mountain Road.** Moderate to strenuous 4 miles, three-hour round trip. **Bass Lake Trail.** Through old orchards and fir forests around shoreline of lake. **Trout Lake Trail.** Moderately strenuous 3.5 miles; very picturesque. **Craftsman's Trail.** Self-guiding, short, cool and labeled; leads from front of Craft Center.

295.9 — 297.2 Julian Price Memorial Park
295.9 — Sims Pond Loop. Moderate two-mile, two-hour walk. Lovely views and variety of scenery.

296.7 — Price Lake Loop Trail. 2.3 miles, easy, flat ground walk.

297.2 — Boone Fork Loop Trail. Fairly strenuous 4.9 miles, interesting terrain.

297.2 — Green Knob Loop Trail. Moderate 2.4 miles, 2½ hours.

305.2 — Beacon Heights Trail. Short, moderate climb. Spectacular view of Grandfather Mountain.

308.1 — Flat Rock Trail. Self-guiding 40-minute trail. Very scenic.

316.5 — Linville Falls Trail. Lovely walk to view of Upper Falls.

316.5 — Linville Gorge Wilderness, entry by permit only. For experienced hikers. Fantastic trails and overnight camping. For permit write P. O. Box 519, Marion, N. C. 28752.

317 — Linville Falls Trail. To unusual views of Lower Falls. In spring the flowers form "hanging gardens." Trail continues to Erwins View along a "heath garden" at the rim of the gorge composed of blueberry, leucothoe, rhododendron, sand-myrtle and others.

320.8 — Chestoa View Overlook. Easy ¾-mile hiking with views of North Cove Valley and Table Rock.

337.2 — Deerlick Gap Overlook. Two-mile easy trail connects with Three Knob Overlook.

339.5 — Crabtree Falls Trail. Moderate 3-mile lovely trail.

355.4 — NC 128 to Mt. Mitchell State Park, interesting trails. **Tower to Mt. Craig.** 1.5 miles. **Mt. Craig to Big Tom,** ⅛-mile. **Big Tom to Balsam Cone,** 1 mile. **Balsam Cone to Cattail Peak,** ½-mile. **Tower to Camp Alice,** 2 miles.

363.4 — Trail to Craggy Pinnacle. From Craggy Dome Overlook. Short, easy trail with outstanding views.

369.6 — Craggy Gardens. Self-guiding trails; one leads to Craggy Flats. Mid-June outstanding purple rhododendron.

BLOWING ROCK, N.C. — Nature Excursions. Appalachian Outfitters, US 321. Trail hiking, rock climbing, backpacking, equipment. 295-3123.

BOONE, N.C. — Appalachian Nature Trail. Center for Continuing Education, ASU.

Mild .8 mile. Marked with 20 stops along the way for a fascinating look at the local environment. Pick up trail booklet at front desk for details. (A good chance to burn up some calories following a delicious luncheon at the Center's dining room.)

BUSICK, N.C. — Black Mountain Campground. Moderate to strenuous 5.5-mile trail to Mt. Mitchell summit.

BUSICK, N.C. — Carolina Hemlock Forest Walk. Carolina Hemlock Campground. Short walk with profusion of wildflowers and plants identified.

LINVILLE, N.C. — Grandfather Mountain. Five varying hikes starting from Visitor Center. Calloway Peak, 3.5 miles, is reached only by trail through a rugged wilderness and connects with the Calloway Trail to Linville Gap at NC 105 and Daniel Boone Scout Trail to Blowing Rock.

LITTLE SWITZERLAND, N.C. — Glen Laurel Hiking Trail. 5-mile trail from post office.

SUGAR GROVE, VA. — Raccoon Hollow Nature Trail. Mount Rogers National Recreation Area. Raccoon Branch Campground. 2-mile scenic trail to Dickey Knob.

TROUTDALE, VA. — Whispering Water Nature Trail at Grindstone Campground. **Hurricane Knob Nature Trail** and other trails at Hurricane Campground. Mount Rogers National Recreation area.

ENTRANCES TO APPALACHIAN TRAIL (AT)

Of the 250 miles of Appalachian Trail in this region, 80 miles of trail run through Pisgah National Forest and parallel the N. Carolina — Tennessee line along the ridge of Bald and Unaka Mountain ranges, and the hiker is privileged to look out on endless panoramic views of mountain ranges. The **AT** also crosses grassy mountain meadows known as "balds" and penetrates through dense stands of evergreens and hardwood trees.

A mile-wide zone flanks both sides of the **AT** route when it runs through national forests and parks. Diamond-shaped metal markers bearing the **ATC** monogram or standard 2 by 6 inch blazes of white paint on boulders or trees mark the **AT** route. Side trails leading to the **AT** are emblazoned with unmistakeable blue paint.

You backpackers who plan to hike along the **AT**, the longest continuously marked trail in the world, write for information on trail trips to Appalachian Trail Conference, 1718 N St., N.W., Washington, D.C. 20036.

DAMASCUS, VA. — Appalachian Trail (AT) information at post office.
ELIZABETHTON, TENN. — AT crosses Roan Mountain Park at Carver's Gap.
ELK PARK, N.C. — AT crossing.
HAMPTON, TENN. — AT crossing.
LINVILLE, N.C. — AT entrance at Linville Gorge.
MARION, VA. — AT entrance at Mt. Rogers National Recreation Area.
MOUNTAIN CITY, TENN. — AT entrance along summit of Holston Mountain.
SUGAR GROVE, VA. — Trail to AT shelter at Raccoon Branch Campground.
TROUTDALE, VA. — Alternate AT route at Grindstone Campground.
UNICOI, TENN. — AT crossing.

13

learning

the

ropes

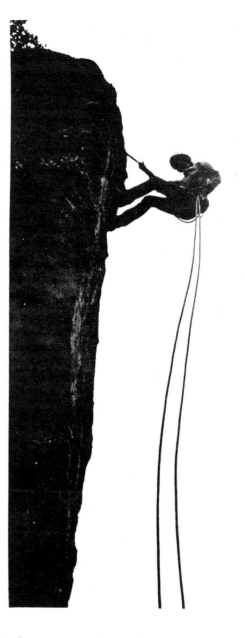

You may not have the sure-footedness or nonchalance of a mountain lion but these qualities sure would help if you're planning to scale the rugged, wild heights of primitive wilderness areas. This high Southern country offers as challenging a "cliff hanger" experience in its perpendicular granite upness, as you'll find anywhere.

Faith alone, however, is not enough to get you from the base to the summit. You must have climbing skills and confidence if you're of the tribe that finds sheer, rocky, steep slopes irresistible, because some of these craggy stone walls are only for the most advanced climbers where ropes are always necessary. Whether amateur or experienced, there are soaring elevations for bold, dauntless, intrepid mountaineers that will excite the imagination and thrill the innards. Steep ridges and precipices overlooking sharp drops and irregular boulders will whet the appetite of any experienced mountain climber.

Hedging on a ledge may be your "cup of tea" for safety as well as rest, while for others just viewing the vertical acreage from the valley floor to the sky above may be sufficiently awesome. But for those who cherish and thrive on moments of engrossing absorption on a granite, unyielding rocky bosom, below are a few of the "free climbing" experiences where using only fingerholds and footholds are all that's necessary to make the "hard" rise to the top; in addition, more difficult ascents are included:

Both sides of the Linville Gorge Wilderness, west of Marion (see Ch. 11), Jonas Ridge on the left and Linville Mountain on the right with 4,000-foot Laurel Knob, offer excellent climbs. There are drops to the river in sheer 600-foot descents. Other areas climbed less often in the gorge are Hawksbill Mountain and Wiseman's View.

The most frequently attempted are The Chimneys (in Linville Gorge) and Table Rock with routes for beginner, intermediate and advanced rock scaler.

A permit is not required for "conquering" 400-foot Table Rock, just outside of the gorge area which has unbolted and bolted routes on conventional face and crack mountaineering.

Shortoff Mountain, south of Table Rock, also outside the Gorge Wilderness Area, offers a 400-foot classic wall with crack climbs on the Gold Coast and Carolina Walls.

Five miles southwest of Roaring Gap, off US 21, at Stone Mountain State Park, are about 15 to 20 different friction climbs to the top of the defoliated dome which has a 600-foot drop.

In advancing to the summit it's well to remember that chocks (aluminum wedges with steel or nylon cables) pushed into cracks leave no unsightly scars as do pitons which should be removed so that the next adventurer will not be robbed of some of the thrilling excitement.

It's a good idea to notify a park official that you'll be climbing if you're in a state or national park even though a permit is not required; entrance to Linville Gorge Wilderness, however, is by permit only. Beginners are advised not to make an ascent unless properly trained and accompanied by experienced rock climbers.

Onward and upward then, for there's plenty of room at the top for those with true grit. Keep in mind, if you don't quite make it the first time — try, try again.

Hugh Morton

14 cascading sculpture

What is it about waterfalls that seems to hold a magnetic attraction for us, that when we discover there are waterfalls anywhere around, drives us miles out of our way to have a look? Is it that the laughter of the waterfalls gives us pause for quiet meditative thought? Or is it that its majesty and peace relieve us of involvement with the world's burdens and turmoil? Or could it be that the unspoiled, wild, unharnessed power of tumbling shafts are symbolic of the eternal, vital energy of "living waters?"

Whatever it may be, you're sure to get quite a thrill out of gazing at any one of the outstanding, spectacular waterfalls listed below. These catapulting, cascading wonders seem to have a fascination for kids and grownups alike making each one glad to be alive!

Some of the waterfalls may be reached only by foot or by horseback through quiet, woodsy paths. Here they are — we dare you to see them all!

ABINGDON, VA. — Northwest on US 19. Near Little Moccasin Gap. 50.

BLOWING ROCK, N.C. — **Glen Burney Falls.** 75 feet. One quarter-mile down gravel road on New Year's Creek; by car on Johns River Road.

BLOWING ROCK, N.C. — **Glen Mary Falls.** Right from Glen Burney Trail.

BLUE RIDGE PARKWAY, N.C. — **The Cascades.** Series of falls, each 30 feet. Milepost 271.9. E. B. Jeffress Park.

BLUE RIDGE PARKWAY, N.C. — **Boone Fork Trail Falls.** 25 feet. Milepost 296.6. Price Memorial Park. Trail begins at picnic area.

BLUE RIDGE PARKWAY, N.C. — **Crabtree Falls.** 60 feet. Milepost 340. Crabtree Meadows.

BLUE RIDGE PARKWAY, N.C. — **Mitchell Falls.** 40 feet. Milepost 349.9. Mount Mitchell State Park.

BLUE RIDGE PARKWAY, N.C. — **Glassmine Falls.** 80 feet. Milepost 361.2. Glassmine Falls Overlook.

BLUE RIDGE PARKWAY, N.C. — **Carter Creek Falls.** 70 feet. Milepost 364.6. Craggy Gardens.

BOOMER, N.C. — **Boone's Falls.** NC 18, on a tributary of Warrior Creek.

BURNSVILLE, N.C. — **Blue Sea Falls.** Directions at Chamber of Commerce.

CRESTON, N.C. — **Longhope Falls.** 300 feet. Just off County Road 1100 (The Tree Top Mountain Road) NC 88.

DAMASCUS, VA. — **Laurel Gorge.** West on US 58. Tumbling cascades.

EDGEMONT, N.C. — **Harper Creek Falls. South Harper Falls.** Pisgah National Forest Road 1358, near Mortimer Recreation Area.

ELK PARK, N.C. — **Elk River Falls.** 85 feet. NC 19E, 2 miles east of Tennessee line at mouth of Shawneehaw Creek.

ERNESTVILLE, TENN. — **Spivey Falls (Upper and Lower).** 60 feet. 7 miles south on 19W. Visible from road.

ERWIN, TENN. — **Buckeye Falls.** 700 feet. Highest falls east of Rockies. Cherokee National Forest, Chigger Ridge across from falls for best viewing.

ERWIN, TENN. — **Rock Creek Falls.** 20 feet. Three separate falls on left prong of Beauty Spot Gap. Accessible only by foot.

ERWIN, TENN. — **Sills Creek Falls.** 60 feet. Cherokee National Forest.

FLEETWOOD, N.C. — **Fleetwood Falls.** 3 miles off US 221, Ashe County. One-half mile of whitewater rapids.

GRANITE FALLS, N.C. — Granite Falls. 35 feet. On Gunpowder Creek, south Caldwell County.

HAMPTON, TENN. — Laurel Falls. 30 feet. Approximately 4 miles southeast on Tenn. 50.

INDEPENDENCE, VA. — Peach Bottom Falls. Power House Road, east of Independence.

LINVILLE FALLS, N.C. — Upper Falls, 12 feet; **Lower Falls,** 90 feet. Off Blue Ridge Parkway, US 221-NC 105.

LITTLE SWITZERLAND, N.C. — Grassy Creek Falls. On private property. 1.5-mile hike from post office.

MARION, N.C. — Buck Creek Falls. On Rock Creek, south McDowell County.

MORAVIAN FALLS, N.C. — Moravian Falls. 35 feet. On Moravian Creek, south Wilkes County.

RIDGECREST, N.C. — Rocky Glenn Falls or Catawba Falls. 200 feet. Southwest McDowell County near Ridgecrest. Water drops over five rocky levels.

SUGAR GROVE, N.C. — Laurel Creek Falls. 85 feet. US 321 on Laurel Creek before joining Watauga River.

Hugh Morton

15   a golfer's dream

Yes! It's here — the challenging, the unique, the excitingly different golf course. It's up among the clouds; it's nestled in the mountains; it's the highest one east of the Rockies. It has winding blue-grass fairways; it has plush native bent grass greens; it has mountain streams and lakes, mountain laurel and rhododendron; it's surrounded by dense woodlands — all providing unmatched scenery which is the only distraction around, if you can call it that. It's a championship course for the scratch player or seasoned pro.

Come and swing your way around these mountain resorts, a different one each day, if you wish, on enchanting, well-manicured public and private courses with more than 800 holes to play — a veritable "buffet" choice — some open all year and others most of the year. There are excellent facilities for dining at the course; there's golf equipment for rent, golf shops for your needs, pros to practice with, and inviting clubhouses.

The altogether restful, uncrowded atmosphere is an experience you'll want to have often.

And for you mini-golf swingers, variety is the name of the game! The price is right! There are no special skills required! Anyone can play it and enjoy it the first time around, and there are no age barriers! For families who like to do things together, miniature golf is wholesome, clean, inexpensive recreation.

Feet Elev.	Location	Club or Course Private or Public	Holes	Open
2057	**Abingdon, Va.**	Glenrochie Country Club (Pr.) (703) 628-3572	18	All Year
5500	**Banner Elk, N.C.**	Beech Mountain Golf Club(Pr.) Resort 387-2372	18	Spring- Fall
5240	**Banner Elk, N.C.**	Sugar Hollow Golf Club (Pr.) Resort 898-4521	18	Spring- Fall
1450	**Blountville, Tenn.**	Tri-Cities Golf and C.C. (Pub.) (615) 323-8521	18	All Year
3600	**Blowing Rock, N.C.**	Blowing Rock C. C. (Pr.) 295-7311	18	April 1- Dec. 1
3600	**Blowing Rock, N.C.**	Hound Ears Golf and C.C. (Pr.) 963-4321	18	April 1- Dec. 1
3333	**Boone, N.C.**	Boone Golf Club (Pub.) 264-8760	18	April 1- Nov. 1
4600	**Boone, N.C.**	Seven Devils Resort and Club (Pr.) 963-5665	18	May 1- Nov. 1
3333	**Boone, N.C.**	Willow Creek Golf Club (Pr.) 963-4025	9	Spring- Fall
1700	**Bristol, Tenn.**	Country Club of Bristol (Pr.) (615) 764-4531	18	All Year
1700	**Bristol, Tenn.**	Holston Valley Golf Course (Pub.) (615) 764-4801	18	All Year
1700	**Bristol, Tenn.**	King College Golf Course (Pub.) (615) 968-2331	9	All Year
1700	**Bristol, Tenn.**	Steele Creek Golf Course (Pub.) (615) 764-6411	9	All Year
1060	**Burnsville, N.C.**	Mount Mitchell Golf Club (Pub.) 675-5454	18	May- Nov.
1060	**Conover, N.C.**	Rockbarn Country Club (Pub.) 464-7430	18	All Year
1600	**Elizabethton, Tenn.**	Elizabethton Municipal G. C.(Pub.) (615) 542-8051	18	All Year
1000	**Elkin, N.C.**	Cedarbrook Country Club (Pr.) 835-6804	18	Spring- Fall
1700	**Erwin, Tenn.**	Buffalo Valley C.C. (Pr.) (615) 743-9957	18	All Year
2400	**Galax, Va.**	Galax C. C. (Pr.) (703) 236-2641	18	All Year
2400	**Galax, Va.**	Gay Hills C. C. (Pr.) (703) 236-9845	9	All Year

Feet Elev.	Location	Club or Course Private or Public	Holes	Open
1200	**Granite Falls, N.C.**	Granada Farms C. C. (Pr.) 396-5311	18	All Year
1200	**Granite Falls, N.C.**	Tri-County Golf Course (Pub.) 728-9935	18	All Year
1200	**Hickory, N.C.**	Catawba Valley Golf Course (Pub.) 324-6304		All Year
1200	**Hickory, N.C.**	Green Valley Golf Course (Pr.) 328-3378		All Year
1200	**Hickory, N.C.**	Huntington Hills Golf Club (Pub.) 328-5010	18	All Year
1200	**Hickory, N.C.**	Lake Hickory C. C. (Pr.) 328-2981	9	All Year
1700	**Johnson City, Tenn.**	Johnson City C. C. (Pr.) (615) 928-9241	18	All Year
1700	**Johnson City, Tenn.**	Lakeview Golf Center (Pub.) (615) 926-5403	9	All Year
1700	**Johnson City, Tenn.**	Pine Oaks Munic. Golf Course (Pub.) (615) 926-5451	18	All Year
1200	**Lenoir, N.C.**	Cedar Rock Country Club (Pr.) 758-4451	18	All Year
1200	**Lenoir, N.C.**	High Hills Golf Course (Pub.) 758-1403	18	All Year
1200	**Lenoir, N.C.**	Lenoir Golf Club (Pr.) 754-4081	18	All Year
1200	**Lenoir, N.C.**	Tri-County G.C., Inc.(Pub.) 728-3560	18	All Year
3800	**Linville, N.C.**	Grandfather Golf and C.C. (Pr.) 898-4388	18	May 1-Oct. 31
3800	**Linville, N.C.**	Linville Golf Club(Pr.) 733-4363	18	May 15-Oct. 15
900	**Maiden, N.C.**	Glen Oaks Golf Club (Pr.) 428-2451	18	All Year
2200	**Marion, Va.**	Holston Hills C. C. (Pr.) (703) 783-7484	18	All Year
1200	**Morganton, N.C.**	Mimosa Hills Golf Club (Pr.) 437-1246	18	All Year
1200	**Morganton, N.C.**	Quaker Meadows Golf C. (Pub.) 437-2677	18	All Year
1000	**N. Wilkesboro, N.C.**	Oakwoods C. C. (Pr.) (919) 838-3011	18	April-Nov.
3600	**Newland, N.C.**	Mountain Glen Golf Club (Pr.) 733-9940	18	April 1-Oct. 30
1000	**Newton, N.C.**	Catawba C. C. (Pr.) 294-3737	18	All Year

Feet Elev.	Location	Club or Course Private or Public	Holes	Open
1000	N. Wilkesboro, N.C.	Rock Creek C. C. (Pr.) (919) 696-2146	9	April-Nov.
1400	Old Fort, N.C.	Old Fort Golf Club (Pr.) 668-4256	9	All Year
3800	Roaring Gap, N.C.	High Meadows Golf Course (Pr.) (919) 363-2221	18	April-Nov.
3800	Roaring Gap, N.C.	High Meadows Golf and C.C. (Pr.) (919) 363-2445	18	April-Nov.
3800	Roaring Gap, N.C.	Roaring Gap Club (Pr.) (919) 363-2211		April-Nov.
2600	Sparta, N.C.	New River C. C. (Pub.) (919)372-4869	9	April-Oct.
2600	Spruce Pine, N.C.	Grassy Creek Golf and C.C. (Pub.) 765-7436	18	May-Oct.
2900	W. Jefferson, N.C.	Mountain Aire Golf Club (Pub.) (919) 877-4716	9	April-Nov.
1000	Yadkinville, N.C.	Yadkin C. C. (Pr.) (919) 679-8590	9	April-Nov.

ANNUAL EVENTS

(Phone sponsor or C. of C. to confirm information. If no area code is shown, use 704.)

MAY

BOONE, N.C. — Blue Ridge Golf Tourney (Ladies). First Tuesday. Held monthly on rotating basis among Boone Golf Club; Hound Ears in Blowing Rock; Cedar Rock, Lenoir; and Oakwoods in N. Wilkesboro. Through October.

BANNER ELK, N.C. — Spring Festival, Golf Tourney. Three days. Banner Elk Area Resort Association (BEARA).

BOONE, N.C. — International Golf Tournament. Boone Golf Club.

JUNE

BAKERSVILLE, N.C. — Golf Tournament. Rhododendron Festival (See Ch. 54.)

JULY

LENOIR, N.C. — President's Cup Golf Tournament. Third weekend. Cedar Rock Country Club and Golf Course.

AUGUST

BLOWING ROCK, N.C. — Grover C. Robbins, Jr. Memorial Golf Tournament. First Sunday.

MORGANTON, N.C. — Burke County Junior Golf Tournament (since 1969). Second week, first three days.

NEWLAND, N.C. — Mountain Glen Invitational Golf Tournament. Second weekend, three days.

BOONE, N.C. — Blue Ridge Pro-American Golf Tournament. Second weekend, Friday — Sunday. Boone Golf Club.

MORGANTON, N.C. — **Burke County Open Golf Tournament for Men** (since 1969). Third Saturday and Sunday.

MORGANTON, N.C. — **Shrine Handicap Tournament.** Last Monday. Quaker Meadow Golf Club.

BOONE, N.C. — **Ladies Day Golf Tournament.** Last Tuesday. Boone Golf Club. Sponsor: Boone Ladies Day Golf Association.

SEPTEMBER
BLOWING ROCK, N.C. — **Grover C. Robbins, Jr. Memorial Golf Tournament** (since 1928). First Sunday. Limited to 25 foursomes. Trophies to top three teams.

GALAX, VA. — **J.C. Golf Tournament.** First weekend, Saturday and Sunday.

BOONE, N.C. — **Blue Ridge Pro-Amateur Golf Tournament** (since 1959). Second week, Wednesday and Thursday. Boone Golf Club. Spectators welcome — no admission.
MORGANTON, N.C. — **Carolina Ladies Golf Tournament.** Last Sunday, Monday, Tuesday. Mimosa Hills Golf Club.

OCTOBER
BOONE, N.C. — **Boone Chamber of Commerce Golf Tournament** (since 1975). Fourth Saturday. Boone Golf Club. Prizes in various categories.

DRIVING RANGES
BOONE, N.C. — **Golfland Driving Range.** Blowing Rock Road at entrance to Boone Golf Course. 25 tees with target flags and greens. 10:00 a.m.—10:00 p.m. daily, all year. 264-5642.

LENOIR, N.C. — **Lenoir Driving Range.** 243 Wilkesboro Blvd. S. E. 759-2492.

MARION, N.C. — **Catawba Valley Recreation Area.** Driving Range.

SPRUCE PINE, N.C. — **Grassy Creek Golf Club Driving Range.** 765-2046.

MINI-GOLF
BLUFF CITY, TENN. — **Putt-Putt Golf.**

BLOWING ROCK, N.C. — **Country Fair,** next to *Tweetsie* Railroad. 264-7234.

BOONE, N.C. — **Jungle Putt Miniature Golf Course.** At entrance to Boone Golf Course. 264-5642.

BOONE, N.C. — **Miniature Golf Putt-Putt.** Polar Palace. Boone Heights Shopping Center. 264-4121.

CROSSNORE, N.C. — **Minigolf.** Nationwide Insurance Building.

CROSSNORE, N.C. — **Minigolf.** Squirrel Creek Road.

ELIZABETHTON, TENN. — **Miniature Golf Course.** (615) 543-4765.

HICKORY, N.C. — **Putting Iron Miniature Golf Course.** Springs Road, opposite Thunderbird Drive-in. 256-7998

MARION, N.C. — **Catawba Valley Mini-Golf.**

16

there's no biz

like snow biz

From around the middle of December through March, the more than 100 inches of natural snowfall that covers these mountains, transforms this area into a winter playground which is a glorious sight to behold. The entire countryside is blanketed under a mantle of white, and trees are laced with a tracery of icicles.

Here at this well-established ski capital of the Southeast, Mother Nature gets an assist — she doesn't have to produce all the glittering white stuff necessary for the down-hill-up-hill sport. (It's not nice to fool Mother Nature...) Efficient snow-making equipment helps to maintain ideal skiing conditions of deeply powdered trails meandering over the graceful slopes.

Ski enthusiasts of all ages and stages — novices, beginners, intermediates, experts, spectators, and those lovers of snow who enjoy relaxing and basking on sundecks, are lured to this winter wonderland in increasing numbers.

For many, the fun continues at the end of the day with the apres-ski activities where conviviality reigns — dancing, entertainment, merriment, warm hospitality, companionship, good food, or simply dreaming by the glow of a romantic, roaring fire. It's really neat how they've put it all together on these Southern mountains — and they're letting it all hang out!

Ski buffs — you have it made! There's a variety of challenging ski runs by day, or by night under a dome of sparkling star "diamonds" scintillating in the dark blue sky augmented by ample artificial lights, transforming the night slopes into day slopes. There are more skiing hours for your delight, plus rental equipment, chic ski shops and boutiques. If you're just starting out, there are lessons in "instant skiing" and for the more advanced there's excellent ski instruction designed to give you confidence, control, poise and assurance with little or no frustration. This is the opportunity to perfect your slaloming, paralleling, styling, and racing performances.

Just bring yourself and a happy consciousness, and take your choice of five excellent winter sports areas — you'll be living exuberantly!

BANNER ELK, N.C. — Beech Mountain, 5,600-foot elevation. Night skiing; snow-making equipment. Seven days a week.

Slopes in feet

Ridge Runner	8200	Snow Fields	1300
Shawneehaw Chute	4700	Snow Lake Run	800
Sky Dive	3900	School Yard	600
Yodeler	2000	Bottom Run	300
Lower Shawneehaw	2000	Try South	

Lifts — Capacity 10,000 skiers per hour. Three double chairs, two triple chairs, two J-bars, three rope tows.

Lessons — Individual and group. Kinder Klub (Ski School Nursery) provides all-day skiing program for primary ages (5-9) at this total skiing day-care center.

Shops — Sports equipment, rental equipment, ski fashions, arts and crafts, cards, candle and gift shops, convenience food store.

Lodging — Chalets and three Mountain Top Inns — Beech Alpen Inn, Top of the Beech and Village Inn. Holiday Beech Villas. Condominiums.

Meals — Beech Tree Inn, Red Baron Room, View Haus.

Apres Ski — Entertainment.

Information — Resort Management Corp., Beech Mountain, Banner Elk, N.C. 28604. 387-4231.

BANNER ELK, N.C. — Sugar Mountain, 5300-foot elevation, 1200-foot vertical drop. Night skiing, snow-making equipment. Seven days a week.

Slopes in feet

Two beginner — Tiny Tim, Ski School.

Three novice — Easy Street, Zoom Yang, Little Hill, 3100.

Three intermediate — Lower Flying Mile, 2400; Big Birch, 4200; Switch Back, 7000.

Two advanced — Flying Mile, 3000; Dead End, 5500.

Lifts — Capacity 5200 skiers per hour. One triple chair, two double chairs, J-bar and rope tow.

Lessons — Individual and group. Ski Nursery.

Shops — Sugar Hollow, ski rental equipment, gift and ski shop, ski repair shop.

Lodging — Sugar Mountain Lodge. Condominiums. Private chalets.

Meals — Resort Center building, dining room and cafeteria.

Apres Ski — Entertainment in Lodge.

Information — Sugar Mountain, Banner Elk, N. C. 28604. 898-4521.

BLOWING ROCK, N.C. — Appalachian Ski Mountain, 4000-foot elevation. Night skiing. Snow-making equipment. Seven days a week.

Six slopes — Advanced 4000-foot with 350-foot vertical drop over a length of 2000 feet. Intermediate 1000-foot with a vertical drop of 130 feet.

Lifts — Double chair, T-bar, rope tows.

Lessons — Individual and group. French-Swiss Ski College.

Shops — Ski shop, rental equipment.

Lodging — Nearby motels and hotels.

Meals — Restaurant and lounge, cafeteria.

Apres Ski — Live entertainment in Lodge Saturday and Sunday nights.

Information — Appalachian Ski Mountain, P.O. Box 617, Blowing Rock, N. C. 28605. 295-3277.

BOONE, N.C. — Seven Devils, Inc. One mile high. Snow-making equipment. Seven days a week. Memberships available.

5 Slopes — Beginners, 700 feet long, 200 feet wide with a 600-foot deluxe rope tow. Intermediate, 3300 feet long. Served by double chair lift, 1000 skiers per hour capacity. Advanced, 2800 feet long with 607-foot vertical drop.

Lessons — Individual and group, technique ski school.

Shops — Rental equipment.

Lodging — Cottages, chalets, condominiums as well as Boone-Blowing Rock area motels.

Meals — Seven Devils Inn and cafeteria.

Apres Ski — Weekend entertainment.

Information — Seven Devils Ski Area, Box 427, Boone, N.C. 28607. 963-4405.

ROARING GAP, N.C. — High Meadows Country Club. Weekend and night skiing. (919) 363-2445.

ANNUAL EVENTS
(Phone sponsor or C. of C. to confirm information. If no area code is shown, use 704)
JANUARY-FEBRUARY
BANNER ELK, N.C. — Watauga-Avery Winter Festival. Watch newspapers for details. ISIA ice skating championships kickoff. Ten days of sports events (basketball, wrestling, ice skating) art exhibits, changing exhibitions, plays and nightclub variety shows.

DECEMBER
BANNER ELK, N.C. — Ski Auction and Sale. Last Saturday. Beech Mountain Ski Equipment Auction. View Haus Building. Great opportunity to purchase winter sports items — skis, clothing, ice skates — or sell them.

17

best fishin'

hot spots

Anyone yearning for the good ole fishin' days had better come up to where the fishin's great and the livin's easy. Our ancestors never had it so good! Would you believe these fish tales: a 26-lb. brown trout, a 25-lb. walleye, an 11-lb. smallmouth bass? All True! Hundreds of well-stocked, fast-flowing, cold mountain streams, ponds, lakes and rivers make fishing conditions better than ever — challenging and highly rewarding — and fishing is an all-year mountain sport.

The jumpingest brook, brown and rainbow mountain trout found in some 4,000 miles of public stream beds (the most and best in all the Southeast) provide an abundance of great fishing and deliciously palatable fish meals. Watch for the frequent "Public Mountain Trout Waters" signs posted along stream banks.

For Blue Ridge Parkway stream and pond fishing, be sure to follow the rules posted around stream banks and lake shorelines. For more information write Blue Ridge Parkway, P.O. Box 7606, Asheville, N.C. 28807.

Two of the most popular questions on trout fishing are "What do you wear?" and "How do you lure the trout?" You certainly don't have to look like the model fisherman in a catalogue — all you really need are ankle boots or tennis shoes with felt glued on the heels and soles to keep you from an unexpected swim. In early spring, when the water is ice cold, you might like hip boots or waders. And any weather-proofed jacket with pockets will do; be sure to have a basket or pail for the big catch.

Although each experienced trout fisherman swears by his own method, most use a fly or spinning rod, or even cut a little birch pole by the stream. Natural bait is popular — red worms, crickets, night crawlers and salamanders. Even corn kernels and marshmallows (yup, that's right) are commonly used. But, in early spring, when the water is high and somewhat cloudy after a rain, artificial spinning lures, small rapalas and flatfish are more effective devices. Do you know that some of the best brown trout fishin' can be enjoyed while it's raining because the rain washes food into the stream? Then there are the fly fishermen who use nymph and dry flies. But if the trout are jumpin', you'll catch 'em no matter what!

To catch the trout it's best to approach quietly without splashing which will "spook" the fish, and to lower your lure or bait in a natural manner without fanfare or much motion. Then watch the satisfying results.

Trout season traditionally opens on most streams the first Saturday in April one-half hour before sunrise. There's a popular annual Opening Day Trout Fishing Derby (since 1973) from daylight to dark, sponsored by the Blowing Rock merchants with exciting prizes in four divisions: Men's Division — 13 and over, Ladies' Division, Boys' Division and Girls' Division — 12 and under. Length is the only deciding factor; trout, however, must be caught from public fishing waters around Blowing Rock. Everyone is invited to participate. Licenses may be obtained at the hardware store.

In the Great Lakes of Tennessee and in large streams there's an abundance of large, small-mouth and white bass, bream and walleye, among others. Trophy-size catches of channel and yellow catfish, spotted rock, bluegill, muskellunge, and sauger are not uncommon. Crappie, despite its name, is especially delicious eating and since it's a "school" fish, a beginner can find success readily and frequently.

Watauga Lake in Tennessee contains 13 species of game fish from bass to salmon. Boy, what fish fries for fisheaters — is your mouth watering? Since these lakes are open all year, they offer some of the finest fishing in the country with best catches reported to be in the spring and early fall. Tailwaters, below the dams at Watauga and South Holston Lakes, are outstanding fishin' hot spots. The best trout fishing is found in the brooks and mountain streams branching off from the lakes. The boast here is that the trout are ALWAYS biting! Boone Lake offers good bream, bass, catfish, crappie and musky.

Virginia waters are also well-stocked by state hatcheries. The superb, natural, unspoiled beauty surrounding the fishing locations in each of the states of this mountain corner is an added lure to participate in this great outdoor activity.

You'll do yourself a favor if you send to:

North Carolina Wildlife Resources Commission, Division of Game, Raleigh, N.C. 27611, for regulations and pamphlets such as *Hunting and Fishing Maps for North Carolina Game Lands*; Tennessee Conservation Department, 2611 West End Avenue, Nashville, Tenn. 37203, for the publication *Tennessee Fishing*; Knoxville Tourist Bureau, P.O. Box 237, Knoxville, Tenn. 37901, for the publication *Fishing and Camping in Eastern Tennessee*.

County maps showing state secondary roads for exact locations of hot-spot streams are available from the State Departments of Transportation and also from the various County Courthouses.

Mid-winter can be the most favorable time of year and perhaps the most fun when you can catch the "braggingest-size" trout and bass. The colder, the better, for a good winter's catch; the trout and bass feed all winter. Just be sure to wear warm woolen clothing.

All three states have excellent boating access areas (Ch. 11) and there's plenty of protection going on in biological research to stock additional species of fish, plus wise management for optimum fishing conditions and fishing enjoyment.

In general, youngsters under 16 are exempt from licenses.

For you guys who prefer a fishing trip that doesn't require much effort or a license and that has no creel limits, commercial trout "catch-out" ponds are the place for you. These places operate on a poundage basis, provide fishing equipment and will clean and package your catch to boot. If there's a restaurant at the spot, you may have your fish cooked to order. Some of these places have outdoor grills and utensils for a "do-it-yourself" meal right then and there. In this way, you just CAN'T miss! These locations are well advertised along the roads; more information about North Carolina fishing spots, however, is available from the Division of Inland Fisheries, North Carolina Wildlife Resources Commission, 325 N. Salisbury St., Raleigh, N.C. 27611.

A few "catch-out" ponds are

Abingdon, Va. — Hidden Valley. Fish for Fun. Route. 6, Va. 19 and 58, 8 miles north.
Boone, N.C. — "Pay-Day" Trout Farm, off Shulls Mills Road. 963-4627.
Boone N.C. — Watauga Trout Ponds (no catch — no pay). US 105 near Tumbling Brook Inn.
Burnsville, N.C. — Hershell Higgins, Route 6, Pensacola Rd.
Burnsville, N.C. — L. B. Troxell, Route 5, White Oak Rd. 675-4087.
Burnsville, N.C. — Mountain Cove Campground, Route 5, Busick Community.
Burnsville, N.C. — Tull Mace, Route 5, Micaville Community. 675-4106.
Elizabethton, Tenn. — Watson Trout Farms, Route 8, (615)543-3223.
Little Switzerland, N.C. — Hoover's Trout Farm, 2.5-acre pond, free bait, poles, ice. Left on Crabtree Creek Rd. 765-6864 or 2217. Closed Sundays.
Little Switzerland, N.C. — Lake Wahoo, County Rd. 1100. Seven days a week. Bass, bream.

Marion, N.C. — Elliott's Trout Ponds, off US 70 on NC 80.
Sparta, N.C. — Peaceful Valley Trout Farm, Route. 4. Pay if you catch.
Sparta, N.C. — Tommy's Fish Lake.

(Confirm fishing information where licenses are issued. Fishing allowed in whole stream or lake unless otherwise indicated. Trout are generally found in all fishin' hot spots; bass and walleye where indicated.)

NORTH CAROLINA

ASHE COUNTY

New River — North Fork: from headwaters to Riverview School Bridge on SSR 1126; Helton Creek from Virginia state line to Little Helton Creek; Big Horse Creek from Virginia state line to Tuckerdale; Little Horse Creek; Buffalo Creek; Big Laurel Creek; Three Top Creek; Hoskins Fork.

New River — South Fork: Cranberry Creek from Alleghany County line to last low water bridge below Piney Branch SSR 1600; Peak Creek; Trout Lake; Naked Creek; Roan Creek; Bear Creek; Obids Creek; North Beaver Creek; South Beaver Creek, headwaters to Ashe Lake; Pine Swamp Creek, all forks; Gap Creek, headwaters to South Fork; Old Field Creek.

AVERY COUNTY

North Toe River — unposted portion from headwaters to Mitchell County line; Jones Creek; Henson Creek; Plumtree Creek; Little Plumtree Creek; Powdermill Creek; Roaring Creek; Squirrel Creek; Birchfield Creek; Horse Creek; Kentuck Creek.

Elk River — from SSR 1306 crossing to Tennessee state line, and from Heaton to Lees-McRae College boundary; Cranberry Creek.

Catawba River (bass)— Gragg Prong; Webb Prong; Coffey Lake No. 1; Archie Coffey Lake.

Linville River — from Sloop Dam to Blue Ridge Parkway boundary; Milltimber Creek.

BURKE COUNTY

Johns River — Carroll Creek from headwaters to SSR 1405 (Adako Road).

Linville River — from first bridge on SSR 1223 below Lake James powerhouse to Muddy Creek.

Lake James — Canal Bridge boating access, two miles northwest of Bridgewater on NC 126 (bass); Linville River boating access, one mile east of Linville River Bridge on NC 126 (bass).

Lake Rhodhiss — Johns River boating access, 3.8 miles north of Morganton on NC 18 (bass).

CALDWELL COUNTY

Yadkin River — Buffalo Creek from headwaters to lower Dahl property line; Rockhouse Creek; Joe's Fork, Watauga County line to Todd's Store.

Johns River — Wilson Creek from Phillips Mill Creek to Browns Mountain Beech Dam.

Lake Hickory — Gunpowder boating access on US 321N, .4 mile north of Catawba River Bridge, east on Grace Chapel road (SR 1758), 3 miles to SR 1757, north 1.3 miles to area (bass); Lovelady boating access on US 321N, .4 mile north of Catawba River Bridge, east on Grace Chapel Road (SR 1758), .3 mile to SR 1757, turn south .9 mile (bass).

Lake Rhodhiss — Castle Bridge boating access, north of Connelly Springs, SR 1001 (bass); Dry Pond boating access, 1 mile southwest of Granite Falls (bass).

CATAWBA COUNTY
Lake Hickory — Oxford boating access, southwest of Oxford Dam, NC 16 and SR 1453 to Lake Hickory Campground Road, 1.2 miles (bass).

Lookout Shoals Lake — boating access near Lookout Dam, 6 miles northeast of Conover on SR 1006 off NC 16.

McDOWELL COUNTY
Catawba River — North Fork: from headwaters to SSR 1571 bridge on US 221; West Fork: Mill Creek from Swannanoa Creek to Old Fort Dam.

Broad River — Cove Creek.

Lake James — boating access, 1 mile north of Nebo off NC 126 on SR 1548 (bass, walleye); North Fork boating access, .5 mile north of US 221-70 intersection west of Marion, SR 1501 and 1552 (bass, walleye).

MITCHELL COUNTY
Nolichucky River — Big Rock Creek from headwaters to fishing club property above A. D. Harrell Farm; Bear Creek, lower two miles; Wiles Creek; Cane Creek from SSR 1219 to Nolichucky; Grassy Creek; Roses Creek.

WATAUGA COUNTY
New River — South Fork (bass): Meat Camp Creek; Norris Fork Creek; Howards Creek; Tater Hill Lake with feeder streams; Goshia Creek: East Fork from Blue Ridge Parkway boundary to New River; Winkler Creek, both forks; Middle Fork from Lake Chetola Dam to New River.

Yadkin River (bass) — Stony Fork; Elk Creek from headwaters to Big Laurel Creek; Joe's Fork.

Watauga River (bass) — from headwaters to NC 194 bridge; Beech Creek; Beaverdam Creek; Laurel Creek; Cove Creek, headwaters to bridge on SSR 1305; Dutch Creek; Crab Orchard Creek; Boone Fork, from headwaters to Blue Ridge Parkway boundary.

Bass Lake and Trout Lake, Moses H. Cone Memorial Park, BRP.

Sims Pond and Price Lake, Julian Price Memorial Park, BRP (bass).

WILKES COUNTY
Roaring River—East Prong: from headwaters to Brewer's Mill on SSR 1943; Garden

Creek; Middle Prong: from headwaters on second bridge SSR 1736; West Prong (Dog Creek): Harris Creek.

Reddies River — North Fork: from headwaters to SR 1570; Middle Fork: headwaters to bridge on SSR 1580; Clear Prong.

Lewis Fork — South Prong: from headwaters to Lewis Fork Baptist Church; Fall Creek, except posted portion.

Stony Fork Creek—from headwaters to Mt. Zion Bridge near intersection of SSR 1155 and SSR 1167.

Elk Creek—Dugger Creek; Little Dugger Creek.

YANCEY COUNTY

Nolichucky River — Cane River: from Pensacola Bridge to 1.5 miles above Bowlen's Creek; Big Creek, lower 2 miles; Bald Mountain Creek, unposted portion from Buck line to Cane River; Price Creek, from junction of SSR 1120 and SSR 1121 to Cane River; Cattail Creek, from Threadgill property line to Cane River.

South Toe River — from Clear Creek to SSR 1152 except for posted portion; Rock Creek, lower 2 miles; Middle Creek, lower 1 mile.

18   **river floating —**

water's
fine
(wild!)

Oh! to be exquisitely lazy...to enjoy the sweet diversion of doing absolutely nothing...to float serenely, meandering through an unspoiled wilderness surrounded by pastoral scenery...to devote a whole morning or whole afternoon or whole day to pondering...to experience a sense of wonder...to inhale the scent of freshness...to listen to the fish jump...to see what is to be seen. Why not...today!

And the best way to learn about the water — to observe just for the sake of observing — is to take to the water in a canoe, a rubber raft, or in a blow-it-up-and-jump-in-boat. Carried along by the current, this can be a terrifically rewarding pasttime. You glide into patches of sunlight and under shady trees slowly enough to scan the scene unhurriedly without disturbing the wildlife and at the same time keeping ears open to the birds serenading you with their rhapsodies. This is a rendezvous with time — the perfect time to study nature in an undisturbed botanical garden.

Everyone needs beauty as well as bread — a sense of total awareness, a feeling of eternity. The timeless serenity of nature is the antidote many are seeking and finding abundantly on these waterways.

An ancient, historic stream, ideally suited for a unique floating adventure, is called paradoxically the "New River." Thanks to an Act of Congress, after years of valiant effort by the people, the river's gracious heritage will remain unspoiled forever. Originating east of Boone the "New" twists through the mountains of North Carolina, Virginia and West Virginia. To the canoe drifter on this natural waterway with its primitive shoreline, it would seem as though nothing in the valley has changed. The universal spirit of relaxation permeates one's being, awakening a peaceful feeling of oneness with all things.

For those more restless souls, for those with a burning desire to experience nature in the raw, for those seeking excitement and challenge on tumultuous waters — crashing massive waves, flying spray, rocks hurtling — for those who enjoy threading their way around house-sized boulders, dipping over the lip of waterfalls — riding the rapids of the spectacular white water Nolichucky River Gorge is a far-out trip. But it is only for the experienced boatman!

Steep walls of sheer rock rising from the water to 2000-foot mountaintops, forming a canyon, unexpected and unsuspected obstacles, a chasm of rock and stone, rushing, boiling, roiling white waters — shooting the rapids with dolphin-like leaps is enough activity to keep anyone tingling with a sense of keen anticipation and enthusiastic sportsmanship. These waters are a raging, rushing, rumbling, glorious, untamed, fantastic turbulence of complicated river gorge, perhaps more so than any other in southeastern United States.

The 11-hour Nolichucky River Gorge trip, sponsored by Wildwater, Ltd., starts at Unicoi, Tenn., five miles south of Johnson City on US 23 and ends near Erwin, Tenn. The Nolichucky is formed at the junction of the Toe River and Cane River near Spruce Pine. These trips are offered only from June through August.

A word of advice: pack dry clothes and other possessions in waterproof bags and wear tennis shoes; one thing is sure — you're bound to get wet or at least damp.

To add to the variety of waters to choose from, there are professional backpacking outfitters who provide expertise for whatever type of water experience you prefer. The Appalachian Outfitters on US 321 in Blowing Rock take all the guesswork out of a river excursion providing a safe, delightful family experience with guides, canoes, transportation, food and equipment for a trip through the remote waters of Ashe and Watauga Counties.

For anyone desiring instruction in white water, flat water, lake and river canoeing, the Carolina Canoe Club, 121 Turner St., Elkin, N.C. 28621 has organized trips led by qualified guides. If you become a member, these canoecades as well as clinics for developing skills are available.

Below is a choice (without a hamburger place in sight) for you to try out your skills plus the ones listed in Chapter 11.

CLINCH RIVER, TENN. — Amateur canoeist, year-round floating, beautiful scenery, US 258, State Highways 33, 66, 94.

CRESTON, N.C. — Access to North Fork, New River SR 1100 bridge, Exit NC 88 bridge west of Clifton. Approx. 3-hr. trip (7 mi.).

ERWIN, TENN. — Access point to Nolichucky River at State Highway 81, year-round floating for amateur canoeists; rafting, riding the rapids for experienced canoeists.

HOLSTON RIVER, TENN. — Amateur canoeist, year-round floating, pastoral scenery, US 11E and 11W, State Highways 1, 92, 66 and County roads.

JEFFERSON, N.C. — Canoeing on S. Fork of New River, 5 miles southeast on NC 88 at intersection of NC 16. Other access points: US 421, 221, NC 163. Year-round floating for amateurs; alternates between farmlands and forest.

NORTH TOE AND TOE RIVERS, N.C. — Access points: US 19E, NC 80, 197, County roads. River flows through Avery, Mitchell and Yancey Counties; scenery: pastoral and wilderness; for amateurs except between NC 197 and 80 which is for experienced canoeists; in dry season, upper regions are low.

UNICOI, TENN. — An 11-hour guided raft trip into the Nolichucky River Gorge for experienced rafters. Reservations required: (803)647-5336. June — August.

WATAUGA RIVER, N.C. — Watauga River Raft Rides. Fifteen miles west of Boone, NC 421, left on 321 then right at sign. 297-3909.

ANNUAL EVENTS
(Phone sponsor or C. of C. to confirm information. If no area code is shown, use 704.)
JULY
ERWIN, TENN. — **Nolichucky and Kayak Race.** Six-mile course from Devil's Looking Glass to just north of Taylor Bridge near Embreeville. Morning: Kayak and solo canoes; 1:00 p.m.: two-person canoes.

W. JEFFERSON, N.C. — **Great Canoe Race** (since 1974) on the New River. Five miles east off NC 163. Begins at entrance to Elk Shoals Methodist Camp; ends at Walters Sheets' Store, at bridge, junction of NC 88 and 16. 1:00 p.m.

SEPTEMBER
MORGANTON, N.C. — **Intercollegiate Canoe Races.** Catawba River II. Intercollegiate and Open Classes: C-1, C-1W, C-2, C-2M, C-2 Jr. Western Piedmont Community College. 437-8685.

19　the tennis racquet

The game of tennis has taken off for outer space, so popular is it with people from all walks of life and all ages. If you're among the group of tennis enthusiasts, you'll find no shortage of tennis courts and tennis tournaments all over the place!

There are vacation package tours, teaching and practice aids, and, indoor tennis in a climate-controlled plastic bubble which makes it always perfect weather for a game. There's a wide variety of private and public courts with experienced instructors. No matter where you travel in this area you'll find public tennis courts under the supervision of the local Recreation Department, and in the Boone area, ASU's tennis courts are always open to the public when not being used by students. The Boone-Blowing Rock region also boasts Beech Mountain, Sugar Mountain, Grandfather Mountain, Hound Ears and Seven Devils, among other private tennis resorts.

If you'd like to join the happy, swinging-racquet crowd, sign up for lessons and after you've hit several thousand tennis balls under expert guidance in a concentrated dose of instruction, you're bound to see good results. By practicing the serve, learning the advanced twist serve, the shot combination, the volley, and "sudden death," you'll enjoy a better game.

It might be your "bag" to develop into a tennis ace or teaching pro. These careers are wide open, especially at tennis camps and tennis clinics continuing to mushroom around the nation in response to the present infatuation with this active, international, healthy sport.

Anyone who wants to learn the game has plenty of opportunities to watch good players in this neck of the woods, amid the grandeur of the mountain beauty.

How about tennis, anyone?

ANNUAL EVENTS

(Phone sponsor or C. of C. to confirm information. If no area code is shown, use 704.)

MAY

BANNER ELK, N.C. — Mountain Homecoming Spring Festival Tennis Tourney. First weekend. Three-day round robin for men and women. Doubles at Seven Devils, Beech and Sugar Mountains.

JUNE

BOONE, N.C. — Watauga Junior Tennis Clinic. ASU Tennis courts. Beginners 16 and under; advanced. Sponsors: Kiwanis Club, Watauga County Parks and Rec. Dept.

JULY

BOONE, N.C. — Watauga Junior Tennis Tournament. Second weekend, Friday, Saturday, Sunday. Awards, trophies. Sponsors: Kiwanis Club, Watauga County Parks and Rec. Dept. 10:00 a.m.

BOONE, N.C. — Mountaineer Open. Third weekend, Thursday, through Sunday. ASU Campus.

AUGUST

HICKORY, N.C. — Greater Hickory Tennis Association Open Tennis Tournament. First Friday. Hickory Foundation Center.

LINVILLE, N.C. — Grandfather Golf and Country Club Invitational Tennis Tournament. Second weekend, Friday, Saturday, Sunday.

SEPTEMBER

BANNER ELK, N.C. — Sugar Mountain Member-Guest Tennis Tournament. Labor Day.

20 open season — conservation hunting

"For everything there is a season..." and the seasons for hunting and trapping are well spelled out in the North Carolina Hunting and Trapping Regulations, the Hunting Regulations of the Tennessee Wildlife Resources Agency, Ellington Center, Nashville, Tenn. 37220. and Commission of Game & Inland Fisheries, P.O. Box 11104, Richmond, Va. 23230.

To enjoy hunting on the fine Wildlife Commission-managed Game Lands you should have (1) a hunting license, (2) a Big Game License if hunting bear, boar, deer or wild turkey, and (3) a Game Lands Use Permit. The local Chamber of Commerce has information on picking up a license from the licensing agent.

If you're writing the North Carolina Wildlife Resources Commission, Raleigh, N.C. 27611 for their regulations, request the highly useful booklet of *Hunting and Fishing Maps for North Carolina's Game Lands.* The most common conservation hunting animals and birds found hereabouts are bear, boar, deer, dove, grouse, quail, rabbit, raccoon, squirrel and turkey. A balanced program of wildlife protection, regulating use of lands, and improving natural habitats is being constantly practiced for the pleasure of sportspeople now and in future generations.

For periodic turkey shoots, watch the local newspapers.

Following, are some of the North Carolina Game lands. You'll also find a list of hunting areas in Chapter 11 describing national and state forests and parks. **Pisgah Game Land** in Avery, Burke, Caldwell, McDowell, Mitchell, Watauga and Yancey Counties covers more than 200,000 acres. **Carson Woods Game Land, Bluff Mountain Game Land** and **Cherokee Game Land** are in Ashe County. **H.M. Bizzell, Sr. Game Land** in Lenoir County, **South Mountains Game Land** in Burke County, **Thurmond Chatham Game Land** in , Wilkes County and **Brushy Mountain Game Land** in Caldwell County cover more than 18,000 acres.

Naturally, shooting with a camera has no restrictions and no exceptions — so fire away!

Hugh Morton

21   high as a kite

There probably isn't a soul anywhere who hasn't had the secret desire to be as free as a bird, flying, floating, soaring and dipping contentedly and serenely in the wide open space between heaven and earth. Hang gliding is a sport that's adding a new dimension to living for many.

The opportunity is readily available for a thrill-of-a-lifetime exhilarating activity, where every breath of air is washed by the mountains, taking off from 1500 feet atop Grandfather Mountain, gazing down on the patchwork quilt scene below. If you're a novice, you can receive private or group instruction in how to manipulate your "flying machine," which resembles a huge, colorful butterfly.

Basically, it's a kite with 180 square feet of sheer nylon and 25 pounds of aluminum wiring and tubing. That's it — no motor, no propellers, no wings, no machinery, only the kite with a steel horizontal bar directional control which becomes an extension of your arms. The student dons a safety helmet, picks up the "kite" and practices a short run before takeoff at one of the hang gliding schools. Then comes the trial hang gliding from a 10-foot vertical hill, progressing to 20 feet, then 50 feet, then 100 feet, and eventually from a mountain top. Most novices fly after the first three-hour lesson. It's safe for those who are properly trained, experienced and careful. Any equipment necessary? A snap: ankle-supporting shoes, long-sleeved shirt, slacks and — that's it!

If you don't believe it, just go and see the phenomenon for yourself. It doesn't take long to learn how to raise the "kite's" nose to fly with the prevailing wind for a smooth takeoff. Soon the student adjusts and responds to the air currents. Then comes the relaxation knowing what it's like to experience the pure freedom, the natural high, and the airy grace of a bird. MAN! IT'S DY-NO-MITE!!! And with the right air currents, it's possible to float along peacefully, effortlessly and joyously for several hours...

If in doubt about trying it yourself, you'll marvel at the hang gliding exhibitions on Grandfather Mountain.

Lessons are given daily all year round at Blue Ridge Hang Gliding School, (704) 264-0616, and at Kitty Hawk Kites, NC 105, weather permitting. For details on the latter call 963-4969.

The increasing interest in hang gliding, fast becoming a major sport, has sparked the formation of the Mountain Gliders Hang Gliders Club, Hamilton National Bank Bldg., Johnson City, Tenn. For information: (615)928-8605.

IT'S A BIRD...IT'S A PLANE...IT'S A BIRD-PERSON!

P.S. For you expert North Carolinian hang gliders, an organization called, "The Order of the Raven" invites you to "join the club." In order to qualify for membership, you "must have soared for more than one hour of continuous powerless flight in a glider launched from the 6,000-foot peaks of Grandfather Mountain, highest point in the Blue Ridge Mountain Range."

ANNUAL EVENTS

(Phone sponsor or C. of C. to confirm information. If no area code is shown, use 704.)

MAY OR JUNE
LINVILLE, N.C. — Grandfather Mountain Hang Gliding Championship. First Saturday and Sunday. Launch site near Mile-High Swinging Bridge. Target, Duration and Free Style categories in three glider classifications: Standard, Rogallo, Open Class (unassisted and assisted), Rogallo and Fixed Wing Glider. 9:00 a.m.

JUNE — NOVEMBER (weather permitting)
LINVILLE, N.C. — Hang Gliding Exhibitions. Grandfather Mountain. 10:00 a.m., 1:00 p.m., 3:00 and 4:30 p.m. daily.

SEPTEMBER
LINVILLE, N.C. — Masters of Hang Gliding. Fourth weekend, Thursday through Sunday. Grandfather Mountain, US 221.

22   crazy over horses!

Riding tall in the saddle, clearing the jump with ease, preparing for the judges, taking the turn before the box seats — it's Horse Show Season getting into full swing from spring through fall. Just about each weekend there's a variety of horse shows, demonstrations and races featuring Appaloosa, Thoroughbreds, Standardbreds, Walking Horses, Pony Hunters, Saddle Horses — attracting visitors from around the country.

There's an air of anticipation and excitement among the horse set — exhibitors, judges, participants, and spectators — all looking forward to enjoying the great horses and horsemanship by local talent as well as outstanding contests (also cowboys and cowgirls, many from Nebraska, Oklahoma, Montana and the East Coast).

Even if horses are not particularly your "bag," the parade of equestrian noble beauty and intelligence — symbol of grace, courage and strength — the superb performances, and the thrill of watching competitions such as bareback bronco riding, will probably keep you at the edge of your seat and bring you to your feet in awe to join the roar of the crowd.

During this season of bustling days of activity, there are main events, neighborhood club competitions and rodeos, all vying for cash and other awards. If you've never attended a horse event, this is Horse Country — so take advantage. Whether it's a Western Horse Show with bronc riding, bull riding, steer wrestling, calf roping, or watching the horses walk, trot, lope, canter, jog, or jump at professional or amateur shows — you'll really find it a HAPPENING!

A combination that's hard to top is the "Miss Horseman's Holiday" competition where young ladies 15 and over are judged on horsemanship, appearance, poise and personality.

The Grandaddy of all Southeast horse shows is the Blowing Rock Charity Horse Show which has not missed a year since 1924. It's the biggest sports and social event of the summer season in Blowing Rock, awarding prizes of more than $25,000 to more than 500 competitors from more than half of the states in the nation. Events include a Jumping Classic as well as Pleasure, Hunter, English and Gaited Horse categories. The week-long show is filled with fun activities and entertainment from parties to horse show ball, fashion shows, golf tournament, square dancing and other events. The permanent Horse Show Grounds, the L. M. Tate Showgrounds in scenic Broyhill Park, on a mountainside, has two rings covered with all-weather sand rock to give excellent footing and there are 400 permanent stalls as well. Small fry under six are allowed in free — lucky!

If you'd like to try horseback riding or would enjoy taking a ride in a horse-drawn carriage as a change from golfing, tennis, swimming or sunbathing, you can rent horses at the stables listed below for as many hours of riding pleasure as you wish. So why not mosey down to the local corral, pardner, for a clippity-cloppity good time along miles of quiet, wooded, scenic trails. You might even venture to participate in the Paradise Ranch Rodeo day's outing on the Blue Ridge Mountain Trail the day before the Fourth of July, if you're around. And don't be too surprised if you qualify for one of the cash awards as one of these: Youngest Rider, Oldest Rider, Horse and Rider From Farthest Away, Most Beautiful Horse or Ugliest Horse. You'll want to be wise, however, in wearing loosely fitting long slacks and in treating and speaking to your horse with kindness and gentleness, relaxing as you ride, and keeping your knees close to the horse's sides while holding the reins loosely.

If you're not too muscle bound at the close of your equestrian experience, there are lots of festivities that go on evenings like barn dances and square dances for a rootin', tootin' good ole time!

RIDING STABLES AND CARRIAGE RIDES

(If no area code is shown, use 704.)

ABINGDON, VA. — G-5 Stables. Clark Extension. (703) 628-5741.

ABINGDON, VA. — Hughes Stables. RFD 6. (703) 628-5354.

BANNER ELK, N.C. — Beech Mountain Stables, Inc. 387-2231 or 4475.

BANNER ELK, N.C. — Sugar Mountain Resort Stables. 898-4521.

BLOUNTVILLE, TENN. — Big Orange Country Stables. RFD 3. (615) 323-4892.

BLOWING ROCK, N.C. — Appalachian Outfitters. Blowing Rock Road. Horses, feed, camping gear, food, sleeping equipment, guides. 295-3123.

BLOWING ROCK, N.C. — Blowing Rock Stables. Mayview Park. Path leads to Moses Cone Memorial Park. 25 miles of wooded trails. Individual and group lessons. 295-7847.

BLOWING ROCK, N.C. — Carriage Rides. Moses Cone Memorial Park. 9:00 a.m. — 4:30 p.m. daily.

BLOWING ROCK, N.C. — Country Fair Livery Stables. Next to *Tweetsie* RR. Blowing Rock Road. 264-7234.

BLUFF CITY, TENN. — Lovedale Stables. Meadow Lark Lane. (615) 538-8113.

BLUFF CITY, TENN. — Rocking C Ranch. RFD 37. (615) 538-8811.

BOONE, N.C. — Seven Devils. Resort stables. 963-4336.

BURNSVILLE, N.C. — Mountain Wilderness. 10 miles south, NC 197. Trailer Park-Campground. 682-3244.

BURNSVILLE, N.C. — Toe River Ranch Campground. 8 mi. southeast on NC 80. 675-4999.

CRESTON, N.C. — New River Saddle Club, Inc. Stables, horse shows.

FERGUSON, N.C. — Powder Horn Riding Stables. RFD 2.   973-3415.

FOSCOE, N.C. — Paradise Ranch. Church Road off NC 105. Fifty miles of trails through 25 acres bordering the Blue Ridge Parkway. Riding instruction, hayrides, tours. 10:00 a.m. — 6:00 pm. 963-5685.

GALAX, VA. — Joe Houk Stables. Coal Creek Road. (703) 236-5062.

JOHNSON CITY, TENN. — Landmark Farm and Stables. 1402 Knob Creek Road. (615) 926-1911.

JONESBORO, TENN. — Millercrest Stables. RFD 11. Instr. (615) 753-2201.

LENOIR, N.C. — Barringer Stables. Clark's Chapel Road. 728-7023.

LENOIR, N.C. — The C-B Ranch. Union Grove Road. Lessons. 728-3356.

LENOIR, N.C. — Foot Hills Stables. Johns River Road. 754-3572.

LENOIR, N.C. — Watts Stables. Pine Mountain Road. 728-3481.

MARION, VA. — Hungry Mother State Park Stables. (703) 783-3422.

MOUNTAIN CITY, TENN. — Mountain View Stables. Rte. 5. (615) 727-7636.

N. WILKESBORO, N.C. — Four Acres Stables. Sparta Road. (919) 838-8689.

TAYLORSVILLE, N.C. — Kellie-Dean Stables. 16 miles east of Lenoir on NC 90. 495-7343.

TROUTDALE, VA. — Fairwood Horse Livery. Mount Rogers National Recreation Area. Virginia Highlands Horse Trail

— longest horse trail in state from Speedwell to Raccoon Branch Campground. Two trails marked by orange blazers. Forest naturalist horseback tours. June through August.

W. JEFFERSON, N.C. — Greenfield Stables. Route 2, NC 149. 246-9671.

ANNUAL EVENTS

(Phone sponsor or C. of C. to confirm information. If no area code is shown, use 704.)

MAY

FOSCOE, N.C. — Watauga County Junior Horse Show. First Sunday. Paradise Ranch Arena, Church Road. Various Halter and Performance Classes. 1:00 p.m. 963-5685.

JUNE

GALAX, VA. — Shrine Club Horse Show.

JOHNSON CITY, TENN. — Country and Western Horse Show. Second Saturday. 15 Classes. 7:00 p.m.

JOHNSON CITY, TENN. — Hawkins County Horse Show. Second Saturday. Rogersville High School Athletic Field. Sponsor: Rogersville Kiwanis Club.

COVE CREEK, N.C. — Cove Creek Horse Show (since 1964). Third Saturday. Junction of US 421 and Vanderpool Road. 30 classes. 12:30 p.m. and 7:00 p.m.

SALTVILLE, VA. — Horse Show. Third Sat. Rich Valley Horse Show Grounds. 1:00 p.m. Contest; 4:00 p.m. Western show.

N. WILKESBORO, N.C. — N. Wilkesboro Rotary Club Horse Show(since 1965). Last Saturday. Memorial Park. 28 Classes. 1:00 p.m. and 6:00 p.m.

FOSCOE, N.C. — Horseman's Holiday. Last Saturday through first Sunday in July (nine days). Paradise Ranch Arena. English, Western and Speed divisions. 264-2277.

JULY

INDEPENDENCE, VA. — Horse Show (since 1966). July 2. Independence High School grounds. 7:30 p.m.

FOSCOE, N.C. — "Miss Horseman's Holiday" crowning. First Saturday.

FOSCOE, N.C. — Blue Ridge Mountain Trail Ride. July 3. Horseman's Holiday activities.

FOSCOE, N.C. — Championship Rodeo. July 4, 5, 6. Paradise Ranch Arena.

ELIZABETHTON, TENN. — Rhododendron Horse Show.

JONESBORO, TENN. — "Jonesborough Days" Horse Show. July 4. Horse Show Grounds. 2:00 — 5:00 p.m.

SPARTA, N.C. — Lions Club Horse Show. July 4. Show of horses from all over North Carolina.

SALTVILLE, VA. — Horse Show. First Friday and Saturday. Rich Valley Horse Show Grounds. 2:00 p.m.

DOBSON, N.C. — Dobson Youth Fellowship Horse Show (since 1959). Third Fri. and Sat. Surrey Central High School. 69 Classes. 7:00 p.m. Fri.; 10:00 a.m. and 7:00 p.m. Sat.

COVE CREEK, N.C. — Watauga Horse Show (since 1968). Third Saturday. Cove Creek Show Grounds, US 421 and Vanderpool Road. ?3 Classes. 1:00 p.m. and 7:00 p.m.

LINVILLE, N.C. — The Linville Horse Show. Fourth Saturday. Horse Show Grounds. For amateur and junior riders; a schooling show. 10:00a.m.—12:30p.m. and 1:30 p.m.

BLOWING ROCK, N.C. — Blowing Rock Charity Horse Show (since 1924). Last Wednesday in July through first Sunday in August. L. M. Tate Showgrounds. Largest in the Southeast. Attracts crowds from all over United States and foreign countries. $25,000 prize awards. 8:30 a.m. — noon daily; 1:30 — 5:00 p.m. daily; 1:30 p.m. Sunday.

AUGUST
BRISTOL, TENN. — The Mountain Empire Horse Show. Bristol International Speedway and Dragway.

LENOIR, N.C. — Lenoir Optimist Horse Show. First Friday and Saturday. Optimist Park. 7:00 p.m. Friday; 7:30 p.m. Saturday.

SALTVILLE, VA. — Rich Valley Fair and Horse Show. Second Wednesday. Rich Valley Horse Show Grounds.

FERGUSON, N.C. — Wilkes Civitan Horse Show. Second Saturday. Noon.

INDEPENDENCE, VA. — The Grayson County Horse Show. Third Saturday. Sponsor: Independence Jaycees.

SALTVILLE, VA. — Rich Valley Fair and Horse Show. Third Saturday. Rich Valley Horse Show Grounds.

SALTVILLE, VA. — All-Western Horse Show. Fourth Saturday. Rich Valley Horse Show Grounds. Sponsor: Saltville Fire Department.

GALAX, VA. — Fairview Ruritan Club Horse Show (since 1969). Last Saturday.

SEPTEMBER
FOSCOE, N. C. — Southeastern Rodeo Association Championship Rodeo. Third Saturday and Sunday. Paradise Ranch, Church Road.

OCTOBER
MORGANTON, N.C. — Bristol Creek Stable Horse Show. Bristol Creek Stables.

23   figure eights and
pirouettes

For participant or spectator, there's plenty of graceful motion on the
skating rinks — and this mountain region is blessed with both ice and roller
skating activities, year round. If you're serious about improving your figure

eights or learning how to dance on skates, professional instruction is at hand.

If you're interested in a good evening's entertainment, just watching the skaters swing by is always a fun show and pleasurable viewing.

Watch the newspapers for dates of professional ice skating spectaculars and hockey games at the Boone Polar Palace. Whether you skate or not you'll have a relaxing time browsing at the nine stores located at The Polar Palace or resting in the gallery during the skating sessions.

So, come on over where the action is...

ICE SKATING

BANNER ELK, N.C. — Open Air Ice Skating at Beech Tree Village. Beech Mountain. Only outdoor facility in Blue Ridge Mountains of western N. Carolina. 387-2251.

BOONE, N.C. — The Polar Palace. Boone Heights Shopping Center. Indoors. Year-round. Two-hour sessions afternoons and evenings. Ice skating school. Two-week courses. Special group rates. 264-4121.

ROLLER SKATING

BOONE, N.C. — The Arena. 176 by 72-foot rink. Blowing Rock Road opposite Holiday Inn. Special group rates. Special sessions Friday, Saturday, Sunday. 7:30 — 10:00 p.m. nightly. 264-4989.

BRISTOL, TENN. — Belmont Skateland. Weaver Pike. (615) 764-5135.

BURNSVILLE, N.C. — Riverside Roller Rink. 682-2651.

GLADE SPRING, VA. — Miller Roller Rink. Ten mi. NE of Abingdon, Va. (703) 429-9085.

HICKORY, N.C. — Skateland. US 64-70. 322-8824.

JOHNSON CITY, TENN.—Skate Inn of Johnson City, Inc. 302 Wesley St. (615) 926-9622.

LENOIR, N.C. — Skyline Skating Rink. Cajan Mountain Road. 728-9944.

MARION, N.C. — Catawba Skateland. US 221. 652-4425.

MORGANTON, N.C. — Skateland Roller Rink. US 70 West. 433-9943.

N. WILKESBORO, N.C. — Wilkes Rollercade. US 268 East. (919) 638-3042.

ANNUAL EVENTS
(Phone sponsor or C. of C. to confirm information. If no area code is shown, use 704.)
JANUARY
BOONE, N.C. — Regional Skating Competition. Jan. 28 through 31. The Polar Palace.

FEBRUARY
BANNER ELK, N.C. — Dogwood Figure Skating Club Ice Show. Beech Mountain. Exhibition skating. 387-2231.

JANUARY — FEBRUARY
BANNER ELK, N.C. — Winter Festival. Last Thursday in January through second Sunday in February. Watch newspapers for details. ISIA ice skating championships kickoff.

24 different strokes for different folks

The reading on the thermometer may deny it but even wintertime is the right time to take the plunge and enjoy the freedom of a satisfying swim. Nautical opportunities abound the year round and if by chance you don't know how to swim, there's a variety of instruction available for tiny tots, children, teenagers and adults (which just about covers everyone except the dog who knows how without even trying). If you know how to swim and would like to improve your swimming skill or diving technique, join one of the classes or take a life-saving course.

Swimming facilities include indoor and outdoor Olympic-size pools as well as loads of natural swimming areas listed in Chapter 11.

At the Watauga County Swimming Pool you can get in on beginner or age-group competitive swimming lessons. Here in the Swim Clinic, the four competitive strokes are taught as well as the mechanics of improving them. If you want to perfect your diving form, sign up at the Diving School.

There's a recreation complex in Boone which includes a junior, a kiddie, and diving pool area. Regardless of weather conditions, the "Welcome" mat is out inviting you to swim under a roof which is retractable and where sliding doors will either let the weather in or close it out.

The Olympic-size outdoor municipal pool at Blowing Rock is open from June to Labor Day and engages excellent instructors who supervise exciting programs for all ages.

So why not make it a special day today — take the plunge and swim your cares away...

(If no area code is shown, use 704.)

Key: H = heated, I = indoor, O = outdoor

BANNER ELK, N.C. — Lees-McRae College. Rhea-Lyon Swimming Pool. H, I. 898-5241.

BANNER ELK, N.C. — Wildcat Lake. O.

BLOWING ROCK, N.C. — Municipal Olympic Pool. H, O. Summer. 295-3700.

BLUFF CITY, TENN. — Underwood Park. O. Summer.

BOONE, N.C. — Seven Devils. O. Lake — summer. 963-4336.

BOONE, N.C. — Watauga County Swimming Pool. H, I. Hunting Lane. 264-0270.

BRISTOL, TENN. — American Legion Pool. O. Wallace Road. Summer.

BRISTOL, TENN. — Clay Pool. O. Edgemont Ave. Summer. (615) 764-4002.

BRISTOL, TENN. — Haynes-Field Pool O. Bluff City Highway. Summer. (615) 764-6554.

BRISTOL, TENN. — King College Swimming Pool. H, I. (615) 968-1187.

BRISTOL, TENN. — Steele Creek Park. O. Sandy Beach. (615) 764-9621.

BURNSVILLE, N.C. — Mountain Wilderness Retreat. O. 10 mi. south on NC 197. 682-3244.

DAMASCUS, VA. — Municipal Pool. O. Summer.

ELIZABETHTON, TENN. — Franklin Club Pool. O. Glantzstoff Hwy. (615) 542-2291.

ERWIN, TENN. — Buffalo Valley Country Club. Members and motel guests. Olympic pool. H, O. (615) 743-9181.

ERWIN, TENN. — Y.M.C.A. H, I. Love Street. (615) 743-3361.

HAMPTON, TENN. — Hillbilly World. O. US 19E. (615) 725-2051.

HAMPTON, TENN. — Lakeshore Resort Marina. O. (615) 725-2223.

HICKORY, N.C. — Lake Hickory. O.

HICKORY, N.C. — Ridgeview Park. O. 11th Ave. SW at 3rd St.

HICKORY, N.C. — W. Hickory Park. O. 330 16th St. SW. Summer.

INDEPENDENCE, VA. — Osborne's Motel. O. (703) 773-3221.

JOHNSON CITY, TENN. — East Tenn. State University. H, I. (615) 929-4112.

JOHNSON CITY, TENN. — Freedom Hall Swimming Pool. H, I. 102 W. Myrtle Ave. (615) 926-3140.

JOHNSON CITY, TENN. — Park and Recreation Board. O. Swimming Pool. Legion Street. (615) 926-3561.

LENOIR, N.C. — Brown Mountain Beach. O. Wilson Creek Road. Lake — summer. 754-9756.

LENOIR, N.C. — Playmore Beach. O. Seven miles south on NC 18. Lake — summer.

LENOIR, N.C. — Powell Road Swimming Pool. I. O. Summer. 758-9194.

MARION, N.C. — Catawba Swimming Pool. O. Summer. 752-3876.

MARION, VA. – Hungry Mother State Park. Hungry Mother Lake. O. Summer. (703) 783-3422.

MILLIGAN COLLEGE, TENN. — Milligan Col. H, I. Field House. (615) 929-0116.

MORGANTON, N.C. — Collett St. Pool. O. Summer. 437-3246.

MORGANTON, N.C. — Optimist Park. O. Twelve miles north on SR 181. Summer. 437-5061.

ROARING GAP, N.C. — High Meadows Country Club. H, I. Plexiglåss-covered swimming pool from which swimmers may observe skiiers. (919) 363-2445.

SPARTA, N.C. — Duncan Recreation Center. Swimming Pool. H, I.

SPRUCE PINE, N.C. — Blue Marlin Swimming Pool. O. Beaver Creek Road.

SPRUCE PINE, N.C. — Safari Campground Pool. O. Safari Campground. 765-7187.

YADKIN RIVER, N.C. — W. Kerr Scott Reservoir. Boomer Road Park. O. Bandits Roost Park. O. Smithey's Creek Park. O. Warrior Creek Park. O. Lake — summer. (919) 921-3390.

25 alley-oops!

What's an ideal family fun sport when you're all together in one place, you're wondering what to do, and you'd like to do something else for a change. There's always the bowling alley for a bit of friendly competition. Special party and family rates as well as bowling instruction are available at some of these alleys. How would you like to improve your game, maintain your score, or get a few inside tips from a local pro? The name of this game is Ten Pins! It will be "music" to hear the thundering crash of spares and strikes!

(If no area code is shown, use 704.)

BRISTOL, TENN. — Belmont Lanes. Weaver Pike. (615) 764-5135.

BRISTOL, VA. — Interstate Bowl. I-81, RFD 4. (703) 669-5942.

ELIZABETHTON, TENN. — Dixie Lanes. W. Elk Ave. (615) 542-5411.

ERWIN, TENN. — Unicoi Lanes, Inc. 119 N. Main Ave. (615) 743-9501.

GALAX, VA. — Gala Bowl. 545 E. Stuart Dr. (703) 236-5951.

HICKORY, N.C. — Colonial Lanes, Inc. US 70 SE. 327-2695, 322-1394.

JOHNSON CITY, TENN. — Brunswick Holiday Lanes. Mountcastle Dr. (615) 926-8182.

LENOIR, N.C. — Glen Bernie Lanes, Inc. 501 S. By-pass. 758-1071.

MAIDEN, N.C. — Town & Country Bowling Lanes. NC 150. By-pass Lincolnton. 755-9046 or 5890.

MARION, N.C. — Woodlawn Lanes. US 221. 756-4334.

MARION, N.C. — Hurricane Bowl. (703) 464-5890.

MORGANTON, N.C. — Mimosa Lanes, Inc. E. Fleming Dr. 437-7044.

NEWTON, N.C. — Twin City Lanes, Inc. US 321. 464-5890.

N. WILKESBORO, N.C. — Wilkes Lanes. Billiard Lounge. NC 268 E. (919) 667-6741.

SPRUCE PINE, N.C. — Oak Lanes. 607 Oak Ave. 7 nights. Music. Free bowling instruction. Bowling apparel and accessories. 765-9545.'

26 king of the track

If stock car racing raises your spirits — Southern style, Grand National stock cars, with exciting action all the way, then you're a fan of one of the top spectator professional sports in the country. There's a full program of weekend races to choose from, testing skills and endurance at three great speedways from March through November.

The North Wilkesboro Speedway (since 1947), originally a dirt track when racing was in souped-up jalopies, is now a paved five-eighths mile, high banked track holding major National Association for Stock Car Auto Racing (NASCAR) events. The size of the track, with its wide sweeping turns, facilitating suspenseful passing, allows a close-up view of what's happening.

Generally, children under 12 are admitted free when accompanied by an adult. Campers are welcome and there's ample free parking. Other special events, such as Agricultural Fairs, Soap Box Derbys and Horseshows are also held at the speedways.

For Hickory Speedway race broadcasts, tune in to WIRC Radio 630 on the AM dial.

For information and schedules of races write or call:

Bristol International Speedway and Dragway, P.O. Box 3029, Bristol, Tenn. 27620. (615) 764-1161.

Hickory Speedway, US 64/70/I-40 Bypass, Hickory, N.C. 28601. 464-3655.

North Wilkesboro Speedway, Old US 421 East, P.O. Box 337, N. Wilkesboro, N.C. 28659. (919) 667-6663.

ANNUAL EVENTS

(Phone sponsor or C. of C. to confirm information. If no area code is shown, use 704.)

MARCH
BRISTOL, TENN. — Southeastern 500. Third Sunday. Bristol International Speedway and Dragway Grand National Stock Car Races, 250 miles. Sanctioned by NASCAR.

HICKORY, N.C. — Hickory 400. Hickory Speedway.

APRIL
N. WILKESBORO, N.C. — Gwyn Staley 400 Grand National Stock Car Race. Second or third Sunday. N. Wilkesboro Speedway. 2:00 p.m.

MAY
HICKORY, N.C. — Hickory Speedway "Wade Stephens Memorial." First Sunday. 200-lap National.

BRISTOL, TENN. — The Tennessee 500. Fourth Sunday. International Speedway and Dragway. 250-mile New Car Championship Race.

JUNE

BRISTOL, TENN. — The Spring Nationals. Third week. International Speedway and Dragway National Championship. Sanctioned by the National Hot Rod Association (NHRA).

BRISTOL, TENN. — Soapbox Derby. International Speedway and Dragway.

HICKORY, N.C. — 100-Lap Sportsman, 100-Lap Limited. Third Saturday. Hickory Speedway.

JULY

BRISTOL, TENN. — Volunteer 500. International Speedway and Dragway Grand National Stock Car Race, 250 miles. Sanctioned by NASCAR.

HICKORY, N.C. — Jaycee Spectacular: 200-Lap National. First Saturday. Hickory Speedway. 8:00 p.m.

HICKORY, N.C. — Powder Puff Derby. Second Saturday. Hickory Speedway. Seven other races included. 8:00 p.m.

HICKORY, N.C. — 200-lap State Championship. 4th Sat. Hickory Speedway. 8:00 p.m.

AUGUST

HICKORY, N.C. — Sunoco 190. First Sat. Hickory Speedway. 8 races. 8:00 p.m.

N. WILKESBORO, N.C. — Wilkes Dragmeet (since 1970). Second Saturday and Sunday. N. Wilkesboro Dragway. 8:00 p.m. Saturday — Elimination; 9:00 p.m. Saturday — Pro-Stock Qualifying; 3:00 p.m. Sunday — Elimination; 4:00 p.m. Sunday — Class Elimination.

HICKORY, N.C. — Permatex 200 — National Championship. Fourth Saturday. Hickory Speedway. 8:00 p.m.

SEPTEMBER

BRISTOL, TENN. — All-American National Drag Championship. Third or fourth weekend, Thursday through Saturday. International Speedway and Dragway. Sanctioned by the American Hot Rod Assn (AHRA).

N. WILKESBORO, N.C. — Qualifying Trials for Sunday's Grand National. Third Friday and Saturday. N. Wilkesboro Speedway.
1:30 p.m. Friday and Saturday; 3:00 p.m. Saturday: 100-Lap Race for Baby Grand Cars.

BRISTOL, TENN. — Volunteer 500. Third weekend, Friday, Saturday and Sunday. International Speedway and Dragway.

N. WILKESBORO, N.C. — Wilkes 400 Winston Cup Grand National Stock Car Race. Fourth Sunday or first Sunday in October. 2:00 p.m.

NOVEMBER

BRISTOL, TENN. — Volunteer 500. First Sunday. International Speedway and Dragway.

27   **grand slam!**

CALLING—ALL—BRIDGE—PLAY—ERS: hours of friendly fellowship and camaraderie are yours if you play bridge, even if you're traveling alone. All you have to do is call in advance for a game and a partner will be arranged. If you're a traveling twosome, partners are welcome at all games. Often, invitational clubs extend this courtesy to visitors. Each club establishes rules of eligibility for playing and you don't have to be a member of the American Contract Bridge League to be in line for master or rating point awards. Here's the scoop:

KEY: O = Open   I = Invitational   N = Novice

ABINGDON, VA. — Abingdon Bridge Club. Sue's Shop and Party House. Saturday **1:00** p.m. (703) 944-3261.

BLOWING ROCK, N.C. — Mountain Club Bridge Club. I. Country Club Road. Tuesday ll:00 a.m. June, July, August, September. 295-3797.

BOONE, N.C. — Boone Bridge Club. O. Lovill Dorm, ASU. Wed. 7:30 p.m. 264-9422.

BRISTOL, VA. — Bristol Duplicate Bridge Club. O. 110 Piedmont St. Tuesday 7:30 p.m. (615) 968-1927.

CONOVER, N.C. — Conover Duplicate Club. O. 101 First St. E. Thursday 10:00 a.m. 464-4156.

ELKIN, N.C. — Cedarbrook Contract Club. I. Friday 10:00 a.m. (919) 835-6804.

GALAX, VA. — Galax Duplicate Bridge Club. Galax Contract Club. O-Wednesday 10:00 a.m. semi-monthly. **O-**Thursday 7:30 p.m. semi-monthly. (703) 236-5841.

HICKORY, N.C. — Hickory Duplicate Club. O. Hickory Foundation. Monday 7:30 p.m., Saturday 1:30 p.m. 322-9220.

JOHNSON CITY, TENN. — Twin City Duplicate Bridge Club. O. Independent Education, Eastern Tennessee State University, Room 205. Tuesday 7:00 p.m., Friday 7:30 p.m. (615) 753-3902.

LENOIR, N.C. — Lenoir Bridge Club. Mulberry Street Recreation Center. **720** Mulberry St. SW. **N.** Thursday 7:30 p.m., **O.** Thursday 7:30 p.m. 754-5573.

MARION, VA. — Marion Duplicate Bridge Club. O. Stage Street. Tuesday, semi-monthly. (703) 783-2360.

ANNUAL EVENTS

(Phone sponsor or C. of C. to confirm information. If no area code is shown, use 704.)

JUNE

BANNER ELK, N.C. — Sugar Mountain Sectional or Bridge Championship. First week, four days: Thursday — Sunday. Sugar Mountain Ski Resort. Main Building. Win-An-Entry Event; Masters' Pairs Event; Mrs. and Women's Pairs Event; Open Pairs Event. 898-4521.

OCTOBER

BOONE, N.C. — Charity Bridge Tournament. Second week. Walker Building, 2nd floor hallway, ASU. Bonus Master Point Awards.

NOVEMBER

BOONE, N.C. — Fall Open Pairs Duplicate Bridge Championship. First week. Walker Building, 2nd floor hallway, ASU. 7:30 p.m.

28 artists galore

How would you like to own an art original capturing an instant in time or become an art collector at your own price? Or, if you're a weekend painter, how would you like to exhibit your own "masterpieces," just to see what the reactions will be? Since art influences the viewer in a variety of ways, are you one who never likes to pass up an opportunity to see an art exhibit by amateurs or professionals? All of these activities are so popular throughout the year that folks just plan their vacations around the dates of scheduled art shows.

A very popular activity is the Art Show in the Park at Blowing Rock which draws thousands of visitors who delight in viewing the ingenuity of artists and craftsmen. You have a choice of being a spectator, a buyer, an exhibitor — or all three, at this highly welcome event which is scheduled on four Saturdays during the summer months. Artists from all over the Southland are featured as well as artists from other regions including Puerto Rico. Not only are paintings in oils and water colors displayed but the traditional mountain crafts are exhibited. This is truly a tremendous family attraction with items for sale from pennies to dollars so that each family member can satisfy a yen for an artistic purchase. Nature's own outdoor gallery is ideally suited for displaying the aisles and aisles of colorful, remarkable oils, watercolors, pottery, candles, and other handcrafted articles under massive shade trees. An eye-catcher is the portrait sketch artist's stall where spectators enjoy either having their portraits done or just watching an artist at work. Exhibitors run the gamut from Sunday painters to professional artists. Anyone 18 years and older wishing to exhibit may register for the Art Show.

In Boone, the Regional Gallery of Art, West King Street (opposite the post office), founded in 1969, is the oldest and largest independently established gallery in western North Carolina. Changing art exhibits are presented monthly and the artists are generally present to discuss their works at the Open House showing.

Also, as long as you're near a university, college or library, you may amply satisfy your artistic urge!

(Contact sponsor or C. of C. to confirm information. If no area code is shown, use 704.)

YEAR-ROUND OR SEASONAL

BANNER ELK, N.C. — Periodic Art Exhibits. J. H. Carson Library, Lees-McRae College.

BLOWING ROCK, N.C. — Art in the Park. Displays of paintings, arts and crafts, beadwork, leather, plastic and woodcraft. A series of Art Shows during June, July and August.

BLOWING ROCK, N.C. — Blowing Rock Auction Galleries, Inc. Main Street. June through October. 295-3280.

BLOWING ROCK, N.C. — Fincke Gallery. Main Street. June thru Oct. 295-3389.

BLOWING ROCK, N.C. — The Collector's Gallery. Sunset Drive. Paintings and antique furniture. 264-7866 or 7470.

BLOWING ROCK, N.C. — Under the Apple Tree (Old Post Galleries). Old Post Office on Sunset Drive. Jewelry, plants. Paintings: still life, landscapes, portraits. Setting is an adorable luncheon-tea room, sidewalk cafe. 295-3777.

BOONE, N.C. — Appalachian Gallery. NC 105 at Valle Crucis Road. Exhibits of professional artists and craftspeople: basket and other weaving, doll making, jewelry making, pottery.

BOONE, N.C. — Country House Village Fine Arts Gallery. Nine miles south on NC 105. 963-5858.

BOONE, N.C. — Dogwood Gallery. Plemmons Student Center, ASU. 262-3030.

BOONE, N.C. — HANDS. NC 105. Paintings, photography, arts and crafts by skilled craftspeople. 264-9743.

BOONE, N.C. — Regional Gallery of Art. W. King Street. Special monthly painting exhibits; pottery, blown glass, jewelry. 10:00 a.m. — :5:00 p.m. Monday through Saturday. 264-2262.

BOONE, N.C. — University Art Gallery. ASU Faculty Apartments Basement. 262-2220.

BRISTOL, VA. — Fine Arts Center. Virginia Intermont College. Series of art exhibits. (703) 669-6035.

EMORY, VA. — Byers Fine Art Center. Emory and Henry College. (703) 944-3121.

HICKORY, N.C. — Hickory Arts Council. Sponsors programs of well-known artists during year.

HICKORY, N.C. — Museum of Art. First Ave. and 3rd St. N.W. An outstanding collection of American art. 327-8576.

HICKORY, N.C. — Lenoir-Rhyne College. Cramer College Center. Periodic student art displays. 328-1741.

JEFFERSON, N.C. — Ashe County Bicentennial Center. Classes in Drawing, Quilting and Creative Writing; variety of art and photography exhibits. (919) 246-5161.

JOHNSON CITY, TENN. — Carroll Reece Museum. East Tennessee State University. Paintings, traveling art exhibits and art objects. (615) 929-4392 or 4283.

LENOIR, N.C. — Caldwell Arts Council. Mulberry Street Recreation Center. Sponsors courses and programs encouraging community arts. 758-7276.

LENOIR, N.C. — Caldwell County Library. Art exhibits.

LITTLE SWITZERLAND, N.C. — The Little Gallery. Paintings of the mountain region, acrylics, oils, watercolors. 765-2153.

MORGANTON, N.C. — Jailhouse Gallery. 115 E. Meeting St. 433-7282.

NEWLAND, N.C. — Morrison Public Library. Periodic art shows. 733-9333.

N. WILKESBORO — The Northwest Art Gallery. NC 105 at Armory Road. Some of finest artists and craftspeople represented. One-man shows. (919) 667-2841.

N. WILKESBORO, N.C. — Wilkes Art Guild. Wilkes Community College. Art lectures, demonstrations and workshops. (919) 667-7136.

SPRUCE PINE, N.C. — Spruce Pine Public Library. Walnut Avenue. Regular displays of paintings and crafts. 765-4673.

ANNUAL EVENTS

FEBRUARY

BOONE, N.C. — Fine Arts Festival. First or second Thursday. First Baptist Church Fellowship Hall. Student and adult art competition in creative expression: crafts, graphic arts, landscapes and seascapes. Sponsor: Junior Woman's Club.

BOONE, N.C. — ASU Women's Art Show. First Sunday. University Art Gallery. Paintings, etchings, photography, tapestries by ASU art students. Works are for sale.

BOONE, N.C. — Appalachian National Drawing Exhibition (since 1975). ASU Art Department. Juried exhibition of drawings from across the land.

APRIL

ELIZABETHTON, TENN. — Elizabethton Art Show. Last weekend, Thursday — Sunday. West Side School PTA.

ERWIN, TENN. — Arts and Crafts Festival.

BOONE, N.C. — Watauga County Spring Festival (since 1974). Fourth Saturday. ASU campus. Art exhibitions, handcrafts. (See Ch. 54.)

MAY

ELKIN, N.C. — Spring Fling. Second weekend.

JUNE

N. WILKESBORO, N.C. — Arts Emphasis Week. Art exhibit, ballet, opera, pops concert, play, tours of homes.

JULY

HICKORY, N.C. — Catawba Valley Arts Show. Second and third weeks. Hickory Museum of Art. Professional and amateur artists exhibiting. 327-8576.

LENOIR, N.C. — Black Arts Festival. Third week. Viewmont Recreation Center. 122 Green Haven Dr. 754-3278.

AUGUST

LITTLE SWITZERLAND, N.C. — Art and Craft Show. Geneva Hall. Sponsor: Little Switzerland Community Assn.

NEWTON, N.C. — Art Show. Third Tuesday — Friday. Sponsors: Northwestern Bank and Newton Arts Guild.

N. WILKESBORO, N.C. — Northwest Outdoor Art Show. Third Saturday. Smoot Park. Sponsor: Wilkes Art Guild. 10:00 a.m. — 5:00 p.m.

BLOWING ROCK, N.C. — High Country Arts, Crafts and Antique Show. Last weekend, Saturday and Sunday. *Tweetsie* Railroad Grounds.

OCTOBER

N. WILKESBORO, N.C. — The Northwest Arts and Crafts Fair. Third Saturday. National Guard Armory. Exhibit of original works by artists, sculptors and craftspeople. Awards. Sponsor: Wilkes Art Guild. 10:00 a.m. — 4:00 p.m.

NOVEMBER

BOONE, N.C. — Printmakers Invitational Exhibition. Last three weeks. RGA Galleries. W. King Street. North Carolina printmakers. 264-2262.

29
beautiful hands, busy fingers

COME TO THE FAIR! COME TO THE FESTIVAL! COME TO THE CRAFTS SHOW! Get in on the action — the year-round craft displays, exhibitions, demonstrations — see how it's made, woven, spun, dyed, braided, hooked, formed, whittled, carved, painted, drawn, sewn, played; see gems cut, shaped, polished, faceted, and see many other work skills demonstrated in the region that's home to a host of expert mountain craftspeople. These artisans are well-known for their exhibitions and demonstrations around the United States. Skills have been handed down from generation to generation and the love of the craftsman for his craft is transmitted somehow to each article which seems to always retain the original glow it had at the time of your purchase. If you should ask a mountaineer for an explanation of how, for example, he carves a bird, he might reply (paraphrasing Michelangelo): "You take a chisel, a mallet, and a tree trunk and cut away anything that doesn't look like a bird!"

Although there are many independent creative craftsmen who sell on their own, there are non-profit craft cooperatives that run wholesale and retail quality sales shows during the year. In this area there are the Appalachia Crafts, Inc., The Blue Ridge Craft Hearthside Association, Cliff Hangers Crafts Association, The Greater Grandfather Arts Guild, "HANDS" Craftsmens Association, Holston Mountain Arts and Crafts Cooperative, Southern Highland Handicraft Guild, and Stone Mountain Crafts.

And wherever there's a fair, festival or show, it's sure to be enlivened by foot-stompin' musicians who've made their own dulcimers, banjos, fiddles, ukeleles or violins. In fact, there's a dulcimer maker whose autographed instruments are a guarantee of recognition and value, prized by collectors and performers alike. Usually, there'll also be colorful square dancers, mountain cloggers, folk dancers and singers, and tellers of tall tales. Oftentimes, you'll have the opportunity to see unique collections of antique agricultural, carpentry, cobbler's and sewing tools.

Would you be interested in a gee-haw, whimmy diddle, a flipperdinger, or a jumpin' jig? How about a moonwinder or an upside down doll, or a corn shuck doll? All of these popular folktoys that are "different" are handcrafted in local homes, more than 50 varieties, and are now marketed around the globe by Jack Guy's Native Crafts Cooperative, in Sugar Grove near Boone. Toys that were made originally by pioneer daddies — " 'cause there warn't nuthin' else around" — have caught the fancy of city and country folk all over.

Because of this ever-increasing demand for handmade articles, you may easily be smitten to "join the club" and turn on to a satisfying hobby, or a satisfying career, or a satisfying pasttime of collecting items with the personal touch which make them really special. They might even become heirlooms. It's not only good therapy but a pleasant way to boost your earnings.

Also, in this area is one of the few craft schools of its kind in the world and one of the oldest in this country (1929) — the Penland School of Crafts — whose purpose is to preserve mountain crafts. Highly trained, producing craftsmen head the programs assisted by noted guest artisans. The school, just six miles northwest of Spruce Pine, is really worth visiting, especially the gift shop. Classes are informal and friendly held in-and-out-of-doors and studios and equipment are open for use round the clock, seven days a week. Minimum age is 18 with no upper limits. (See Ch. 37.)

See the sample listing of year-round and summer craft shops open for delightful, pleasurable browsing and gift selections. Included are choice annual and seasonal craft shows you won't want to miss!

For gem and rock shops see Ch. 34.

ABINGDON, VA. — The Cave House Craft Shop. 279 East Main St. An old Victorian structure. Displays of corn shuckery, quilting, chair caning, block printing, sculpting, knitting, musical instruments, weaving, wood carving, leather work, etc. Their motto: "If we don't have it, we can make it." Sponsor: Holston Mountain Arts and Crafts Corp. (703) 628-7721.

ABINGDON, VA. — Cumbow China Decorating Company. 436 East Main St. Showplace for internationally famous Ruskin china created by owner; skillful restoration of fine china guaranteed to last forever. (703) 628-2471.

BAKERSVILLE, N.C. — Roan View Gift Shop. Roan Valley. Mountain crafts by local craftsmen: quilts, pottery, dolls, beads, silk screening, macrame, windmills, metal sculpture.

BANNER ELK, N.C. — Beech Mountain Craft Shops. Leather tooling, glass blowing, jewelry making, sign carving. Mid-June through October.

BANNER ELK, N.C. — "The Cheese House." Arts and Information Center, NC 184. Demonstrations and exhibits of various crafts by local craftspeople. During a typical month there were demonstrations and displays of weaving, bark and berry basketmaking, mountain toys, musical instruments, rug hooking, wrought iron, candle and soap making, butter churning, mountain cooking and vegetable dyeing. Sponsor: The Greater Grandfather Arts Guild.

BANNER ELK, N.C. — Covered Bridge Crafts. Halfway up Beech Mountain. Professional craftsmen in residence offering fine quality items including clocks, scrimshaw, woodcarving, carved signs and pottery. 898-5788.

BANNER ELK, N.C. — Everything Scottish, Ltd. Woolens, tartans by the yard, kilts, kilted skirts, ties, scarves, sweaters, Buchan thistleware pottery, bagpipes, practice chanters, cookbooks and other literature, shortcake, jams and more goodies. Shop is a reproduction of 16th Century "tallbooth" or town hall in Invershiel, replica of Scottish village. 898-4414.

BANNER ELK, N.C. — The Kiln Room. NC 105. Original works designed and produced by skillfully trained artists. Pottery created while you browse in the rustic gallery salesroom. "Friendly" clay animals. 963-5865.

BLOUNTVILLE, TENN. — Holston Mountain Arts and Crafts, Inc. Route 2.

BLOWING ROCK, N.C. — The Apple Tree, Ltd. Main Street. Handcrafts, jewelry, custom quilts, pewter. 295-3155.

BLOWING ROCK, N.C. — Blowing Rock Crafts, Inc. Cornish Road near traffic light on US 321 By-pass. Early American weave shed of Goodwin Guild. Demonstrations and displays of weaving, native crafts, tablecloths, napkins, placemats, potholders, afghans in Scotch and star plaids; family collection of over 530 coverlet patterns. 295-3577.

BLOWING ROCK, N.C. — Blue Ridge Gift Shop. Main Street. Mountain handcrafts, lamps, pictures, clocks, gifts from around the world. 295-7390.

BLOWING ROCK, N.C. — The Farm House, Inc. Shopping Promenade, South Main Street. Handcrafts, jewelry, dulcimers, souvenirs. 295-3131.

BLOWING ROCK, N.C. — The Hayes House. Main Street. Silver, turquoise jewelry, pewter. **Needle Nicely** all kinds of art needlework. 295-3313.

BLOWING ROCK, N.C. — Herbert Cohen. Linville Road. Pottery, ceramics. 295-7246.

BLOWING ROCK, N.C. — Minerva's. Main Street. Mountain crafts. 295-7830.

BLOWING ROCK, N.C. — The Mountain Craftsman. Blowing Rock Road. Native crafts, Shaker furniture, home-baked goodies. 295-3198.

BLOWING ROCK, N.C. — The Mountain Shop. US 221, Linville Road. Handcrafts, souvenirs, homemade jams and jellies, mountain honey. 295-7521.

BLOWING ROCK, N.C. — The Pewter Shop. US 221, three miles south. Beautiful array of handcrafted candlesticks, trays, plates, tankards and art objects. 295-3368.

BLOWING ROCK, N.C. — The Rain Forest. Blowing Rock Road. Plants 'n Things. Craft shop features custom leather work, pottery, turquoise jewelry, blown glass. 295-3826.

BLOWING ROCK, N.C. — The Rock Gift Shop. US 321 at The Blowing Rock. All kinds of attractions in handcrafts. 295-7111.

BLOWING ROCK, N.C. — The Silver Tree. Main Street in The Apple Tree. Original handcrafted jewelry in gold and silver, custom designs. 295-3155.

BLUE RIDGE PARKWAY, N.C. — Brinegar Cabin. Milepost 238.5. Handcraft exhibits and fascinating local lore.

BLUE RIDGE PARKWAY, N.C. — Cherry Hill. Milepost 257. Native handcraft shop.

BLUE RIDGE PARKWAY, N.C. — Northwest Trading Post. Milepost 258.6. Glendale Springs. Quaint country store. More than 250 handmade crafts from 500 producers. Eleven counties represented. Also jellies, relishes, hams, baked goods, antiques and old furniture. April 15 through October 31. Sponsor: Northwest Development Assn.

BLUE RIDGE PARKWAY, N.C. — For Friends & Lovers. Milepost 270. Handcraft and gift gallery — leather, jewelry, home furnishings, candles.

BLUE RIDGE PARKWAY, N.C. — Parkway Craft Center. Milepost 294. Moses H. Cone Memorial Park. Mountain handcraft such as baskets, wood carvings, brooms, hooked rugs, conecraft, pottery, hand-woven goods, iron work, enamels, copper, dolls, silver jewelry and furniture. Demonstrations of rug making, weaving and other crafts. May to November. Sponsor: Southern Highland Handicraft Guild. 295-7938.

BOONE, N.C. — Crickside Mountain Crafts and Antiques. Linville Road. 264-8133.

BOONE, N.C. — The General Store. Blue Ridge Cottage Industries, Inc. The Country House Village, NC 105. A lovely complex of shops, apartments and restaurant around a gushing little stream and village green. Wholesale and retail handcrafts, designer collection of patchwork furniture covers, Christmas tree balls, wreaths, stockings and trees, dolls, toys, baskets for fern stands and planters. 963-5858.

BOONE, N.C. –HANDS. NC 105, next to Ramada Inn. Handcrafted candles, dulcimers, furniture, jewelry, needlework, pottery, paintings, plants, quilts, sculpture and photography. Sponsor: "HANDS" Craftsmen's Association. 264-9743.

BOONE, N.C. — House of Creative Crafts. Blowing Rock Road. Mountain handcrafts: leather goods, decorative wall plaques, hand-forged fireplace accessories, bark bird feeders and houses, calico bonnets, dulcimers, vegetable-dyed burlap rugs, hand-loomed placemats, woven baskets, handhooked chair pads and rugs, beeswax candles and wooden candle holders, sterling silver jewelry, handmade furniture of solid woods. 264-9078.

BOONE, N.C. — The Glass Barn. Blowing Rock Road. Handcrafted and handblown glass of an amazing variety, handmade candles. 264-4174.

BOONE, N.C. — "Horn in the West" Gift Shop — Crafts Unlimited. "Horn in the West" grounds. Handcrafted items, knits, large number of handmade items and souvenirs. Sponsor: Boone Worthwhile Woman's Club. Open during play season before performance. Noon to 11:00 p.m. Mondays, noon to 6:00 p.m. 264-3285.

BOONE, N.C. — The Log Haus. Blowing Rock Road. Large selection of handcrafted items. 264-5664.

BOONE, N.C. — Lost Scotsman Silver Mine. 603 E. King St. Custom designing turquoise jewelry, leather. 264-0820.

BOONE, N.C. — Mountain Top Ceramics. 1707 E. King St. Greenware, free lessons. 264-0226.

BOONE, N.C. — Watauga Handcrafts (since 1930). Hardin Street, US 321 and 421. A varied collection of regional handcrafts including corn cob and corn shuck dolls, quilts, placemats, ceramics, glassware, jewelry, framed nature pictures, brooms, toys, hooked chairmats. Weaving instruction (seven looms). May — October. 10:00 a.m. — 8:00 p.m. Monday through Saturday; 1:00 — 8:00 p.m Sunday.

BRISTOL, TENN. — Loretta Abston, Pottery. 1100 Florida Ave. Hand-thrown pottery custom made. (615) 764-4943.

BRISTOL, TENN. — Brynfield of London. Tri-City Airport. Handcrafts and unique gifts for all occasions. (615) 323-6202.

BRISTOL, TENN. — Hall's Handicrafts. Edgemont Shopping Center. (615) 968-1911.

BRISTOL, TENN. — The All American Country Garden Store. 2825 Volunteer Parkway at Bristol Speedway. Handcrafts, old-timey gifts, country furniture, plants, antiques. (615) 968-7932.

BRISTOL, VA. — The Guild Gallery. 501 State St. Weaving, ceramics, woodworking by craftsmen from mountain areas of nine states. Sponsor: Southern Highland Handicraft Guild. (703) 669-0821.

BURNSVILLE, N.C. — Ce-Nan's Ceramics. Main Street. Greenware, kiln instruction, paints, gifts. 683-3728.

BURNSVILLE, N.C. — Barbara Grenell. Celo Farm, Celo. Vegetable Dyed Yarn: "a beautiful organic reminder of the treasures found in nature." Come smell the natural dyes simmering over a wood fire in late summer and early fall.

BURNSVILLE, N.C. — Hemlock Hills Homecrafts. NC 80 at Celo. Handmade articles by North Carolina craftspeople. Ceramics, dolls, baskets, pillows, pine cone crafts, quilts, nature plaques, local jewelry and attic treasures. 675-4902.

BURNSVILLE, N.C. — Lamp Post Shop. US 19E, West Main Street. In addition to lamps: handcrafts, candles, needlepoint and kitchen items. 682-2444.

BURNSVILLE, N.C. — Laurel Mountain Crafts. Two miles south of Micaville.

BURNSVILLE, N.C. — McWhirter Pottery. NC 80 at Celo.

BURNSVILLE, N.C. — The Candle Light. NC 80 at Celo. Largest candle shop in the East. Old farm house. Original handcrafted designs, ancient craft of glass mosaic called "Gloom Chasers" and an interesting collection of old candle sticks. 675-4189.

BURNSVILLE, N.C. — The Hillbilly Craft Shop. Bolems Creek Road, 1109 off Pensacola Hwy. Bicentennial china dolls and crafts. 682-3527.

BURNSVILLE, N.C. — The Pendulum Shop. East Main Street at the surrey with the fringe on top. Signs, designs, old pieces, crafts, custom framing, odds and ends.   682-2463.

BURNSVILLE, N.C. — Ruby's Permanent Flowers & Gifts. Main Street. Unusual gifts. 682-3600.

BURNSVILLE, N.C. — Toe River Craftsmen. Seven miles south of Micaville, NC 80 at Celo. Area craftsmen displaying free-blown glass, weaving, stained glass, prints, sculpture, batik, stitchery, pottery, crochet and photography.

BURNSVILLE, N.C. — Yancey County Country Store. At the lovely town square. Allow plenty of time for browsing through this rambling store jam-packed with old and new: pottery, calico, family pitchers, patterns, dolls, folk toys, sealing wax, moustache cups, clocks, placemats, puzzles, hammocks and loads more. Play a game of checkers or shell some corn — it's a fun place! 682-3779.

CONOVER, N.C. — The Pepper Tree House of Arts and Crafts. Near Hickory, RFD 2, across from Catawba Mem. Hospital. Unique handmade items, plaster crafts. 322-6654.

CROSSNORE, N.C. — Crossnore Sales Store. Across from Post Office. Handcrafted articles and used clothing. Proceeds help support Crossnore School, Inc. Ceramics and handsewn articles also sold. Visit school weaving room and fabric shop. 733-4305.

DEEP GAP, N.C. — Ward's Produce & Gift Shop. Near Boone, eight miles east. Handcrafts, glassware, bedspreads, novelties, souvenirs. 264-6888.

ELIZABETHTON, TENN. — The Scarecrow. Pine & East Street. Assortment of mountain crafts: wooden toys, quilts, dolls and critters, patchwork. (615) 543-2200.

ELK PARK, N.C. — Wee Loch Gift Shop. Folk toys and musical instruments. 733-5301.

GALAX, VA. — New River Pottery (John Frantz). Fries, 3 mi. north on Va. 94 to SR 737, Route 1, Box 351. Earthenware and stoneware pottery made to order. (703) 744-2716.

GALAX, VA. — Rooftop of Virginia Crafts. 206 N. Main St. Needlework, pottery, woodcarving. (703) 236-9511.

HICKORY, N.C. — A. A. Brinkley, Metalsmith. 464 7th St. SW. Fireplace accessories, logholders, pincers and pokers. 328-1563.

HICKORY, N.C. — Collectors Studio. 2763 N. Center St. 322-1846.

HICKORY, N.C. — Godfrey's. Hildebran, five miles west of Hickory. Craft shop, copperware, collector's items, bowls and teardrop swirl enamel plates, as well as handcrafted items by other craftsmen. These unusual pieces have been displayed in Egypt, India and the Smithsonian Institute.

HICKORY, N.C. — Hobnob Corner. 10 23rd Ave. NE. 322-1846.

HICKORY, N.C. — J J's Crafts N' Things. 918 3rd Ave. NW. 328-4658.

HICKORY, N.C. — Hyalyn Porcelain Showroom. Old Lenoir road. Colorful display of hostess serving items, lamp bases, vases, ashtrays. 322-6413.

INDEPENDENCE, VA. — Padgett House. (703) 773-4981.

JOHNSON CITY, TENN. — Lady Bug Gallery. 208 E. Main St. Handmade Tennessee crafts. (615) 926-2931.

LAUREL BLOOMERY, TENN. — iron mountain. Near Mountain City. On Tenn. 91 towards Damascus, Va. The only high-fired stoneware dinnerware plant in the U.S. Take a fascinating tour, Monday through Friday. Seconds available. Sundays 11:00 a.m — 6:00 p.m. (615) 898-4414.

LENOIR, N.C. — Crafts Unlimited, Inc. 907 College Ave. SW. Hand-woven baskets and planters. 758-7377.

LINVILLE, N.C. — Bear Den. US 221. Handcrafts.

LINVILLE, N.C. — Martin's Handcrafts. Junction US 221 and NC 184.

LITTLE SWITZERLAND, N.C. — Skyline Craft Shop. Skyline Motor Motel and Restaurant. Great selection of souvenirs and gifts. 765-9394.

LITTLE SWITZERLAND, N.C. — The Tulip Tree. Authentic mountain crafts.

MOUNTAIN CITY, TENN. — The Craftsman's Concept. US 421, 15 miles west of Boone. (615) 727-9721.

NEWLAND, N.C. — Elaine's Ceramics & Gifts. Handmade quilts, dolls, leather crafts, jewelry, ceramics, bisque, greenware and much more. 733-9896.

OLD FORT, N.C. — Kitt Elliott Table Shop. US 70, six miles east.

PENLAND, N.C. — Penland School of Crafts Gift Shop. Three miles west of Spruce Pine, right on NC 80 three miles, left on SR 1164. School is one mile on right. Handcrafted articles: metal enameling, glass blowing, hand weaving, jewelry, plastics, pottery, vegetable dyeing and woodworking. 765-2359.

ROAN MOUNTAIN, TENN. — The Hack Line Shop. Mountain crafts, primitive furniture like pie sofas, meal chest, blanket chest and round tables.

ROAN MOUNTAIN, TENN. — The Scarecrow. Assortment of mountain crafts: wooden toys, quilts, dolls and critters, patchwork. (615) 543-2200.

SPARTA, N.C. — Arzetta's Art Shop. (919) 372-4346.

SPARTA, N.C. — Choate's Antiques — Arts and Crafts. (919) 372-8841.

SPARTA, N.C. — Pat's Craft Shop. (919) 372-5353.

SPRUCE PINE, N.C. — Bea Hensley's Forge. Five miles south on NC 226. Wrought iron work.

SPRUCE PINE, N.C. — Mayland Technical Ceramic Guild. Mayland Technical Institute. 765-7351.

SPRUCE PINE, N.C. — Ron Propst Pottery. Two miles on Penland Road off US 19E, west of Spruce Pine. Originally designed handmade stoneware pottery. 765-4060.

SPRUCE PINE, N.C. — Clyde F. Smith. Two miles west on Burnsville Highway US 19E. Handcrafted signs. 765-2104.

SPRUCE PINE, N.C. — Jim Sockwell's Pottery. NC 226 and Blue Ridge Parkway. Handthrown stoneware designed by Sockwell.

SPRUCE PINE, N.C. — Thayer Artcrafts, Inc. Route 1, Marion Road. Inlaid marquetry pictures, handcrafted items. 765-2988.

SPRUCE PINE, N.C. — Woody's Chair shop. Three miles south on NC 226, Marion Road. Handmade chairs, Colonial design. 765-9277.

SUGAR GROVE, N.C. — Jack Guy's Native Crafts. Beech Creek, US 421 and US 321. Five miles on right toward Johnson City. More than 50 kinds of handcrafted popular folk toys. 297-2650.

TRAPHILL, N.C. — Stone Mountain Crafts. State Road 1002, north of Wilkesboro. Meet the craftspeople, watch them work and try your hand at crafting. Quilts, bonnets, deer-antler knives, baskets, knitted shawls and sweaters, honey and dried fruits from nearby farms. Sponsor: Blue Ridge Opportunity Commission. May through October.

TROUTDALE, VA. — Fairwood Craft Center. Mount Rogers National Recreation Area. Near Gindstone Campground, five miles west on Va. 603. Woodcarving, pottery, needlework. Operated by Forest Service — summers.

VOLNEY, VA. — Grayson-Highlands State Park Crafts Center. Wide variety of crafts made by local craftsmen. Authentic mountain cabin. Summers. Sponsor: Virginia State Park Commission and Rooftop of Virginia, CAP.

W. JEFFERSON, N.C. — Cliff Hangers Association. Handmade quilts, afghans, bonnets, ponchos, woven apparel, toys, mountain dolls, woodcrafts. Sponsor: Blue Ridge Opportunity Commission. (919) 246-9874.

W. JEFFERSON, N.C. — Virginia's. Pottery, wood products, candles. (919) 246-2856.

ANNUAL EVENTS

(Contact sponsor or C. of C. to confirm information. If no area code is shown, use 704.)
FEBRUARY
SPRUCE PINE, N.C. — Arts and Crafts Festival. Third Thursday. United Methodist Church, East King Street. 100 or more art, craft and needlework items. Sponsor: Senior Woman's Club.

MARCH
HICKORY, N.C. — Needlework Fair. Middle of month — Friday, Saturday, Sunday. Workshops for adults and children in needlepoint, embroidery and pulled thread techniques; demonstrations, needlework competition with prize awards. Sponsor: Western Piedmont Symphony Guild.

APRIL
BOONE, N.C. — Watauga County Spring Festival. Fourth Saturday. ASU Varsity and Broome Kirk Gyms. Displays of weaving, pottery, dulcimers, handcrafts, puppet shows, art exhibit, clogging, folk singing. 10 a.m. — 5 p.m.

ERWIN, TENN. — Art and Crafts Festival.

MAY
ABINGDON, VA. — "Spring Sampler." Memorial Day Weekend. Cave House Craft Shop, 279 E. Main St. Craft demonstrations. Sponsor: Holston Mountain Arts and Crafts Coop.

JEFFERSON, N.C. — May Day Festival (since 1976). Last Saturday. Ashe County Park. Crafts a'plenty and Bluegrass, Country and Gospel music; square dancing, too, and games for everybody! Sponsor: Blue Ridge Creative Activities Council. 262-1026.

JUNE
N. WILKESBORO, N.C. — Northwest North Carolina Arts and Crafts Fair. Third Saturday. National Guard Armory, Hwy. 115 at Armory Road. Open to all artists, craftspeople, sculptors. Sale of original art works. Awards. Sponsor: The Wilkes Art Guild. 10:00 a.m. — 4:00 p.m. (919) 667-2841.

ELKIN, N.C. — Spring Festival (since 1964). Craft exhibits. Sponsor: Northwest North Carolina Extension Homemakers.

MORGANTON, N.C. — Burke Arts and Crafts Festival. Second week, Wed. to Sun.

NEWLAND, N.C. — Avery County Crafts Fair (since 1975). Fourth weekend, Friday and Saturday or first weekend in July. Newland Elementary School Gym. Demonstrations by more than 50 craftspeople. Fri.: 1:00 — 9:00 p.m.; Sat.: 10:00 a.m. — 9:00 p.m.

JULY

BANNER ELK, N.C. — Covered Bridge Crafts. July 3-6. Halfway up Beech Mountain. Craft demonstrations: clock making, pottery, carved signs, taxidermy, woodworking.

JONESBORO, TENN. — "Jonesborough Days." Independence Day weekend. Art show, craft exhibits, paintings and sculpture sale, flea market. (See Ch. 54.)

BANNER ELK, N.C. — Arts and Crafts Show (since 1974). Third week. Lees-McRae College.

BANNER ELK, N.C. — Beech Mountain Folk Festival. Third Saturday. Lees-McRae College. Craft show, paintings, dulcimer and banjo music, storyteller.

BOONE, N.C. — Mountain Arts Festival (since 1976). *Horn in the West* grounds. Arts, crafts, demonstrations, watercolors, music, dancing, games and entertainment all day! Sponsor: Blue Ridge Creative Activities Council. 262-1026.

MARION, VA. — Hungry Mother Arts and Crafts Festival (since 1974). Third weekend. Hungry Mother State Park. More than 130 exhibits and demonstrations by artists and craftspeople from southeastern United States. Folk art, painting, sketching, etc. Sponsor: Art League of Marion, and the Virginia Division of State Parks.

SPRUCE PINE, N.C. — Handmade Crafts Exhibit and Sale. July 31 and August 1. Deyton Elementary School. Sponsor: Mitchell County Extension Homemakers.

AUGUST

BURNSVILLE, N.C. — Mt. Mitchell Crafts Fair (since 1957). First weekend, Friday and Saturday. Exhibits and demonstrations of baskets, candles, ceramics, decoupage, handmade toys, wood carving, doll furniture, gems, weaving, glassblowing, pottery, needlework. Also contests and performances. (See Ch. 43.) Sponsor: Yancey County C. of C. 682-2312.

BOONE, N.C. — Boone Craftsmen's Festival (since 1972). Second week, Wednesday through Sunday. Varsity Gym, ASU. More than 70 demonstrating craftspeople and entertainment. Glassblowing, sand candles, batiks, gourd art, gold and silver wire, crewel embroidery, coppersmith and loads more. Sponsor: Blue Ridge Hearthside Crafts Assn., Inc. 262-1026 or 264-2225.

ABINGDON, VA. — The Virginia Highlands Arts and Crafts Festival. August 1 — 15. Continuous exhibits. Speshul happenin's: Senior Citizens Day, Youth Day, craft demonstrations, sidewalk art shows, an antique car show, guitar building. A memorable take-in, especially the flea market. Sponsor: Historical Society of Washington County.

YADKINVILLE, N.C. — Sunbonnet Festival. Second Saturday and Sunday. Yadkinville

School Grounds and Buildings. More than $1500 in prizes in the arts, crafts and writing. Band music, Dixieland, gospel singin' and mountain cloggin'. For entry forms write Yadkin Arts Council. Enclose stamped envelope. (919) 679-2941.

BANNER ELK, N.C. — Youth Arts and Crafts Festival. Third weekend, Friday, Saturday, Sunday. Beech Tree Village, Beech Mountain. Southeastern artists and craftspeople up to and including 16 years-of-age. Prizes. Talent contest and lotsa fun things.

BLOWING ROCK, N.C. — High Country Arts and Crafts Show. Last Saturday and Sunday. Tweetsie Railroad, Blowing Rock Road. 264-9061.

SEPTEMBER
BOONE, N.C. — Craftsmen's Fair (since 1976). Weekend preceding Labor Day, Friday and Saturday. King Street between Water and Appalachian Streets. 8:00 a.m. through the day; 8:00 p.m. square dancing.

BOONE, N.C. — HANDS Craft Fair (since 1976). First Friday and Saturday. Parking Lots — Dog Patch and Marvin's Garden. 10:00 a.m. — 8:00 p.m. 264-9743.

LENOIR, N.C. — Crafts Fair. Second weekend. Agricultural Center. Sponsor: Lenoir Homemakers.

OCTOBER
ABINGDON, VA. — Virginia Highlands Community College Mountain Crafts Festival. Second Friday and Saturday. Loads of crafts. Watch apple butter, molasses and lye soap being made. Herbs for sale. Country music and square dancing. Sponsors: Vaten School of Crafts, Holston Mountain Arts & Crafts, Corp., Inc.

BLOWING ROCK, N.C. — High Country Arts and Crafts Show. Second Sat. & Sun. Tweetsie Railroad, Blowing Rock Road. 264-9061.

JONESBORO, TENN. — National Storytelling Festival. Second weekend, Sat. & Sun. Demonstrations in Arts and Crafts. Mountain folk music.

NEWTON, N.C. — Arts and Crafts Festival. Community Center. Sponsor: Senior Citizens Club.

ROARING GAP, N.C. — The Autumn Leaves Arts and Crafts Festival. Second Saturday and Sun. Original woodcrafts, painting, decoupage, ceramics, Christmas decorations.

N. WILKESBORO, N.C. — Northwest North Carolina Arts and Crafts Fair. Third Saturday. National Guard Armory, Hwy. 115 at Armory Road. Open to all artists, craftspeople, sculptors. Sale of original art works. Awards. Sponsor: The Wilkes Art Guild. (919) 667-2841.

NOVEMBER
VALLE CRUCIS, N.C. — Community Art Festival. Valle Crucis Elementary School. Art works of students and parents, craft demonstrations and exhibits, talent show by students, baked goodies for sale. Sponsor: PTA

DECEMBER
BOONE, N.C. — Crafts Festival Exhibition. RGA Galleries, W. King Street.

BOONE, N.C. — Mountain Greens, Inc. 123 W. Howard St. Natural Christmas decorations, wreaths, etc., made by local mountaineers, shipped all over U.S. 264-4009.

30   sold to the highest bidder!!!

G-O-I-N-G ONCE, G-O-I-N-G TWICE...SOLD to the young man with the Afro and sunglasses! You'll never know what's in store for you until you "live dangerously" by bidding at an exciting, suspenseful auction sale, 'cause auction-fever is contagious! There's something for everyone!

At the bang of the auctioneer's gavel, you may find yourself the proud owner of a sparkling diamond from "one of the world's finest estates" if you're at the Blowing Rock Auction Gallery or the Fincke Gallery in Blowing Rock. Shades of Ft. Lauderdale, Fla., and the Boardwalk at Atlantic City . . . would you believe bidding for Oriental rugs or precious objets d'art in the little mountain town of Blowing Rock? Landmarks on the Main Street of the town, these galleries attract hundreds of people daily (except Sundays) at 10:30 in the morning and again at 7:30 at night from mid-June to mid-October. Family entertainment, presented with a natural flair probably as good as some national television network comedy, there's no end to the good-humored bantering and joking at these auctions, going strong since 1952. Bids are exhorted sometimes from the most conservative. So watch out!

And at country home or estate auctions, everything is sold regardless of price, from old crank telephones, wooden churns, butter molds, picture frames, hand-made tables, clocks, ice boxes, to ... horse-drawn buggies with the fringes still on top! There are musical instruments, brass and iron beds, old tools and books, wood or oil cook stoves, rocking chairs, old glass and all kinds of scales, bargains, sometimes in need of repair, just for you!

If you are one of those who just loves anything old whether it's a sinister-looking glass bottle, or outmoded rings, brooches and earrings; or if you are one for the practical antique like an old oil lamp or lantern, now being rediscovered for nostalgic as well as useful purposes, you'll find them in every conceivable size, shape and price up here.

There just seems to be something about old gewgaws (junk to some folks and treasures to others) that make them good sellers, especially in this area. As Falstaff put it, "some smack of age, some relish of the saltiness of time," and they seem to hold enormous appeal, oftentimes transforming ugliness to charm. There's always the possibility there might just be that certain rarity that will make you rich! Anyway, you'll enjoy lotsa sociability.

Some of the "junk" of yesteryear that you can pick up cheaply will undoubtedly become the hot collector's items of tomorrow, like early aviation "literature," cold cream jars, travel clocks, even canceled checks — so hang on to those prized collectible objects of tomorrow. If you happen to be a sports collecting "nut" it's always possible to make a trade in game programs, team yearbooks, bubble-gum and baseball cards. It's sports memorabilia time, and collectors come in all sizes, shapes and ages.

For another kind of auction event, come and listen to the sing-song chant of the tobacco auctioneer ringing out loud and clear from November on with mountains of Burley tobacco stretched out as far as you can see at the Farmer's Burley Warehouse or Big Burley Warehouse, both in Boone — it's really a happening for the eyes, nose and ears! And, if you're around for a livestock sale, you'll soon be caught up in the drama of horses, cows, bulls and sheep changing owners!

Now, if you're just browsing at one of the numerous Flea Markets or local Yard or Garage Sales that go on from spring through fall, you're bound to be ahead with a purchase you didn't even plan to make, especially, as is usually the case, when there are homemade breads, cakes, pies, cookies, jams, preserves, pickles, jellies and honey for sale. You'll have to watch the newspapers or listen to radio announcements to stay abreast of the church, organization and private flea market activities.

Perhaps foremost among all the ancient clutter, your best find may be books! There seems to be a never-ending supply of discarded ones, and perhaps one of them may open a whole new way of life for you — and only you will be the judge of that!

So be careful when you're bidding, 'cause any motion of fingers or body, or a change of facial expression, a flick of the eye, (or heavy breathing) may result in your becoming the proud owner of something you never wanted!!!

(Phone sponsor or C. of C. to confirm information. If no area code is shown, use 704.)

YEAR-ROUND AND SEASONAL

BLOWING ROCK, N.C. — Blowing Rock Auction Galleries, Inc. June through October. Main Street. Auctions held daily except Sunday. 295-3280.

BLOWING ROCK, N.C. — Fincke Gallery. June through October. Main Street. Auctions held daily except Sunday. 295-3389.

BOONE, N.C. — D & W Auctions. US 421, Zionville, by old milk-processing plant. Old and new, odds and ends. 297-3841 or 2930.

BOONE, N.C. — Tobacco Market. Farmer's Burley Tobacco Warehouse and the Big Burley Warehouse. Bristol Road. 264-8460.

BOONE, N.C. — Watauga Livestock Market. Six miles east on US 421. Yearling and calf sales. 264-3061.

BOONE, N.C. — Yard Sale. The Boone United Methodist Church. 341 E. King St. Loads of goodies throughout the year. 264-3825.

DEEP GAP, N.C. — Wildcat Flea Market. May through Oct. US 421, eight miles east of Boone. All kinds of antiques, crafts, jewelry, quilts, lots of surprises. Auctions held first and third Saturday in Auction Barn year round. 264-7757.

ELK PARK, N.C. — Wee Loch Flea Market. Each weekend. 933-9770.

E. JEFFERSON, N.C. — Flea Market Auctions. NC 16, R.D. Barker's Store. Sat. 7:00 p.m.

LENOIR, N.C. — Flea Market. Across from Singer Plant No. 6.

LINVILLE, N.C. — Linville Village Flea Market (Indoors). Crafts, antiques, treasure and junque. 10:00 a.m. — 6:00 p.m.

NEWLAND, N.C. — Flea Market and Auction. Four days, Thursday — Sunday. Smokey Straight, Newland Auction House. 7:30 p.m. Saturday Auction. Sunday Flea Market, glassware, new and used furniture, antiques.

SALTVILLE, VA. — Kell's Trading Post. Buy, trade, sell anything; antiques, Indian relics.

SALTVILLE. VA. — Swap and Shop. June, July, August. On the streets.

SPARTA, N.C. — Glade Valley Antique Auction.

SPRUCE PINE, N.C. — Pap's Trade Day and Flea Market. US 19E. Saturdays 6:00 a.m. — 6:00 p.m. Free Bluegrass music show, 2:00 p.m.

TERRELL, N.C. — Antique Auction Sale. Third Saturday, 11:00 a.m. **Flea Market.** Fourth Sunday, 9:00 a.m. — 5:00 p.m. Lake Norman Music Hall. NC 150.

ANNUAL EVENTS

FEBRUARY

JOHNSON CITY, TENN. — East Tennessee Antique Dealers Assn. Sale and Show. Last

Fri. and first Sat. and Sun. in March. National Guard Armory, Fri. and Sat. 11:00 a.m. — 10:00 p.m. The Miracle Mall, Sun. 1:00 — 6:00 p.m.

ABINGDON, VA. — Tri-State Livestock Market. Second Friday. Mountain Hereford Bull Sale. 1:00 p.m. Bulls weighed, graded, inspected. (703) 628-5111.

MARCH

SPRUCE PINE, N.C. — Tri-County Flea Market. Third weekend. West on Burnsville Hwy. 19E at Tri-County Drive-in. Noon — 5 p.m. Sat.; 1:00 — 6:00 p.m. Sun.

SPRUCE PINE, N.C. — Spring Rummage Sale. Last Friday and Saturday. Grassy Creek Firehouse, three miles south on NC 226. Clothing and household items. 765-9277.

APRIL

JEFFERSON & WILKESBORO, N.C. — Spring series of state-sponsored Stocker Cattle Sales. Demonstration Sales. Sponsors: N.C. State University, N.C. Cattlemen's Association, N.C. Department of Agriculture.

ABINGDON, VA. — Stocker Cattle Sale. Sponsor: Tri-State Livestock Market, Inc.

BOONE, N.C. — Auction (since 1967). First Saturday. Watauga High School. All kinds of merchandise. Sponsor: Watauga County Emergency Rescue Squad. 2:00 — 5:00 p.m. and 7:00 p.m. 264-0033.

N. WILKESBORO, N.C.– Wilkes Antiques Fair (since 1967). First week. National Guard Armory, Highway 115. Antique dealers from eastern seaboard displaying furniture, coins, clocks, firearms, pictures, books, glassware, silverware, jewelry and other articles. Home-made food served continuously. Sponsor: N. Wilkesboro Kiwanis Club. Friday and Saturday, 10:00 a.m. — 10:00 p.m.; Sunday, noon — 6:00 pm.

BOONE, N.C. — Junior Woman's Club Garage Sale. Third Saturday. Watauga High School. Musical instruments, clothing and other items.

JOHNSON CITY, TENN. — East Tennessee Antique Dealers Association Sale and Show. Last weekend starting Thursday. 10:00 a.m. — 10:00 p.m, Thursday, Friday, Saturday; 1:00 — 6:00 p.m., Sunday.

MAY

FOSCOE, N.C. — Auction Sale. Fourth Saturday. Field Day (See Ch. 33). Sponsor: Volunteer Fire Department.

JUNE

JOHNSON CITY, TENN. — East Tennessee Antique Dealers Association Sale and Show. Second weekend, Thursday — Sunday.

BLOWING ROCK, N.C. — Flea Market. Second Saturday. Elementary School parking lot, Sunset Drive.

BLOWING ROCK, N.C. — Russell's Antique Show and Flea Market (since 1957). Last weekend, Friday and Saturday. Sunset Drive. 295-7871.

BOONE, N.C. — Community Flea Market. Last Saturday. City parking lot between Burgess Furniture Store and Northwestern Bank, E. King Street. Big bargains for all ages. 8:00 am. — 1:00 p.m.

VALLE CRUCIS, N.C. — Flea Market. Last Saturday. Community Club, Elementary School.

JULY
BOONE, N.C. — Boone-Blowing Rock Antique Show Sale. First Wednesday to Saturday. Holiday Inn Conference Center.

BLOWING ROCK, N.C. — Flea Market. First Friday and Saturday. Elementary School. Sponsor: Garden Club.

BLOWING ROCK, N.C. — Rummage Sale. First Friday and Saturday. American Legion Building. Sponsor: Garden Club.

INDEPENDENCE, VA. — Auction, Dairy and Beef Show. Fourth of July Celebration. Athletic Field. (See Ch. 52).

JONESBORO, TENN. — Historic "Jonesborough Days" Flea Market. Four-day Independence Day Celebration. (See Ch. 52.)

BANNER ELK, N.C. — Flea Market. Last Saturday. Fire Department Building. Baked goods, books, clothing, vegetables, odds and ends. Sponsor: Grandfather Home Alumni Assn.

AUGUST
ABINGDON, VA. — Flea Market and Crafts Festival. First Saturday. The Virginia Highlands Arts and Crafts Festival. (See Ch. 29.) Sponsor: Historical Society of Washington County.

BLOWING ROCK, N.C. — Flea Market. Third Friday and Saturday. Elementary School parking lot, Sunset Drive.

OCTOBER
BOONE, N.C. — Purebred Show and Sale. Second Saturday. US 421, five miles east, New Purebred Sale Barn. All polled Herefords and heifers sold to the highest bidder. Sponsor: Watauga Hereford Breeders Association. 9:30 a.m. show, 1:00 p.m., sale.

MORGANTON, N.C. — Bargain Fair of the Service League. Second Saturday. Recreation Center, Collett Street.

BOONE, N.C. — Antique Show and Sale. Third weekend, Friday, Saturday, Sunday. Holiday Inn. Sponsor: Worthwhile Women's Clubs, Boone-Blowing Rock. Noon — 10:00 p.m., Friday, Saturday; noon — 6:00 p.m., Sunday.

HICKORY, N.C. — Antique Show and Sale. Third weekend. Sponsor: Hickory Service League.

PINEY FLATS, TENN. — Antique Show and Sale. Third week, Tuesday to Thursday.

NOVEMBER
BOONE, N.C. — Pumpkin Pie Contest. Just before Thanksgiving Day. King Street. Sponsor: Downtown Merchants Association.

DECEMBER
(See Ch. 53.)

Hugh Morton

31 our fine-feathered friends

Ah-h-h! What a thrill there is to birdwatching, a hobby that's different from any other experience. What would the world be like if there were no birds? Awakening to a symphony of birdsong and watching the flight of gay plumage can make your day special.

Birdwatching is a perfect way to enjoy nature, particularly while on a birdwalk with the sky as your roof, flowers blooming, and the freedom and freshness of the out-of-doors. Birdcalls will serenade you as your feathered neighbors carol out their innermost hearts with the sheer joy of living bringing meaning to the hours of the day. Just listen to the sound of the birds and see if you don't feel as peaceful as though you were back in the Garden of Eden, millions of miles away. You'll lose all track of time as you enter a universe of simple, soul-cleansing activity!

Pleasurable possibilities unfold — locating areas where birds are attracted — learning to identify them by sight and by call — following nature trails with experts — all are an enormous delight. Listening to recorded bird songs in advance of a trip will greatly enhance your pleasure in being able to identify birds by their calls. Joining an Audubon Society group for illustrated lectures and walks will help you learn quite a bit about these beautiful creatures.

But the easiest way to watch birds is to hang feeders outside your windows, using binoculars (8 x 40 is a good size) and a bird guidebook, and study them as they come for meals.

Special treats for the birds will lure particular species. The sweet, pink syrup (dissolved sugar in water with red food coloring) in a tube-like feeder will attract ruby-throated hummingbirds. This tiniest of all birds with a long, needle-like bill that's one-half its body size, will hover in midair sipping nectar from flowers or syrup from the vial, with wings fluttering so rapidly they become a blur. And you should see them fly backwards! Their eggs are so small that four of them can fit into a teaspoon! And this bird winters from Florida to South America, miraculously flying all those miles and back. Incidentally, a visit to ASU's Rankin Science Building Museum to see the extensive birds' egg collection will fascinate you!

Up here birds may be watched all seasons of the year. If you have a preference for cardinals, just sprinkle sunflower seeds around. Of course, you may also attract blue jays, titmice, chickadees, towhees, mourning doves, sparrows, brown thrashers and nuthatches. If you'd like to attract bluebirds, mocking birds, woodpeckers, chickadees and wrens, just mix peanut butter and grease, or leftover cooked cereal, laced with grease and nutbutter for the feeders. Provide any kind of shallow pan with about an inch of water set on the ground or on a table for them and just see the birds of a feather flock together. Note how they add color to the scene as you observe them bathing. You might like to keep a record of how many in the following list you can spot:

Common Name	Where Found
YEAR-ROUND	
American Goldfinch	Near ground
Barn Owl	Tree hollows, old barns and buildings
Black-capped Chickadee	Rotted stumps
Blue Jay	Fork of evergreens
Bob White	Combination of tall grasses and thicket
Cardinal	Thick bushes
Crow	Trees, preferably pine
Downy and Hairy Woodpecker	Dead tree limbs
Eastern Bluebird	Hollow trees
Field Sparrow	Fields
Great-horned Owl	Large pines
Grackle	Evergreens
House Sparrow	Any place over five feet above ground
Loggerhead Shrike	Thorny hedges
Meadow Lark	Meadows and green fields

Mockingbird .... Shrubs and vines
Mourning Dove .... Conifers for nesting
Pigeon .... Open ground
Red-headed Woodpecker .... Holes in trees, posts and poles
Red-winged Blackbird .... Low bushes
Robin .... Woods or open country
Ruffed Grouse .... Brushy woodlands, open fields
Screech Owl .... Tree hollows, holes
Starling .... Tree hollows
Tufted Titmouse .... Tree stumps
Vesper Sparrow .... Dry ground
White-breasted Nuthatch .... Tree cavity
Wild Turkey .... Small clearings in forests
Yellow-shafted Flicker .... Dead trunk cavities

SUMMER

Baltimore Oriole .... Fruit trees
Black and white Warbler .... Tree trunks
Blue-gray Gnatcatcher .... Tree tops
Brown Thrasher .... Bushes and brush
Carolina Wren .... Brushy undergrowth
Catbird .... Dense shrubbery
Chimney Swift .... Chimney tops
Chipping Sparrow .... Hedges
Common Night Hawk .... Open fields
Great-crested Flycatcher .... Holes in posts
Indigo Bunting .... Shrubbery
Purple Martin .... Cavities in trees
Red-eyed Vireo .... Branch forks
Ruby-throated Hummingbird .... Trees
Rufous-sided Towhee .... Ground
Wood Thrush .... Saplings
Yellow-billed Cuckoo .... Orchards and thickets
Yellow Warbler .... Shrubbery or low trees
Yellow Throat .... Shrubbery

WINTER

Brown Creeper .... Deep woods
Brown-headed Cowbird .... Everywhere
Cedar Waxwing .... Fruit trees
Fox Sparrow .... Open fields
Golden-crowned Ringlet .... Evergreens
Hermit Thrush .... Near ground — usually pine and hemlock
Purple Finch .... Pine woods
Slate-colored Junco .... Ground
Song Sparrow .... Shrubbery, fields
Swamp Sparrow .... Lakes and swamps
White-crowned Sparrow .... Thick grass
White-throated Sparrow .... Ground
Yellow-bellied Sapsucker .... Dead or live trunk cavities

Hugh Morton

32   dancing flowers

Why not come to the high country once to watch the wildflower blossoms dancing? As waves of wind currents cause them to sway and bend tossing their heads and blending their colors, you'll smile inwardly with a joyous feeling. Just meander down a country road at dusk and watch the yellow evening primrose pop open wafting its heavenly perfume in your direction. There's a continuous colorful unfolding of gay wildflowers from winter, while snow is still on the fields, to well into the last of autumn — almost all year long! But the two periods when you'll see the greatest variety and profusion are from mid-April to mid-May and again from mid-June to mid-July.

Approximately between June first and the fifteenth, depending on the elevation, is the peak bloom period for the mountain laurel, flame azalea and rich purple rhododendron. The showiest purple rhododendron displays are to be found at Craggy Gardens, 600 acres along the Blue Ridge Parkway, and, of course, on the incredible Roan Mountain (see Ch. 11).

Growing rhododendron is Big Business in twenty counties in these parts with over 800 rhododendron nurseries producing one million plants a year! It's Avery County's largest cash crop. And, naturally, there's a Southeastern Chapter of the American Rhododendron Society. The three popular varieties are: Catawbiense, used in hybridizing, able to withstand temperatures down to minus 25 degrees; Carolinianus, distinguished by a small leaf and early blooming growing in high elevations; and the Maximus with long leaves, which is the most common.

An open air botanical paradise of more than 1500 species of native plants, flowering herbs, trees and shrubs is yours for viewing and enjoying. There are at least 30 trees bearing colorful blossoms: black cherry, pin cherry, serviceberry, redbush, several magnolias, many hawthorns, plums, several buckeye, tulip poplar, flowering dogwoods, white and pink-flowering locusts, black haw, yellowwood, mountain ash, crabapple, several lindens, sourwood, fringe trees, silverbell, witchhazel, and Hercules' club.

You can take yourself on Self-guiding Nature Trails (see Ch. 11) conveniently placed for admiring the richness and delicate beauty of the display at close range or you may take advantage of annual wildflower pilgrimages, guided by the experts. One such pilgrimage has been going on since 1962, the Annual Roan Mountain Naturalists' Rally sponsored by the Roan Mountain Citizens Club, the first weekend in September. Starting on Friday with highly interesting slide-illustrated talks by authorities in the fields of botany and ornithology, it is continued on Saturday with a choice of exciting Field Trips. Incidentally, at this time of year blueberries are ripe for picking (it's allowed). Not only are wildflowers in bloom but a marvelous assortment of clubmosses, lichens, ferns and mushrooms await scrutinizing. Other field trips specialize in discovering the world of salamanders and insects.

Another annual wildflower tour that has become increasingly popular since 1958, is the Carter County Wildflower Tour. Sponsored by the Carter County Chamber of Commerce in Elizabethton, Tenn., the first weekend in May, devotees come from neighboring states to enjoy the enormous variety of upper East Tennessee wildflowers.

Because these mountains are a billion years "young" there's a wide flower mixture from subtropical orchids to northern types of flora such as wood sorrel and witch-hobble. And when you're driving from the foothills to the mountain heights, it will be equivalent to driving a thousand miles north as far as plant life zones are concerned; so imagine a two-hour trip as equal to driving from North Carolina to Canada. If you've missed a particular favorite flowering period, don't despair, chances are you'll see your darlings blooming at a higher elevation.

Nowhere else in the world, outside of China and Japan, are there as many species of wildflowers as are found here, covering entire mountainsides. In fact, many of the plants found in this area have relatives in the Orient. Does that make us "kissin' cousins?" And here, too, is found that mysterious little plant, ginseng called "sang" which is used in the U.S. and exported to China and other lands for its "curative" powers.

For an extraordinary introduction to native plant families, visit the Daniel Boone Native Gardens, a stroller's delight, adjacent to the *Horn in the West* Amphitheatre. Take time out for a restful, unhurried treat to relish the beauty of this small but extensively landscaped six-acre tract, not just once but at each season, if possible. You'll discover other very lovely gardens in many of the communities covered in this guidebook.

Should you be interested in greenhouse gardening, plan a visit to Montezuma, on the Newland Road near Linville, where Patterson's Greenhouses grow not only the largest carnations (up to six feet high), but the greatest number in all of the Southeast. You can feast your eyes on pink, white, yellow, dusty tangerine, yellow tinged with red, totally red, wine, flamingo, peppermint green, and rose, a remarkable and delightful spectrum of color with the white variety the most fragrant. The longest lasting of all flowers, carnations need cool, moist summers and protection in winter. It takes three to four months before they start to bloom and they need to be pinched back to encourage bushiness. Then, there's continual blooming with each plant producing as many as 20 flowers. The plants are kept only for two years but each day, thousands of blooms are cut. You'll also see 'mums, azaleas and roses in these well-known greenhouses.

Did you know that western North Carolina provides three-fourths of the world's supply of galax plants primarily to florists for longlasting leaves which are used in floral arrangements? The galax, red in spring with cloud-white blooms of from six to eight inches above the plant in early June, in summer have the shiniest, waxiest-looking heart-shaped green leaves, and turn radiant-bronze, then wine-red in fall.

And now for a fairly complete "menu" of magical moments, what you may expect to see in wildflowers, flowering bushes, vines and trees:

SPRING FLOWERING

American Beech	Blackberry	Blue Cohosh
Arrow Leaf	Black Cherry	Blue-eyed Grass
Arrow-Wood	Black Cohosh	Bluets
Baneberry	Black Locust	Buckeye
Beard Tongue	Blazing Star	Buttercup
Bellwort	Bleeding Heart	Butterfly Weed
Birdfoot Violet	Bloodroot	Cattail
Bitter Cress	Blueberry	Cinquefoil

Clinton's Lily
Columbine
Crabtree
Crested Dwarf Iris
Cross Vine
Cucumber Tree
Daisy
Dandelion
Dutchman's Breeches
Elderberry
False Foxglove
False Solomon's Seal
Field Pansy
Fire Pink
Flame Azalea
Flowering Dogwood
Fly Poison
Fringed Phacelia
Galax
Giant Chickweed
Goat's Beard
Goat's Rue
Golden Alexander
Golden Club
Golden Ragwort
Grass Pink
Halberd-leaved
    Yellow Violet
Hawthorn
Hawkweed
Heart Leaf
Henbit
Hepatica
Hobble Bush
Honeysuckle
Houstonia
Indian Cucumber
Indian Hemp
Indian-Physic
Indigo Bush
Jack-in-the-pulpit
Large Flowered Trillium
Larkspur
Leather Flower
Leucothoe
Lily-of-the-valley
Lousewort
Lyre-leaved Sage
May Apple

Meadow Beauty
Meadow Rue
Milkweed
Miterwort
Mock Strawberry
Moss Pink
Mountain Andromeda
Mountain Holly
Mountain Laurel
Mountain Maple
New Jersey Tea
Ninebark
Nodding Trillium
Painted Trillium
Partridge Berry
Passion Flower
Pennywort
Phlox
Pinesap
Pink Moccasin Flower
Pink Spiderwort
Pink Wood Sorrel
Pinxter-flower
Poke
Princess Tree
Purple Honeysuckle
Purple Rhododendron
Pussy Toes
Queen Anne's Lace
Redbud
Robin's Plantain
Rosebud Orchid
Sassafras
Scarlet Oak
Sedum
Serviceberry
Sheep Laurel
Silver Bell
Skull Cap
Slender Ladies' Tresses
Smooth Sumac
Soapwort
Solomon's Seal
Sourgrass
Sow Thistle
Spring Beauty
Squaw Root
Squirrel Corn
Staghorn Sumac

Strawberry Bush
Sundrops
Swamp Rose
Sweet Shrub
Sweet Leaf
Thimbleweed
Toothwort
Trailing Arbutus
Trout Lily
Tulip Tree
Turkey Beard
Umbrella Magnolia
Venus Looking-glass
Veronica
Virginia Creeper
Wake Robin
Water Leaf
White Oak
White Violet
Wild Columbine
Wild Ginger
Wild Geranium
Wild Hydrangea
Wild Strawberry
Wind Flower
Witherod
Wood Anemone
Wood Sorrel
Yarrow
Yellow Buckeye

SUMMER FLOWERING
Arrow Leaf
Arrowwood
Barnyard Grass
Basswood
Beard Tongue
Bell Flower
Black Cohosh
Black-eyed Susan
Black Locust
Blazing Star
Bleeding Heart
Blue-eyed Grass
Blue Haw Vibernum
Bluets
Bush Dogwood
Buttercup

Butterfly Pea
Butterfly Weed
Button bush
Cardinal Flower
Cattail
Chestnut
Chicory
Chinquapin
Clinton's Lily
Common Clematis
Cone Flower
Coreopsis
Crimson Bee Balm
Daisy
Dandelion
Dodder
Elderberry
Evening Primrose
False Foxglove
False Hellebore
False Solomon's Seal
Filmy Angelica
Fire Pink
Fireweed
Flame Azalea
Flowering Raspberry
Fly Poison
Fringed Loosestrife
Galax
Giant Chickweed
Goat's Beard
Goat's Rue
Golden Ragwort
Goldenrod
Grass Pink
Hawkweed
Hawthorn
Heartleaf
Hedge Nettle
Henbit
Hobble Bush
Honeysuckle
Houstonia
Hypericum
Indian Cucumber
Indian Hemp
Indian Paint Brush
Indian Physic
Indian Pipes

Ironweed
Joe-Pye Weed
Leather Flower
Leucothoe
Lobelia
Lily-of-the-Valley
May Root
Meadow Beauty
Meadow Rue
Milkweed
Miterwort
Mock Strawberry
Monkey Flower
Morning Glory
Moth Mullein
Mountain Andromeda
Mountain Ash
Mountain Holly
Mountain Laurel
Mountain Maple
Mountain Mint
Myrtle
New Jersey Tea
Nine Bark
Obedient Plant
Ox-eye
Pale-jewel Weed
Partridge Berry
Partridge Pea
Passion Flower
Phlox
Pinesap
Pink Moccasin Flower
Pink Spiderwort
Pipsissewa
Poke
Purple Gerardia
Queen's Lace
Rabbit Tobacco
Ramp
Rattlesnake Plantain
Robin's Plantain
Rosebud Orchid
Sedge
Sedum
Sensitive Briar
Sheep Laurel
Skull Cap
Slender Ladies' Tresses

Smooth Sumac
Soapwort
Sour Grass
Sourwood
Sow Thistle
Spiderwort
Spreading Dogbane
Squaw Root
St. Joan's Wort
Stiff Gentian
Strawberry Bush
Sundrops
Sunflower
Sweet Pepper Bush
Sweet Shrub
Tea Berry
Trumpet Creeper
Tulip Tree
Turkey Beard
Turtle Head
Venus Looking-glass
Veronica
Virginia Creeper
Virgin's-Bower
Water Leaf
White Rhododendron
White Snakeroot
Wild Geranium
Wild Hydrangea
Wild Strawberry
Wintergreen
Witherod
Wood Sorrel
Yarrow
Yellow-eyed Grass

FALL FLOWERING
Aster
Barnyard Grass
Bell Flower
Blazing Star
Cardinal Flower
Chicory
Common Clematis
Cone Flower
Coreopsis
Dodder
Evening Primrose
False Foxglove

Fireweed
Gerardia
Goldenrod
Indian Pipes
Ironweed
Joe-pye Weed
Leather Flower
Lobelia
Marigold
May Root
Meadow Beauty
Milkweed
Mock Strawberry
Monkey Flower
Morning Glory
Moth Mullein
Obedient Plant
Ox-eye

Pale-jewel Weed
Partridgeberry
Pinesap
Pink Spiderwort
Poke
Purple Gerardia
Queen Anne's Lace
Rabbit Tobacco
Sedge
Sedum
Sensitive Briar
Slender Ladies' Tresses
Sneeze Weed
Soapwort
Stiff Gentian
Strawberry Bush
Sunflower

Turtlehead
White Snakeroot
Witch Hazel
Wood Sorrel
Yarrow

WINTER FLOWERING

Dandelion
Hazel Alder
Hepatica
Mock Strawberry
Skunk Cabbage
Spring Beauty
Trailing Arbutus
Weeping Willow
Winged Elm

33 'a pretty girl . . .'

There is not a month of the year around these mountains when there isn't a fair, festival, pageant or contest of some kind going on. They're not all strictly beauty pageants, however. Skill and sportsmanship play a large role in judging winners in such contests as the crowning of Miss Horseman's Holiday at Foscoe. Whereas, at the Watauga County Junior Miss Pageant, scholastic ability and contribution to family and community, among other attributes, are rated.

Even if you're not acquainted with the contestants, pageants and contests can be "spine-tingling" for both participant and on-looker with loads of excitement generated.

Come and see a mountain-style pageant-festival and judge for yourself!

ANNUAL EVENTS

(Phone sponsor or C. of C. to confirm information. If no area code is shown, use 704.)

FEBRUARY
BANNER ELK, N.C. — Winter Carnival Festivities. Second week. Lees-McRae College. Crowning of Winter Carnival Queen. Winter Carnival Fashion Show. 898-5513, ext. 27.

APRIL
BRISTOL, TENN. — Dogwood Coronation and Play. Last Friday. King College. Crowning of King and Queen and presentation of a pageant in their honor. And, of course, the dogwood trees are festive in their full bloomery of white and pink at this time (for the occasion)! 8:00 p.m. (615) 968-1187, ext. 66 or 72.

MAY
FOSCOE, N.C. — Crowning of Miss Foscoe Fire Department. Fourth Saturday. Field Day and Auction Sale. Sponsor: Foscoe Volunteer Fire Department.

JUNE
BAKERSVILLE, N.C. — Rhododendron Festival and Crowning of Festival Queen. Third or fourth week. Bowman High School. Final judging and crowning of Queen Saturday night. Sponsor: Bakersville Lions Club. 688-3113.

ELIZABETHTON, TENN. — Roan Mountain Rhododendron Festival and Crowning of Miss Rhododendron. Third or fourth week. (Preliminary to Miss Tennessee Pageant). Sponsor: Roan Mountain, Tennessee Citizens' Club. (615) 543-2122.

JULY
FOSCOE, N.C. — Crowning of Miss Horseman's Holiday. First Saturday. Paradise Ranch Arena. Church Road and NC 105. Young ladies 13 and over judged on horsemanship, poise, personality, appearance. 264-2277.

JONESBORO, TENN. — Miss Historic and Little Miss Historic "Jonesborough" Pageant. First Saturday. Old Jonesboro High School, Main Street. 7:30 p.m. Historic "Jonesborough Days", P. O. Box 294, Jonesboro, Tenn. 37659.

LENOIR, N.C. — Miss Caldwell County Pageant and Little Miss Caldwell County. Last Saturday. 8:00 p.m. Sponsor: Lenoir Jaycees.

JOHNSON CITY, TENN. — Miss Park and Recreation Beauty Pageant (Since 1973). July 31. Rotary Park. Wee Miss 2—4; Tiny Miss 5—7; Little Miss 8—10; Junior Miss 11—13; Miss Park and Recreation 14 and over. 7:00 p.m.

AUGUST

NEWTON, N.C. — Little Miss Reunion Pageant 8 — 9. **Miss Reunion Pageant** 10 — 14. **Junior Miss Reunion Pageant** 15 — 18. First Thursday and Friday. Elementary School Auditorium. Entertainment each night. 8:00 p.m.

ELKIN, N.C. — Miss Elkin Valley Pageant. Second Friday and Saturday. Dixon Auditorium.

MOUNTAIN CITY, TENN. — Miss Johnson County Pageant. Third Saturday. Johnson County High School. Preliminary to Miss Tennessee Pageant. 8:00 p.m.

BURNSVILLE, N.C. — Miss Mayland Beauty Contest. Third Saturday. Parkway Playhouse (date and place varies yearly). Sponsors: Yancey and Avery Counties, Spruce Pine Jaycees.

BANNER ELK, N.C. — American Sweetheart Pageant. Third Weekend. The Land of Oz, Beech Mountain. Contestants' costumes represent home states.

IOHNSON CITY, TENN. — Senior Fairest of the Fair Pageant. Third Th. and fourth Sat. Appalachian District Fair. Fairgrounds at Gray, six miles northwest. 7:30 p.m.

HICKORY, N.C. — Miss Hickory Pageant. Fourth Saturday. P. E. Monroe Auditorium. Preliminary to Miss North Carolina Pageant.

OCTOBER

BOONE, N.C. — Harvest Queen Crowning. First Saturday. Farmers Harvest Festival. Watauga County Farmers' Market, *Horn in the West* grounds. (See Ch. 54.)

LENOIR, N.C. — Miss Caldwell County Pageant. Third week. Caldwell County Fair Grounds. High Schools' Beauty Contest.

BOONE, N.C. — Watauga County Junior Miss Pageant (since 1973). Fourth Saturday. Watauga High School Auditorium. Judged on scholastic ability, poise, appearance, youth fitness, talent, awareness, capability in human relations, and contribution to family and community. Sponsor: Boone Jaycees.

BOONE, N,C. — Appalachian Homecoming Queen. Last Saturday. Conrad Stadium, ASU. Half-time of football game.

NOVEMBER

BOONE, N.C. — Miss Appalachian State University Pageant. Third Friday. Judged in four categories: swim suit, evening wear, talent and interview. Winner competes in Miss North Carolina Pageant in June.

34 rockhounding

Got a bit of adventure in your blood? Want to try something on the unusual side, perhaps even extraordinary? Are you game for a new activity? Then why not join the growing legion of gem-fever amateurs who "dig" collecting some of the earth's hidden treasures?

With more than 300 amazing varieties of minerals and rocks, (one of the largest concentrations in the country), it's no wonder the Tar Heel State is. called "Nature's Sample Case of Gems." Incidentally, did you know that gold was discovered first in this state in 1799 and that there were more than 700 gold mines here long before the California Gold Rush began? And some of the many famous collections of the world, like the Metropolitan Museum of Art and the Museum of Natural History contain choice emeralds and aquamarines from this very region.

The tri-state mountain corner offers a number of attractions that rate prime billing, but none more captivating perhaps than digging for or viewing the incomparable beauty of gemstones and mineral crystals, nature's underground glories. Gems, blossoming in the rocky depths of the earth, are aptly described by the Latin term "gemma" originally meaning "bud." Just reflecting on the millions of years it took for rocks and minerals to be formed and fashioned atom by atom is to stand in hushed awe at the ordered perfection and symmetry of these creations.

At the Museum of North Carolina Minerals on the Blue Ridge Parkway, Milestone 331, Gillespie Gap, you'll see a fabulous collection of one-of-a-kind, unique art works of nature. Among them: gold, amethyst, crystal, golden beryl, garnet, and sapphire. Also, there are fascinating exhibits of the many practical uses of minerals in our everyday living. For example, there's mica used principally for insulation and in rubber and paint; tungsten, which has the highest known melting point, about 3400 degrees C. (34 times the heat necessary to boil water) used in light bulb filaments and high speed tools; feldspar used in manufacturing glass and porcelain; and kaolin, a prime ingredient in the clay used to form china. Corundum, next to the diamond in hardness, also found here is used for sandpaper, emery wheels and other abrasive instruments. Ancient rocks have formed colorful gems such as sapphires, crystals (rubies, purple amethyst), emeralds and topaz, often cut and sold as cabochons (convex, highly polished, unfaceted gems).

Fluorescent minerals are on view in a special display booth where they glow weirdly in the dark. The Museum offers stimulating field trips, lapidary and craft demonstrations, and a guided tour of an informative array of exhibits.

Now here's where the adventurous part comes in — there are still vast quantities of treasure awaiting the rockhounder. Dream of what is yet to be found . . . ! At the end of this chapter is a partial listing of old mines open to the public, where for a small fee (equipment is provided) you may "dig it, man" and keep whatever you find. The kids will think this is "outta sight!" especially when you have a local craftsman transform your stones into objects of beauty.

Be sure you wear clothing you won't mind discarding after digging, when you head for the mines. Who knows, you may find enough gems to pay for your vacation or to start or add to a valuable collection. Practically no one goes away empty-handed!

There are other excellent places to explore like highway digs (the local Highway Department may supply locations) or freshly plowed fields, old mine dumps, gullies, along railroad ties, even stream banks and stream beds! You won't need much in the way of equipment, just a prospector's hammer (hammerhead on one end and a pick head on the other) for splitting rocks and for removing crystals from them, a cold chisel, a fine screen, a magnifying glass (8x to 10x) for identifying small crystals and for examining sands, and a collecting bag stuffed with newspapers for wrapping specimens carefully and labelling them. Just be sure you're not on private property without permission . . .

One event you shouldn't miss is the annual four-day July and/or Aug. Mitchell County Chamber of Commerce Mineral and Gem Festival in Spruce Pine, going since 1959. The Spruce Pine Mineral Kingdom is internationally known because more minerals and gems have been found here than in any area this size in the world. It encompasses some 225 square miles and is located in the center of three grand mountains: Grandfather, Roan and Mitchell. Activities include field trips to local mineral deposits and lectures by famous mineralogists. Known as the Queen of Mineral Shows, this is a fascinating attraction where you'll be tempted to buy tumbled, polished stones, cutting material, fine jewelry (are "diamonds a girl's best friend?"), supplies for clubs and collectors, findings, cut gem stones, fossils, scupltures, and sand paintings. You'll be able to watch sandpainters, faceting and other lapidary demonstrations, and for do-it-your-selfers there are infinite possibilities to explore. And if you have anything to swap, this is the place to meet the most intriguing swappers anywhere. It'll be a learning-for-fun experience all around for everyone!

If you really become "hooked" on the subject, a fine way to learn quickly about good finds and what to look for is to get in touch with local rockhound clubs. Drop by the Mitchell County Chamber of Commerce for more information, particularly about gemsmith shops and gift shops for browsing among the dazzling, scintillating displays.

This pursuit is one hobby where "finders keepers" is the name of the game!!!

Check at the local Chamber of Commerce for mines located in Ashe, Avery, Burke, Mitchell, Watauga and Yancey Counties. All have yielded and are yielding many varieties of minerals and gemstones. In fact, if you're a skilled prospector there's placer gold (small particles of gold in sand or gravel that can be washed out) still to be found in the streams!

ROCKHOUND SITES

(Following is a list of mines, their location in relation to Spruce Pine, NC., and the minerals which may be found in them.)

BANJO BRANCH MINE —One mile east on US 19E, right on 1122 for one-half mile. Actinolite, apatite.

BIG CRABTREE EMERALD MINE — Five miles south on NC 226, right on Blue Ridge Parkway to Little Switzerland, right on 1100 to church, 2.5 miles on 1104. Emerald, tourmaline.

BURLESON MOONSTONE MINE — Thirteen miles east on NC 19E, left on 1132 Roaring Creek Road for .5 mile, inquire at house trailer on left. Moonstone.

CHALK MOUNTAIN MINE — Two miles west on US 19E, left on unmarked road, about .4 mile. Road is closed when mine is not in operation. Hyalite, torbenite, autonite.

CHESTNUT FLATS MINE — 4.2 miles north on NC 226, right on rough, unmarked road for 2.5 miles. Garnets, quartz, uranium.

DEER PARK MINE — Four miles west on NC 226, left on Penland Road, 1162 for two miles, left .5 mile on 1163. Garnets, thulite, uranium.

GUDGER MINE — Three miles north on NC 226, left on private, rough road. Apatite, garnets, mica, thulite.

HARRIS CLAY MINE — Three miles east on US 19E, right on private road. Kaolin.

HAWK MINE — Ten miles west on NC 226 to Bakersville, right for six miles on 1211; mine is at junction of 1210 and 1211. Black tourmaline, garnet, oligoclase, thulite.

HENSON CREEK MINE — Ten miles north on US 19E, left on Henson Creek Road, two miles to brick church, right on gravel road, .2 mile on left. Aquamarine, beryl, garnet.

INTERNATIONAL MINERALS — 1.5 miles north on NC 226, right on 1150. Autunite, hyalite, torbenite.

LAWSONS MINE — Two miles north on NC 226 to Mimpro, right on private road. Amazonite, autonite, garnet, hyalite, torbenite.

McHONE MINE — .5 mile south on NC 226, right on 1120 for one mile beyond end of pavement. Amazonite, beryl, fluorite.

McKINNEY MINE — Five miles south on NC 226, right on Blue Ridge Parkway to Little Switzerland, right on 1100, about 2.5 miles to mine. Columbite, garnet, sphalerite, uranium.

OLD NO. 20 FELDSPAR MINE — 4 miles west on US 19E, left on 1002 (Crabtree Road) for 3 miles, right on 1176 for .5 mile. Amazonite, beryl, hyalite, mica, uranium.

OLIVINE MINE — Seven miles west on US 19E, right on NC 80 one-fourth mile. Chromite, olivine.

OLIVINE MINE — Twelve miles west on US 19E, right on NC 197 for four miles. Olivine, chromite.

RAY MINE — Thirteen miles west on US 19E to Burnsville, left on NC 197 for .7 mile, left on 1109 for 1.4 miles, left on 1192. Apatite, beryl, columbite, garnet.

ROAN MOUNTAIN FLOWER GARDEN — Twelve miles north on NC 226 to Bakersville, right on NC 261 for 12 miles. Epidote, unakite.

SINK HOLE MINE — 7.6 miles west on NC 226, left on Mine Creek Road (1191) for 1.7 miles, left on NC 80 for 2.5 miles. Mine is on left above road with small dump. Apatite, garnet, thulite.

SULLINS MINE — One mile north on NC 226, right on 1146. Autunite, garnet, pitchblend, thulite.

WISEMAN MINE — Two miles south on NC 226, left on Carter's Ridge Road 1117, for one mile, sign on right. Aquamarine.

OTHER AREAS

CRANBERRY IRON MINE — Avery County, one mile from Cranberry. Epidote, garnet, magnetite, uralite.

LENOIR, N.C. — Playmore Beach. Seven miles south on NC 18. Sluices at beach site for prospecting; bring wash basin to pan for flecks of gold, quartz with gold, limonite and pyrite. Lots more doing there for recreation.

GEM AND ROCK SHOPS

BAKERSVILLE, N.C. — Gems by Roby. Route 4, Hawk. Open year round.

BAKERSVILLE, N.C. — Roan View Gift Shop. Route 1, Roan Valley.

BURNSVILLE, N.C. — Mineral and Gem Shop. W. Main Street. 682-7378.

FOSCOE, N.C. — Miller's Antiques. NC 105. 963-4859.

LITTLE SWITZERLAND, N.C. — Swiss Christmas Shop. Chalet Motor Lodge.

MICAVILLE, N.C. — Floyd Wilson's Mineral Shop.

SPRUCE PINE, N.C. — Baker's Mineral & Gift Shop. US 19E. 765-9344.

SPRUCE PINE, N.C. — Lee's Mineral & Gem Shop. Three miles south on NC 226.

SPRUCE PINE, N.C. — The Gem Shop. Three miles east on US 19E. 765-4613.

VALLE CRUCIS, N.C. — Webb's Rock Shop. NC 194.

35 jams and jellies from the vine

If you're a do-it-yourself person, or if you like to stretch the dollar (and who doesn't), you can really have a great time picking your own fruits and vegetables from spring through fall while sightseeing. Wild strawberries are plentiful on country road banks or meadows from mid to late June. Try 'em, you'll like 'em, and when you find yourself a good pickin' patch, keep on going back for the daily harvest. They're so flavorful on cereal with cream or in jams and jellies or in pies and over ice cream!

Have you ever eaten the delicious, green transparent apples, native to this area? The season for them is rather short, but there's an abundance during peak pickin' time which is from the end of June through July. Listen to "Swap Shop" on WATA radio, Boone from 10:15 a.m. to 10:30 a.m. for ads on where you may pick the apples, "buy" a cherry tree for pickin', gather fresh vegetables — or, place your own ad (free) and you'll get responses, more than you'll know what to do with. And even if you pick the apples off the ground and have to trim spots, it's still tremendously worthwhile! Help the farmer while you help yourself.

At blueberry, huckleberry and blackberry time, you'll find many along roadsides and in the state and national parks, where you ARE allowed to pick (that's it, though, nothing else). But for a blueberry picker's paradise, go to Blue Ridge Blueberry Farms, 1.5 miles north of junction NC 194 and 184 in Banner Elk. During the month of August and part of September, on a 12-acre farm, huge, pretty-as-a-picture, mouth-watering blueberries, carefully and lovingly tended, await your fond caress. From 7:00 a.m. to dusk, seven days a week, in fresh mountain air and sunshine, you can pick comfortably but wear a head covering. The bushes grow just the right height for pickin' and eatin'. You'll want to take home several gallons to keep in your freezer. Give them a call first, though, just to make sure they are allowing the fruit to be picked that day since there's a rest period periodically. Phone 898-4747.

To complete the fruit pickin' season, go to Hayes Apple Orchard at Elk Park, seven miles east of Banner Elk, for red and yellow starks in the fall.

For picking your own vegetables, the State Department of Agriculture or County Farm Agent should have a listing of "pick-your-own" farms.

Then enjoy the fruits of your labors in the applesauce, jams and jellies you'll be eating and the tasty squash, beans, tomatoes, cukes and other vegetables — a good remembrance of the sun-fun-filled days you spent up in the mountains!

36 hi-ho, come to the farmers' market

See the mouth-watering pyramids of fresh, high quality, "blue ribbon" sweet corn, tomatoes, cukes, lettuce, peas, beans, onions, peaches, green transparent apples (for the best, slightly tart, applesauce this side of heav'n), watermelon, berries, whatever's in season — picked the evening before, or that morning, including fresh eggs — mountain produce at its best! No ordinary, tourist attraction but a wholesome one, these homegrown, colorful vegetables and fruits, wild and cultivated flowers and plants, homemade breads, pies, cakes, rolls, ham biscuits with real country ham, jams, jellies, preserves, a variety of honey, cider, apple butter — will surely satisfy your tastebuds and make you a regular customer! And even if you have all your meals out, some of these items are great to have around for a delicious snack. You'll readily agree that there's a vast difference between the taste of fresh fruits and vegetables, homemade breads, pies and other produce and foods that have been hanging around for awhile. Go on and indulge — spoil yourself. . .

The merchandise — including genuine mountain crafts, handmade jewelry, furniture, lamps, fancy pillows, calico bonnets, quilts, hanging flower baskets, scarves, candles — rests on wooden planks supported by cinder blocks or on the tailgates of station wagons or in pickup trucks. There's an air of gaiety as singers accompanied by dulcimer, banjo or harmonica add to the hospitable, friendly, cooperative, informal manners and activities at the marketplace. It's a great opportunity to meet a native!

For getting your money's worth in buying fresh produce and baked goods — it's directly from the farmer to the consumer — it's just like in the days before refrigeration. And there are many young people creating their own gardens, baking their own specialty, or doing their own thing while earning some money for school or for a special hobby. It's an old-fashioned revival, that's what.

The Watauga County Farmers' Market at *Horn in the West* grounds opens in May, stays open through October.

Mitchell Farmers' Market in Spruce Pine runs from July through October. There's also one in Morganton — The Burke County Farmers' Market — and — there are others for you, yourself to discover.

Be sure to take in the following annual event:

OCTOBER

BOONE, N.C. — Harvest Festival. First Saturday. *Horn in the West* grounds. Mountain craft displays, music, flea market, delicious produce and goodies for sale. 8:00 a.m. — 5:00 p.m. Sponsor: The Watauga County Farmers' Market.

37 you don't have to be a high school grad

"Esse Quam Videri," the North Carolina motto meaning "to be rather than to seem," has a deep message if you read between the lines. It may be, however, just for those who are willing to try something new, who are eager for self-discovery, who want to live in the HERE AND NOW!

It doesn't matter how far you've gone in school or what age you are, this area offers loads of opportunities to explore a new activity or to continue studying in a favorite field. To whet your appetite, the schools listed below give a suggestion of the fringe benefits of living or vacationing in college towns. There's alway something going on from bagpipe playing and Scottish dances to gem cutting, from skiing, to learning how to play an instrument, sing, dance or paint. There are day and evening classes year-round for everyone from the adult age of three up, to pursue a hobby, improve skills, or to take a special interest course.

You don't have to be a high school grad to take advantage of the marvellous variety of courses where you can learn just for fun. For example, have you heard of the world-famous craft school that was started in 1929 to preserve mountain crafts called the Penland School of Crafts just six miles from Spruce Pine on the North Toe River, 2500 feet high? Highly trained, producing-craftspeople lead the programs and in addition, noted experts and scholars in their fields visit informally to give valuable suggestions and inspiration. Not only is Penland one of the oldest schools of its kind in the country, but one of the biggest. It offers beginning and advanced instruction in hand-weaving, ceramics, jewelry, pottery, metalsmithing, enameling, photography, glass blowing, plastics, woodworking and vegetable dyeing. Classes are quite informal and friendly, creatively overflowing outdoors; in the distance, one can hear students play on shepherd's pipes. Minimum student age is 18 but there are no upper limits agewise.

You're always welcome to visit school libraries, museums, art exhibits, craft festivals, concerts, lectures, sports events and to stargaze at university observatories (see individual chapters).

Community colleges and technical institutes, a true boon to society, generally offer two-year college transfer programs, two-year technical programs, one-year vocational trade, and a wide variety of adult continuing-education courses tailored to suit a minimum of ten students.

For all you sports fans out there, here's what you may expect to watch in towns and cities and at the schools and colleges in this vicinity: football, soccer, basketball, baseball, field hockey and volleyball games, gymnastics, golf and tennis matches, wrestling, skiing and swimming competition. As a matter of fact, ASU has one of the best well-rounded athletic programs and inter-collegiate competition in the Southeast. And if you see "YOSEF" (a contraction for "Yourself") appearing in full regalia at campus athletic events and functions, the ole bearded mountaineer, wearing tattered overalls and smoking a corn cob pipe, will remind you of the importance of being YOURSELF.

Watch the newspaper or call the information office of the school or university, and listen to local radio stations for announcements of the calendar of sports and other events.

It's always up to YOU!

APPALACHIAN STATE UNIVERSITY FACILITIES

ART EXHIBITS — Dogwood Gallery, Plemmons Student Center. 262-3030. **University Art Gallery,** Faculty Apartments Basement. 262-2220.

ARTIFACTS MUSEUM — Appalachian Room, Belk Library. Tools, kitchen utensils, weaving loom, grandfather clock, crafts, handmade spreads, films, ballads, books, maps. 272-2186.

ARTIST LECTURE SERIES — Campus Auditoriums. See Ch. 40.

BRIDGE — Lovill Dormitory. Locust Street. 262-2272.

CHILDREN'S DAY CAMP — Camp Broadstone. June — August. Arts, crafts, campcraft, nature study. 262-3045.

CONCERTS — Cannon Music Camp. July — August. Faculty, students, guest artists. I. G. Greer Auditorium. 262-3020.

COURSES — Art, Music, Folklore (you name it). 2, 4, 6 and 10-week terms. 262-3654.

DINING — Center for Continuing Education. Bull & Bear Buffet. Candlelight dinners. Superb view! 264-5050.

MOVIES — D. J. Whitener Hall (Students). Wednesday and Sunday. 262-3030.

MUSIC LISTENING — I.G. Greer Music Library. 262-2292.

PLAYS — See Ch. 44.

RECREATIONAL FACILITIES — Broome-Kirk Gymnasium. Basketball, volleyball, weightlifting (students). 262-3140.

READING — Belk Library. Periodicals, books, microfilm, special bicentennial collection. Newspapers: 9 N.C., 14 out-of-state, 7 foreign. 262-2186.

SCIENCE EXHIBITS — Rankin Science Building. Displays on each floor. Biology, geology, physics, minerals, stuffed animals, bird eggs, seashells. 262-3090.

SPECIAL EVENTS — Pioneer Week, Fall Festival. 262-2084.

SPECTATOR SPORTS — Varsity Gymnasium. Conrad Stadium.

STAR GAZING — Physics Department Observatory. 262-2090.

SWIMMING — Indoor Pool. Broome-Kirk Health and Physical Education Building, (students). 262-3019.

TENNIS — 23 courts, Rivers Street. 262-2040.

Be sure to take a tour of the beautifully landscaped campus! (See map "Walking Tour ASU Campus")

HOBBY AND OTHER COURSES

ABINGDON, VA. — Virginia Highlands Community College. Two-year program. Day and evening continuing adult education courses. (703) 628-6094.

BANNER ELK, N.C. — Bagpipe Lessons. Everything Scottish, Ltd., Invershiel. 898-4414.

BANNER ELK, N.C. — The Greater Grandfather Arts Guild. Arts and Crafts classes for young people and adults in the Cheese House; December course, "Making Things for Christmas." 898-5911.

BANNER ELK, N.C. — Lees-McRae College. Two-year Presbyterian liberal arts college; 3740-feet elevation, highest college campus east of Mississippi. 898-3513, Ext. 27.

BLOWING ROCK, N.C. — The French-Swiss Ski College. Appalachian Ski Mountain. Two, four, five and nine-week courses. 295-3277.

BLOWING ROCK, N.C. — The Community School. Large variety of cultural, educational, recreational and social programs for people of all ages.

BOONE, N.C. — Creative Hours for Children (ages 3-9). I. G. Greer Building, Room 224, ASU. 10:00 a.m. — noon.

BOONE, N.C. — Appalachian State University. Bachelor, Master, and Ph.D. degree programs. Short summer courses in art, crafts, music, foreign languages, painting, sculpture. Competitive swimming and diving school: April — May. Art Workshop — studio art and art appreciation, courses in fabric design, painting, sculpture and silk screen printing for high school students; two weeks in July. Ceramics, mixed media, jewelry, photographic design, miniature sculpture for high school-age art students, one-week courses: August. Cannon Music Camp, intensive training in music theory for high school students with individual lessons in major instruments, group experience; entrance based on audition and school recommendation: four weeks, July — August. 262-3036.

BOONE, N.C. — Caldwell Community College and Technical Institute. Year-round. Watauga Learning Center, 101 Rivers St. All kinds of hobby courses. 264-4292.

BOONE, N.C. — Mountain Top Ceramics, 1707 E. King St. Classes for handicapped persons and for all children. 264-0226.

BOONE, N.C. — Polar Palace Ice Skating School. Boone Heights Shopping Center. Six-week courses, private or group instruction in free style, dance: couples, adults, children. 264-4121.

BRISTOL, TENN. — King College. Four-year, coed. (615) 968-1187, Ext. 72.

BRISTOL, VA. — Virginia Intermont College. Two-year women's liberal arts program (703) 669-6101.

BURNSVILLE, N.C. — Painting in the Mountains. Rustic mountainside studio, one mile from Town Square. Instruction in painting, watercolor, oil, acrylic, pastel, representational drawing, landscape classes, portrait and still life. All-day painting trips to scenic areas. Minimum reservation — one week. Spring class two weeks in May; summer class: July and August; fall class: October. Scholarships for young Burnsville residents. Box 182, Burnsville, N.C. 28714.

CROSSNORE, N.C. — Crossnore School, Inc. School for mountain children where weaving and handicrafts are taught; articles for sale. School of Scottish Arts — Highland dancing, drama and bagpipes. 733-4305.

EMORY, VA. — Emory and Henry College. 4-yr. liberal arts program. (703) 944-3121.

HICKORY, N.C. — Catawba Valley Technical Institute. Two-year programs. Day and evening continuing adult education courses. 327-9124.

HICKORY, N.C. — Lenoir-Rhyne College, 4th Ave. and 8th St., N.E. 4-yr. coed college of the North Carolina Synod of the Lutheran Church of America. 328-1741.

JOHNSON CITY, TENN. — Eastern Tennessee State University. Bachelor, Master, and Ph.D. degree programs. Wide variety of short summer courses. (615) 929-4342.

LENOIR, N.C. — Caldwell Community College and Technical Institute. Two-year college programs. Day and evening continuing adult education courses. 728-4323.

LINVILLE FALLS, N.C. — Linville Falls Art School. 765-7844.

MARION, N.C. — McDowell Technical Institute. Two-year programs. Day and evening continuing adult education courses. 652-6021.

MILLIGAN COLLEGE, TENN. — Milligan College. Two and four-year degree programs; teacher certification program; two-year secretarial program; pre-med, pre-law and pre-engineering programs. (615) 928-1165.

MORGANTON, N.C. — Western Piedmont Community College. Two-year programs. Day and evening continuing adult education courses. 437-8688.

NEWLAND, N.C. — Alexander School of Dance. Adult clogging and square dancing. 733-2122.

PENLAND, N.C. — Penland School of Crafts. Late May to mid-September. Living and working community of students from 18 upward. Beginning and advanced instruction in ceramics, metal enameling, glass blowing, hand weaving, photography, plastics, pottery and many others. Two and three-week sessions. 765-2359.

SPRUCE PINE, N.C. — Mayland Technical Institute. Two-year programs. Day and evening continuing adult education courses. 765-7351.

WILKESBORO, N.C. — Wilkes Community College. Two-year programs. Day and evening continuing adult education courses. Wilkes Art Guild holds workshops, lectures, demonstrations and exhibits by leading artists and educators as well as art lessons. (919) 667-7136.

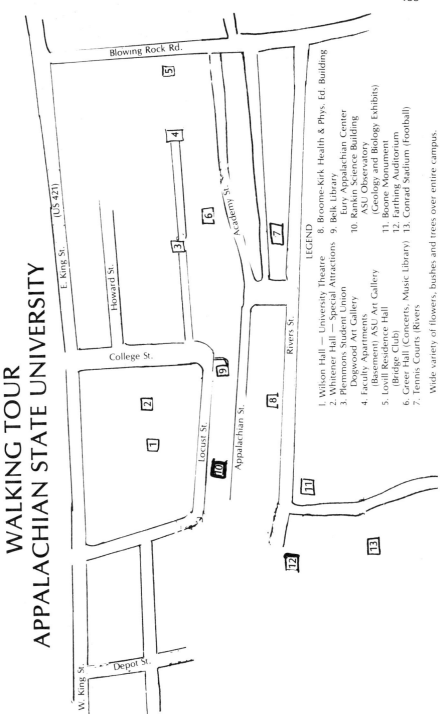

WALKING TOUR
APPALACHIAN STATE UNIVERSITY

LEGEND

1. Wilson Hall — University Theatre
2. Whitener Hall — Special Attractions
3. Plemmons Student Union
   Dogwood Art Gallery
4. Faculty Apartments
   (Basement) ASU Art Gallery
5. Lovill Residence Hall
   (Bridge Club)
6. Greer Hall (Concerts, Music Library)
7. Tennis Courts (Rivers

8. Broome-Kirk Health & Phys. Ed. Building
9. Belk Library
   Eury Appalachian Center
10. Rankin Science Building
    ASU Observatory
    (Geology and Biology Exhibits)
11. Boone Monument
12. Farthing Auditorium
13. Conrad Stadium (Football)

Wide variety of flowers, bushes and trees over entire campus.

38 love story at the library

You must come see what's new at the library besides books. In addition to fascinating displays of hobbies and a variety of arts and crafts, you may borrow recordings, sculptures, oil and water color paintings, power tools, toys, jigsaw puzzles, and movies, just to name a few items. You can trace your family tree, see a free movie, learn how to belly dance, tap dance, ballroom dance or how to do yoga exercises. You can learn how to be a gourmet cook, how to make out a will, how to be an ideal parent, and how to find peace of mind and serenity through the art of meditation. Just borrow a book on any of these subjects or others that may titillate your curiosity. There's a smorgasbord of learning tapes on such courses as English, foreign languages, and mathematics, as well as listening tapes on stories and music. You may even comfortably watch TV with headphones on or listen to informative speakers from the library Talent Bank whose talents include rock-collecting, woodcarving, astronomy, playing musical instruments, storytelling — a gamut of hobbies. Just nose around the local library or university library — you'll be amazed at the potpourri of activity and information.

And some libe, no doubt, will be showing the outstanding Civilisation film series which easily bears viewing more than once.

Little ones may climb onto floor cushions or curl up with a book in a rocking chair in appealing, colorful surroundings or they may participate in wonderful, adventurous programs in their niche of the libe.

Love is always in bloom when you visit the library thanks to the wealth of expanding services that keep on unfolding and luckily, you don't have to travel far to reach one. Most ambitious of all library undertakings now underway, is the nationwide computer network for exchanging books and cataloguing information. What a bonanza for every one of us!

You'll be delighted to learn, however, that no matter how far automation goes, the kind souls at the library who offer loving assistance in researching any question bugging you, are here to stay! Why not, while you're here, delve into the adventurous, romantic stories of the mountain people and their culture, and how they founded their independent "nation," the State of Franklin. One of the top collections anywhere is in Boone at the Eury Appalachian Center, second floor of the ASU Belk Library. It's a storehouse of more than 5000 books on biography, history, folklore, handcrafts, geography, literature, social and economic conditions, artifacts, films, the largest collection of authentic performances of mountain music, the Guy collection containing more than 1000 hours of taped folk music — single note and claw-hammer banjo strumming — recordings of Church harmony, Blue Grass music, and "Jack-tales" those tall tales that have come down through generations. And if you'd like to see a part of the tree where the famous words, "D. Boon cilled a bar on this tree in year 1760," were carved, that's here, too. All this and much, much more to delve into for as long as you desire.

Lovers of all kinds of music will find favorite recordings at college and university music libraries, as well as at public libraries — with a pair of headphones you're in a world of your own — NIRVANA.

Best of all, at a number of libraries you don't have to be a resident of a community to enjoy borrowing privileges.

There's no time like a vacation to catch up on your reading and since it's no longer necessary to load your suitcases with reading matter, make yourself right at home when you stop by for some quiet browsing at the library. There's a "Welcome" sign out for you.

ABINGDON, VA. — **Virginia Highlands Community College.** (703) 628-6094.

ABINGDON, VA. — **Washington County Public Library.** (703) 628-2971.

BAKERSVILLE, N.C. — **Mitchell County Public Library.** 688-2511.

BANNER ELK, N.C. — **James H. Carson Library,** Lees-McRae College. 898-5513.

BLOUNTVILLE, TENN. — **Sullivan County Library.** (615) 323-5301.

BLOWING ROCK, N.C. — **Blowing Rock Community Club Library,** Main St. 295-7951.

BLUFF CITY, TENN. — **Bluff City Library,** 513 Park Worley Ave. (615) 538-5341.

BOONE, N.C. — **Bernhardt Library and Lounge,** Center for Continuing Education, ASU. Small library containing leading daily newspapers, magazines, journals, some books and reference works. 264-5050.

BOONE, N.C. — **Carol Grotnes Belk Library,** Appalachian State University. 262-2186.

BOONE, N.C. — **William L. Eury Appalachian Collection,** Appalachian State University Belk Library. 262-2186.

BOONE, N.C. — **I. G. Greer Music Library,** Appalachian State University. 262-2292.

BOONE, N.C. — **Watauga County Public Library,** Water Street. 264-8784.

BRISTOL, TENN. — **Avoca Library,** Volunteer Parkway. (615) 968-9663.

BRISTOL, TENN. — **Bristol Public Library,** 701 Goode St. (615) 669-9444.

BRISTOL, TENN. — **E. W. King Library,** King College. (615) 968-1187.

BRISTOL, VA. — **Hicks Memorial Library,** Virginia Intermont College. (703) 669-6101.

BURNSVILLE, N.C. — **Yancey County Public Library.** 682-2600.

ELIZABETHTON, TENN. — **Public Library.** (615) 542-4841.

ELKIN, N.C. — **Northwestern Regional Public Library,** 11 N. Front St. 835-5586.

EMORY, VA. — **Frederick T. Kelly Library,** Emory and Henry College. (703) 944-3121.

ERWIN, TENN. — Library of Unicoi County. (615) 743-6533.

GALAX, VA. — Vaughan Memorial Library, 608 W. Stuart Dr. (703) 236-2351.

GRANITE FALLS, N.C. — Granite Falls Public Library, 18 Crestview St. 396-7703.

HICKORY, N.C. — Albert Ivey Memorial Library. 327-6241.

HICKORY, N.C. — Rudisell Library, Lenoir-Rhyne College, 4th Ave. and 8th St., N.E. 328-1741.

INDEPENDENCE, VA. — Wythe-Grayson Regional Library. (703) 773-4524.

JEFFERSON, N.C. — Ashe County Public Library. (919) 246-2041.

JOHNSON CITY, TENN.— The Sherrod Library, East Tenn. State U. (615) 929-4303.

JOHNSON CITY, TENN. — Mayne Williams Public Library. Summer programs for children; monthly programs for all ages. (615) 928-3522.

JONESBORO, TENN. — Washington County Public Library. (615) 753-4841.

LENOIR, N.C. — Caldwell County Public Library. 758-8481.

MARION, N.C. — McDowell County Public Library, 100 W. Henderson. 652-3858.

MARION, VA. — Smyth Bland Library. (703) 783-2323.

MILLIGAN COLLEGE, TENN. — Milligan College. (615) 928-1165.

MORGANTON, N.C. — Burke Public Library, 204 S. King St. 437-4505.

MOUNTAIN CITY, TENN. — Johnson County Public Library. (615) 727-6544.

NEWLAND, N.C. — Avery County Public Library, Avery Square. 733-9393.

NEWTON, N.C. — Catawba County Library, North College Ave. Children's films shown. 464-2421.

N. WILKESBORO, N.C. — Wilkes County Public Library, 913 C St. Framed art reproductions may be borrowed by residents and non-residents. Story hour for children through grade three plus short films. (919) 838-2818.

OLD FORT, N.C. — McDowell County Public Library. 668-7111.

PERKINSVILLE, N.C. — Green Valley School Library, NC 194, five miles northeast of Boone. 264-3606.

SPARTA, N.C. — Alleghany County Library. (919) 372-5573.

SPRUCE PINE, N.C. — Spruce Pine Public Library, Walnut Avenue. 765-4673.

TAYLORSVILLE, N.C.— Alexander County Public Library, 115 First Ave., S.W. 632-4058.

VALDESE, N.C. — Valdese Library, Germain Ave. 874-2421.

WILKESBORO, N.C. — Wilkes Community College Library. (919) 667-7136.

YADKINVILLE, N.C. — Yadkin County Public Library. (919) 679-8792.

39 treasure troves

Where would you go to find a priceless collection of handmade bedspreads and coverlets? Where would you find recordings of folk music, folk tales and folk ballads, or Carl Sandburg's zither, or a hummingbird's eggs, or an active beehive, an antique steam engine or a sausage stuffer? The answers to all these questions and to many more are found in the many museums included in this chapter.

Whoever thinks museums are boring places doesn't get around much anymore. "Especially for you" should be written above the portals of each of these museums for their contents have been carefully selected and prepared for your appreciation and enjoyment.

And you never know what may spark you or the children to start holding on to articles that may become collector's items or maybe to resume a fascinating hobby that will provide you with countless pleasurable hours.

If you'd like to become a collector of precious stones, gems, rare rock and other minerals, visit the mines listed in Ch. 34. And, of course, in practically every town of any size you'll find gem shops with dazzling displays of stones in every color of the rainbow and in all shapes and sizes.

But one thing is sure, whether you become a collector or not, a visit to any of these museums is a visit that will long be remembered, for an infinitely greater appreciation not only of the facts you've learned but for the collections you've seen!

(If no area code is shown, use 704.)

BANNER ELK, N.C. — Blue Ridge Taxidermy Studio. Lees-McRae College campus. Animal museum: stuffed mounted bobcat, wild boar, fox, owl, game birds, deer heads, 486-pound black bear, squirrels, skunk. 898-4659.

BLUE RIDGE PARKWAY, N.C. — Frances L. Goodrich Pioneer Museum. Milepost 294. Parkway Craft Center, Moses H. Cone Memorial Park. May — October. Display of utensils used by early pioneers: spinning wheel, loom, potter's wheel, basketry, furniture, tools of mountain artisans, many of which are still used in production of handcrafts, and other articles of interest. 295-7938.

BLUE RIDGE PARKWAY, N.C. — Museum of North Carolina Minerals. Milepost 331. Gillespie Gap. May — October. Visitor Center: Exhibits and collections of North Carolina minerals — precious and semi-precious stones — emeralds, garnets, rubies and others; lapidary and craft demonstrations, tours. 765-2761.

BLUE RIDGE PARKWAY, N.C. — Mount Mitchell State Park Nature Museum. Milepost 349.9. (Closed in winter). 675-4611.

BOONE, N.C. — Eury Appalachian Center, Belk Library, ASU, second floor. Eight thousand volumes. Outstanding collection of materials about the Appalachian Region of Alabama, Georgia, South and North Carolina, Tennessee, Kentucky, West Virginia, Virginia, Maryland and Pennsylvania. Artifacts, clippings, crafts, films, maps, manuscripts, microfilm, periodicals, pictures, tools, and numerous books on history, geneology, biography, geography, literature, social and economic conditions. **Tatum Collection** of furniture and household utensils and tools of pioneer vintage including the loom of Dan'l Boone's mother (still working). **Fry Collection** of handmade spreads and coverlets tufted, crocheted, fringed and knotted. **Guy Collection** of folk music and folk tales, recordings. **York Collection** of ballads and folksongs. University archives of bulletins, programs, wills, deeds. Carl Sandburg's zither, unusual dulcimers and antique grandfather clock — just to name a few items! Don't miss replica of switch-back train at Shull's Mills. 262-2186.

BOONE, N.C. — 1921 Buggy used by Dougherty Brothers, founders of ASU. Restored by Industrial Arts and Technical Education Dept. Above entrance to Center for Continuing Education.

BOONE, N.C. — Anthropological Museum. Whitener Hall, Room 109, ASU. Displays of artifacts from Appalachia, Mexico, Yugoslavia, the New River area and Watauga County. **Geology Museum.** Rankin Science Building, ASU. Splendid collection of native gems and minerals of North Carolina as well as from other parts of the United States. First floor. 262-3049. **Biology Museum.** Rankin Science Building, ASU. Display of stuffed animals and wide variety of bird eggs from hummingbird to ostrich. Second floor. 262-3025. **Meteorology and Geography Museum.** Rankin Science Building, ASU. Various displays, seashells and rocks. Fourth floor. 262-3000.

GALAX, VA. — T. J. Mathews Museum, 608 W. Stuart Dr. Indian artifacts, antique farm instruments, coin collection. 2:00 — 4:00 p.m

HICKORY, N.C. — Creative Museum for Youth, Inc. Includes The Star Ceiling, exhibits of minerals, shells, fossils, dinosaurs, microscopic specimens, mounted animals, wild plants, primitive man; also a live ant farm and bee hive, an Evolution Chart, an Early Cultures Map, a Cherokee Indian Hut, a slide program on many life forms, an art studio, an aquarium with over 20 species of tropical fish, a crafts center, The Geology Module, and a dark room where children may learn basic photographic skills. 9:00 a.m. — 5:00 p.m. Thursday — Saturday; 2:00 — 5:00 p.m. Sunday. 322-8169.

JOHNSON CITY, TENN. — Carroll Reece Museum, East Tennessee State University. Period art, history displays, contemporary one-man shows (traveling exhibitions), guided tours, concerts and films; arts and crafts of regional artists for sale. 12:45 — 4:45 p.m. Monday through Friday; 1:00 — 5:00 p.m. Saturday, Sunday. (615) 929-4392.

MARION, VA. — Hungry Mother State Park Nature Center. All year. Pioneer utensils, Indian artifacts, stuffed animals and other displays. (703) 783-3422.

MARION, VA. — Smyth County Historical Society and Museum. (703) 783-5585.

NEWTON, N.C. — Catawba County Historical Museum, 306 S. Main St. Catawba County history, costumes, customs, utensils of 1800's portrayed in exhibits and displays. 465-0383.

OLD FORT, N.C. — Mountain Gateway Museum, Water Street. Artifacts of early life in this area, cooking ware, maps, pottery, musical instruments, home remedies, log cabin. Guided tours May 1 to October 31, Tuesday through Saturday, Sunday afternoon.

PINEY FLATS, TENN. — Rocky Mount. April to November 1. Brick Museum of pioneer artifacts. Operated by Rocky Mount Historical Assn. 10:00 a.m. — 5:00 p.m. Monday through Saturday; 2:00 — 6:00 p.m. Sunday. (615) 538-7396.

SPARTA, N.C. — Maxwell's Museum. Antique cars, steam engines. (919) 372-8581.

VALDESE, N.C. — Waldensian Museum, Old Colony Amphitheatre. Open before performances (July — August). Artifacts of Waldenses including antique steam engine, outdoor stone oven, tools, cider press, corn sheller and grindstone. **Church Museum** contains history of religious group who founded town of Valdese in 1893. Presbyterian Church. 6:30 — 8:30 p.m. Thursday through Sunday. (919) 874-0176.

WILKESBORO, N.C. — Old Wilkes Jail Museum. Old candle molds, apple peeler, cherry seeder, antique child's chair, sausage stuffer, pewter coffee pot, powder horn, Revolutionary War canteen, an original lock from jail. On loan to the museum are four antique lamps, chest of drawers, cherry and oak pie sofa, blanket chest (pine), hand-painted sewing table and a walnut corner cupboard. Sponsor: Old Wilkes Jail Society.

40   that's entertainment!

One of the best buys you can get around these parts — a *real* bargain, and who doesn't love bargains in these days of high prices — is the artist-lecture series sponsored by schools, colleges and universities during the school year for just a nominal charge or no charge at all, for individual events.

AND, other hard-to-top take-ins are the naturalist programs held in city, state and national parks and forests. These summer illustrated, interpretive nature and area talks, as well as folk music and dancing programs, on the Blue Ridge Parkway and state and national park amphitheatres, are first-rate and free of charge. How can you beat that! (See Ch. 11 for locations.)

Just to give you an idea of the caliber of cultural opportunities available, here's a recent year of an Artist and Lecture Series at Appalachian State University in Boone: five major Fine Art Series — Charlotte Symphony, Tokyo String Quartet, Burgess Meredith, Mimi Garrard Dance Company, Houston Ballet; five-major lecture series, — a literary treat — Boston Tea Party, Richard Wordsworth, Art Buchwald, Gene Rodenberry and the well-known naturalist, Euell Gibbons; a five chamber music series, a feast for the music lover — Panocha String Quartet, Robert Hill, Harpsichordist, Clarion Wind Ensemble, Jean Ritchie, Folk Singer, and Ars Musica playing Baroque music. Most of these events take place at the Arts Complex housing an outstanding multi-purpose auditorium and Fine Arts Department which includes art, music, theatre and speech. (See Ch. 37 for other colleges and universities sponsoring similar entertainment including debates, films and literary readings as well as programs by poets, historians, concert artists, authors, performers, and other special well-known celebrities!)

All these programs are for the sole purpose of life enrichment and life enjoyment here, where nature and culture meet.

Broadening your horizon in this way may be a step toward "opening out a way for the imprisoned splendor to escape." 'Cause THAT'S ENTERTAINMENT!

(Phone sponsor or C. of C. to confirm information. If no area code is shown, use 704.)

SCHOOL YEAR — SEPTEMBER TO JUNE
BOONE, N.C. — Artist and Lecture Series. Appalachian State University. 262-2090.

BRISTOL, TENN. — Lecture Series. Memorial Chapel, King College. (615) 968-1187.

BRISTOL, VA. — Series of Lectures and Poetry Readings. Fine Arts Recital Hall, Virginia Intermont College. (703) 669-6101.

HICKORY, N.C. — Lecture Series. Lenoir-Rhyne College. Deals with subjects of great magnitude. 328-1741.

JOHNSON CITY, TENN. — Lecture Series, Poets, Artists, Concerts. The University Center Program Committee, East Tennessee State University. (615) 929-4342.

JOHNSON CITY, TENN. — Freedom Hall Performing Arts Series. The Freedom Hall Civic Center. (615) 929-1171.

MILLIGAN COLLEGE, TENN. — Concert-Lecture Series. Milligan College. Performing artists, entertainers and lecturers on various subjects of current interest. (615) 929-0116.

WILKESBORO, N.C. — Wilkes Art Guild Workshops, Lectures and Demonstrations. Wilkes Community College. Leading artists and educators of North Carolina present monthly programs free to the public. (919) 667-7136.

JUNE TO SEPTEMBER
LITTLE SWITZERLAND, N.C. — Summer Lecture Series. Geneva Hall. Sponsor: Little Switzerland Community Assn.

AUGUST
ABINGDON, VA. — Art and Other Lectures. August 1 — 15. Virginia Highlands Festival. (See Ch. 54.) Sponsor: Historical Society of Washington County.

SEPTEMBER — NOVEMBER
BANNER ELK, N.C. — Film Discussions. (Following Great Film Series). College credit or audit. Carson Library Auditorium, Lees-McRae College. 7:00 p.m. 898-5241.

41   flick favorites

Have you been to a movie lately? Or do movies turn you off these days? Would you like to know where there are some fine films for youngsters? How about looking in on some really great professionally produced film fare both for grownups and children? Schools, universities, libraries, churches and art galleries show films many of which are outstanding not only as entertainment but also in script and photography — and — mostly they're free of charge.

Lasting values are subtly and interestingly interwoven into the plots of many children's films that will provide guideposts for a child to grow into a responsible adult.

For adults, thought-provoking classics are scheduled regularly as well as inspirational art classics such as the Civilization Series narrated by Sir Kenneth Clark. Among the art films shown in the past have been *Pursuit of Happiness,* a classical music feast featuring the sounds of Bach, Handel, Hayden and Mozart and depicting examples of rococo architecture. Each one of these great films is marvellous for viewing more than once and for discussion afterwards.

The entire family will thrill to the splendors of our wildlife resources and the beauty of nature, birds, insects and flowers photographed by famous naturalists. Films such as *Migration Mysteries* illustrating the east-west route of the redhead duck and the loop flight of the petrel or *Antillean Adventure* are artistic natural masterpieces. This caliber film has been shown at Audubon Society or Sierra Club meetings or at the amphitheatres in the national parks and state forests.

Then, there are also excellent travel movies and many worthwhile, inspirational Hollywood classics you may have missed and would like to see.

The Watauga Public Library in Boone sponsors varied monthly films of more than passing interest such as *Carl Sandburg, William Shakespeare, The British Isles, Music Makers of the Blue Ridge,* a guided tour of western North Carolina with traditional folk melodies, dance and verse, and *Jefferson's Monticello,* an example of fine Colonial architecture. Many of these excellent movies will heighten the mood for your stay in the Land of the Clouds.

Watch the local newspaper announcements for these NOT "X" or "R"-rated film showings at nearby public and private schools and organizations.

(Phone sponsor or C. of C. to confirm information. If no area code is shown, use 704.)

YEAR-ROUND

BANNER ELK, N.C. — Great Film Series (followed by discussion). Carson Library Auditorium, Lees-McRae   College. College credit or audit (no test!). 7:00 p.m. Mondays. 898-5513.

BOONE, N.C. — Film Series. Hollywood movies and others, Whitener Hall, Appalachian State University (students only). 262-3030.

BOONE, N.C. — Audubon Wildlife Film-Lecture Series. Rankin Science Building, Room 379, ASU. Sponsor: ASU Artist and Lecture Series and Grandfather Mountain Chapter of Audubon Society. 262-3025.

BOONE, N.C. — Young People's Film Series. Watauga Library, Children's Room. For ages 4 — 12. 3:30 p.m. weekly.

BOONE, N.C. — Adult Film Program. Watauga Library Browsing Room. Films on art, music, nature, and old classics. 7:00 p.m. Thursday. 264-8784.

BOONE, N.C. — Historical Films Series. Edwin Duncan Hall, ASU. 262-2282.

BRISTOL, VA. — Film Series. Virginia Intermont College. (703) 669-6101.

JOHNSON CITY, TENN. — Adult Film Series. Eastern Tenn. State U. (615) 909-4317.

NEWTON, N.C. — Children's Films. Nature, adventure, classics. Catawba County Library, North College Avenue. 464-2421.

N. WILKESBORO, N.C. — Art Film Series. Wilkes Community College, Hayes Building, Room 312. Sponsor: Wilkes Community College and Wilkes Art Guild. (919) 667-7136.

JUNE THROUGH LABOR DAY
STATE PARKS, FORESTS AND BLUE RIDGE PARKWAY — Extraordinary Naturalist Movies and Slide Programs. Amphitheatres. 8:30 or 9:00 p.m. (sundown). Programs available at area Visitor Centers.

JUNE THROUGH AUGUST
BOONE, N.C. — Children's Matinee. Weekly. Chalet Theatre. Sponsors: Boone Junior Woman's Club and Chalet Theatre.

PUBLIC PARKS AT VARIOUS LOCATIONS — Films for Children. Blowing Rock, N.C.; Boone, N.C.; Cove Creek, N.C.; and Mabel and Parkway schools in Boone. Sponsor: Watauga County Public Library. 264-8784.

42   fascinatin' rhythm

If you've got a pair of feet that can't be still when there's music in the air, you've come to the right place. Whether it's folk dancing, flat footin', buck dancin', Hoot 'n Nanny, clogging, ballroom dancing, Highland fling, ole timey street dancing, dancing in the park, or festivals including loads of other goodies, the mountaineers have got it all together for you no matter when you come.

There's great ballet to watch as well as square dancing and clogging exhibitions — visual delights with sensational sounds. There are all kinds of dance lessons available and dance workshops for all ages as well as dance spots to "trip the light fantastic."

No matter what your hang-up, dancing is a great way to loosen up the muscles when the band starts playing and let it all hang out! Whether it's the Hustle, the Cumbia, Rock'n Roll, the Hully Gully, Latin beats, or good ole "Swing", grab your partner and head for the dance floor of your choice and let the fascinatin' rhythm take over!

(Contact sponsor or C. of C. to confirm information. If no area code is shown, use 704.)

SQUARE DANCE CLUBS

ABINGDON, VA. — Burley Twirlers. First and third Sat. 4-H Center. 8:00 p.m.

BRISTOL, TENN. - VA. — Twin City Swingers. First and third Friday. Camp Waldo Miles.

BRISTOL, TENN.-VA. — Bristol Pea Pickers. Second and fourth Saturday. Y.M.C.A., Edgemont Avenue.

COVE CREEK, N.C. — The Cove Creek Swingers. Wednesday. WAMY Community Center.

CROSSNORE, N.C. — Shawneehaws. Second and fourth Friday. Old High School gym. 8:00 p.m.

ELIZABETHTON, TENN. — Betsy Squares. First and third Friday. National Guard Armory.

ERWIN, TENN. — Circle Left Squares. Second and 4th Sat. Evans Elementary School, Mohawk Road. 8:00 p.m.

HICKORY, N.C. — Hickory Nut Squares. Second and fourth Saturday. Longview Recreation Center. 8:00 p.m.

JOHNSON CITY, TENN. — Johnson City Grand Squares. Second and fourth Friday. 8:00 p.m.

LENOIR, N.C. — Caldwell Squares. Second Sat. and fourth Fri. Mulberry Street Recreation Center. 8:00 p.m.

MORGANTON, N.C. — Mimosa Squares. First and third Saturday. Collett Street Recreation Center. 8:00 p.m.

NEWTON, N.C. — Newton Twirlers. Second and fourth Saturday. Mary Hardister Recreation Center. 8:00 p.m.

SPRUCE PINE, N.C. — Swinging Pines. Second and fourth Saturday. Deyton Elementary School. 8:00 p.m.

TAYLORSVILLE, N.C. — Alexander Squares. First and third Saturday. Ellendale Community Center. 8:00 p.m.

VALDESE, N.C. — Brown Mountain Lite

Steppers. First and third Friday. Valdese Community Center. 8:00 p.m.

W. JEFFERSON, N.C. — Highland Squares. Second and fourth Saturday. BROC Building. 8:00 p.m.

ALL YEAR
BANNER ELK, N.C. — Tamarack Inn. Dine and Dance. 898-4201.

BLOWING ROCK, N.C. — Villa Maria Restaurant. Monday, Thursday, Friday 9:30 p.m. — 1:30 a.m. Dine and Dance. 295-3146.

BOONE, N.C. — Ramada Inn. Saturday night. Dine and Dance. 8:00 p.m. till midnight. 264-1000.

BRISTOL, TENN. - VA. — Ballet Company Series.

HICKORY, N.C. — The Hickory Ballet Series. 464-3512.

INDEPENDENCE, VA. — Square Dance. VFW Building.

JOHNSON CITY, TENN. — Folk Dancing. Thursday. Memorial Gym, Room 108, Eastern Tenn. State U. 7:00 p.m.

N. WILKESBORO, N.C. — Dancing. Wilkes Recreation Center, US 268 East.

SPARTA, N.C. — Square Dancing. Saturday. VFW Building.

ANNUAL EVENTS
APRIL
BOONE, N.C. — Watauga County Spring Festival Clogging Exhibition. Fourth Saturday. Varsity or Broome-Kirk Gym, ASU. 10:00 a.m. — 5:00 p.m.

MAY
BANNER ELK, N.C. — Spring Festival — Clogging. First weekend. Lees-McRae College.

MARION, N.C. — Mountain Clog Dance Show. Second Saturday. East

McDowell High School. Children under six free. Individual competition from 4:00 to 6:00 p.m.; team performance at 7:00 p.m.

LENOIR, N.C. — Lenoir Academy of Dance. Recital — Ballet. Fourth Sat. Hibriton High School Gym. 8:00 p.m

BOONE, N.C. — Spring Folk Dance Festival. Third or fourth weekend, Friday, Saturday, Sunday. ASU Varsity Gymnasium.

JUNE 1 — OCTOBER 15
BLOWING ROCK, N.C. — Dine and Dance Green Park Hotel. Every night. 295-3141.

BURNSVILLE, N.C. — Square Dancing. Saturday night. "Hootin' Owl Hall." Toe River Ranch and Campground, eight miles southeast. Live country music for all ages. 7:30 p.m.

BURNSVILLE, N.C. — Square Dancing. Saturday night. "Wilderness Hall." Mountain Wilderness, ten miles south on NC 197. Live band. 8:30 p.m.

JUNE — SEPTEMBER
LITTLE SWITZERLAND, N.C. — Square Dancing. Saturday night. Geneva Community Hall. 7:30 p.m. to midnight.

MARION, VA. — Fireman's Jamboree. Saturday night. Opposite Courthouse. 8:00 p.m. to midnight.

NEWLAND, N.C. — Jamboree Street Dance. Second Saturday. Clogging, buck dancing, cakewalks. 7:30 p.m.

JUNE
N. WILKESBORO, N.C. — Arts Emphasis Week — Ballet. Sponsor: Wilkes Art Guild.

ELIZABETHTON, TENN. — Country River Days. Third week. Square dancing, clogging, contests. Doe River Bridge in center of town.

BAKERSVILLE, N.C. — Rhododendron Festival Square Dance. 3rd or 4th week.

JULY

BLOWING ROCK, N.C. — Independence Day Festival Dance. Town Park. 8:00 p.m.

INDEPENDENCE, VA. — Independence Day Celebration Square Dance. Tennis Court. 9:00 p.m. to midnight.

NEWLAND, N.C. — Street Dance. First Saturday. Sponsor: Newland Volunteer Fire Department. 7:30 p.m.

TERRELL, N.C. — Fiddler's Convention. First Saturday. Lake Norman Music Hall, NC 150. Buck dancing and clogging.

JONESBORO, TENN. — "Jonesborough Days" Square Dancing. July 4 and 5. 8:00 — 10:30 p.m.

BANNER ELK, N.C. — Informal Ceilidh. Second Friday and Saturday. Hayes Auditorium, Lees-McRae College. Dance preview of Grandfather Mountain Gathering of the Scottish Clans. 8:30 p.m. Friday, 7:30 p.m. Saturday.

BOONE, N.C. — Summer Dance. Third Saturday. Holiday Inn Convention Center. Sponsor: Boone Junior Woman's Club. 9:00 p.m. — 1:00 a.m.

MARION, VA. — Hungry Mother Art and Crafts Festival. Third weekend, Friday, Saturday, Sunday. Mountain Clogging and Square Dancing. (See Ch. 29) 10:00 a.m. — 6:00 p.m.

BLOWING ROCK, N.C. — Dancing in the Park (during Annual Horse Show Days). Last Friday in July or first Friday in August. Sponsor: Blowing Rock Recreation Department. 8:00 p.m.

SPRUCE PINE, N.C. — Street Dancing (at Gem Festival). Last week in July or first week in August. Thursday and Friday. Spruce Pine Parking Lot behind Sullins Music Center. 9:30 p.m.

AUGUST

ABINGDON, Va. — The Virginia Highlands Arts and Crafts Festival — Square Dancing. August 1 — 15. (See Ch. 29.)

BURNSVILLE, N.C. — Yancey Youth Jamboree (since 1968). First Thursday and Friday. Loads of dancing! East Yancey High School. Sponsor: Yancey C. of C. 7:00 p.m. 682-2512.

BURNSVILLE, N.C. — Mt. Mitchell Crafts Fair (since 1957). First Friday and Saturday. Square Dancing. Town Square.

BLOUNTVILLE, TENN. — Blountville Country Hoe Down. Mid-August. Clogging, street dancing, square dancing. (See Ch. 54) 5:30 — 10:00 p.m.

BLOWING ROCK, N.C. — Benefit Arts Ball (since 1975). 2nd Fri. Blowing Rock Country Club. Sponsor: Blue Ridge Creative Activities Council. 262-1026.

SEPTEMBER

BOONE, N.C. — Pep Rally and Square Dance. First Thursday. ASU Driver' Training Lot. 7:00 p.m.

HICKORY, N.C. — Western Piedmont Symphony Hall Dinner Dance. First Friday. Lake Hickory C.C. 324-8603.

UNION GROVE, N.C. — Clogging "Square-Up" (since 1970). First Friday, Saturday, Sunday. Fiddler's Grove. Workshops in traditional mountain clogging.

BLOWING ROCK, N.C. — Festival in the Park — Dance. Second Sat. 8:00 p.m.

OCTOBER

ABINGDON, VA. — Burley Tobacco Festival and Farm Show (since 1950). Second weekend, Saturday, Sunday, Monday. Saturday night square dance to end festivities. (See Ch. 54.)

DECEMBER

BOONE, N.C. — New Year's Eve Dance. Sponsor: Jaycees. 9:00 p.m. to 1:00 a.m.

43   'play it again, sam'

Are you a "high-brow," "low-brow," or "middle-brow" when it comes to music? Have you ever been to an old-time fiddler's convention, a Bluegrass music festival, a religious sing-in on a mountaintop which attracts such singing personalities as Johnny Cash and Bob Hope? How would you like to build your own simple musical instrument, a mountain dulcimer and learn how to play it in ten minutes — or have a banjo made to suit your taste?

In this Land for All Seasons, you'll discover a treasury of musical entertainment programmed for your pleasure. There's a continuous succession of year-round joyful activities (see sample listing), providing unique opportunities to listen to top musicians from folk to symphonic music. Particularly at the college campuses, if you feel like listening to music — hundreds of excellent recordings are available at the music libraries for private listening, and, shades of Broadway, a bountiful variety of live musical happenings are offered to on-and-off campus music lovers.

For musical youngsters, Appalachian State University runs the Cannon Music Camp each summer offering individual lessons, practice and music theory classes and most valuable — an opportunity to perform publicly with faculty musicians — and the public loves it!

For the finest Hillbilly, Blue Grass and Country Western vocalists, guitarists, banjo players, this heah's the home of Hillbilly Music. Watch the competition for cash prizes, trophies and ribbons at a foot-stompin', heel-tappin', hot, swingin' fiddler's convention (see how many there are).

For the "highbrow," one of the finest of chamber music series, a four-concert event, takes place each summer at Burnsville, called "Music in the Mountains." The setting, the sounds, the ambiance, will undoubtedly lure you here each summer.

To add a sweet note to your vacation or business trip, if you happen to be a musician who plays chamber music, there's an excellent directory available listing chamber music players, amateur or professional. They're in a variety of professions, occupations and ages. Whenever and wherever you travel, the directory of the non-profit Association of Chamber Music Players, Inc., Box 66A, Vienna, Virginia 22180, should prove indispensable to having a satisfying musical event. Take it with you when you travel abroad, too.

If you find yourself in Elizabethton in June, join the townspeople for one whole week to celebrate "Country Music Days," you'll have one whale of a time!

A popular musical activity is gospel singing which you are warmly welcome to join at local churches. Just watch the newspaper for time and place.

For an unusual, one-of-a-kind, Scottish music bash, along with colorful pageantry and athletic contests, don't miss the nation's largest yearly tribute to a distant motherland — Scotland — The Highland Games on Grandfather Mountain in July (See Ch. 54.) 'Nuf sed!

And just a word about the Farm House Lodge, a groovy dining spot with a "rave notice" mountain view in Blowing Rock. Have a meal and be entertained by the waiters and waitresses each of whom is a college music major. You'll rate the highly competent musicianship and acting performances as first-class entertainment. Don't miss it!

And how does one describe the harmony of Barbershop Quartets and Sweet Adelines — all one can say is that music, the universal language, hath great charm for different moods and varying occasions!

(Phone sponsor or C. of C. to confirm information. If no area code is shown, use 704.)

YEAR-ROUND
ALTAMOUNT, N.C. — Blue Ridge Opry. Saturday. Pine Cone Gift Shop, US 221. Midway between Crossnore and Linville. Bluegrass music, country music. Children under 12 free. 8:00 p.m. 733-2452 or 4526.

BOONE, N.C. — Gospel Singing and Concerts. A regular part of area church programs. See newspapers for location and date.

HAMPTON, TENN. — Country and Blue Grass Music. Friday, Saturday and Sunday. Hillbilly World.

HICKORY, N.C. — Unifour Symphony Orchestra. Annual concert series.

JOHNSON CITY, TENN. — Johnson City Symphony Orchestra. Milligan College.

LENOIR, N.C. — North Carolina Bluegrass Association. Tuesday, semi-monthly. American Legion Hall, North Main Street. Concerts 7:30 p.m.

MOUTH OF WILSON, VA. — Music Recitals. Concert, choir, instrumental. Oak Hill Academy.

N. WILKESBORO, N.C. — North Carolina Symphony Orchestra. Concerts and operas. Sponsor: N. Wilkesboro Musical Arts Club.

TERRELL, N.C. — Bluegrass, Country and Gospel Music. Lake Norman Music Hall Family Entertainment Center.

YADKINVILLE, N.C. — Concert Series. Sponsor: Yadkin Arts Council. (919) 679-2941.

JANUARY
BOONE, N.C. — Bluegrass Music Week. Second week. ASU Plemmons Student Union and Varsity Gym. Fiddlers, mandolins in concert. 264-2000.

FEBRUARY
BOONE, N.C. — Northwestern North Carolina Band Clinic (since 1950). Second Friday, Saturday, Sunday. Three concerts. ASU. Symphony band, brass choir, woodwind choir, percussion ensemble.

MARCH
LENOIR, N.C. — Bluegrass Festival (since 1975). Third Saturday (sometimes April). Caldwell Community College, Student Lounge. Competition and prizes for banjo, mandolin, fiddle, guitar, dulcimer and bass fiddle. All-day concerts for 11 hours.

UNION GROVE, N.C. — Old-Time Fiddlers Convention (since 1925). Easter weekend, Thursday, Friday, Saturday and Sunday (sometimes April). Old-time and traditional Bluegrass music.

APRIL
BOONE, N.C. — ASU Symphonic Band Spring Concert. First Wednesday. Greer Auditorium. 85-member band plus the University Chamber Singers. 8:00 p.m.

BOONE, N.C. — Watauga County Music Festival (since 1975). First Tuesday. ASU,

Farthing Auditorium. Five hundred children performing in orchestra, band and chorus from grades four through eight.

BOONE, N.C. — All-County Spring Music Concert. First Friday. Watauga High School Gymnasium. Choral and instrumental, grades six, seven, eight, nine. Includes bands, orchestral strings, guitars.

UNION GROVE, N.C. — Old-Timers Fiddlers World Championship and Bluegrass Festival (since 1923). Second weekend, Thrusday, Friday, Saturday.

BOONE, N.C. — Barbershop Harmony Week. Third week. Appalachian State University. Sponsor: SPEBSQSA in America, Inc. (Society for the Preservation and Encouragement of Barber Shop Quartet Singing in America, Inc.)

BOONE, N.C. — Contemporary Music Festival. Five days, Wednesday — Sunday. Appalachian State University.

BOONE, N.C. — Watauga County Spring Festival. Fourth Saturday. ASU, Varsity and Broome-Kirk Gyms. Folk singing. (See Ch. 29.)

GALAX, VA. — North Carolina Little Symphony Spring Concert (sometimes in May). Galax High School.

MAY

BANNER ELK, N.C. — Spring Festival. First weekend, Friday, Saturday, Sunday. Lees-McRae College. Pickin' and Singin' (See Ch. 54.) Sponsor: BEARA.

ELK PARK, N.C. — Western North Carolina Gospel Singing (since 1969). First Friday. Avery County H.S. Gymtorium. Sponsor: Avery County Rescue Squad. 8:00 p.m. ·

MILLIGAN COLLEGE, TENN. — Chorale Spring Concert. First Friday. Milligan College, Seeger Memorial Chapel. 8:00 p.m. (615) 928-1165, Ext. 47.

BOONE, N.C. — Spring Concert. Last Sunday. Watauga High School Concert Band.

HUDSON, N.C. — Spring Concert (since 1949). High School Gym. Band and choral. 8:00 p.m.

UNION GROVE, N.C. — Ole Time Fiddlers and Bluegrass Festival (since 1923). Memorial Day weekend, Friday, Saturday, Sunday. Invitational (write Box 11).

N. WILKESBORO, N.C. — Spring Concert (since 1948). High School Gym. 8:00 p.m.

LENOIR, N.C. — Commencement Concert. Last Friday. Cook Stadium (in case of rain, High School Auditorium). 8:00 pm.

NEWLAND, N.C. — Whispering Pines Bluegrass Festival. Last Friday and Saturday. US 221, five miles south. Friday, 6:00 p.m. to midnight; Saturday, 4:00 p.m. to midnight.

JUNE THROUGH AUGUST

BLOWING ROCK, N.C. — Singing Waiters and Waitresses. Farm House Restaurant & Villa, South Main Street. Musicals, concerts, loads of entertaining fun! Interesting shops on lower level. 295-7361.

JUNE

N. WILKESBORO, N.C. — Arts Emphasis Week. Pops concert, opera.

WATAUGA LAKE, TENN. — Singing on Watauga.

LENOIR, N.C. — Gospel Singing (since 1969). Second Friday. Hibriten High School. Sponsor: Whitnel Optimist Club. 728-6838.

CHILHOWIE, VA. — Oldtime Fiddlers and Bluegrass Convention (since 1969). Third Thursday, Friday, Saturday. (703) 783-3161.

ELIZABETHTON, TENN. — Country Music Days in Elizabethton. Third week. Fiddle playing and dancing, beard contest, parade, all at the Doe River Bridge, center of town.

ELIZABETHTON, TENN. — Bluegrass Music Festival. Last weekend, Thur., Fri., Sat. Slagle's Pasture, Bristol Highway, US 19E. (Children under 12 free). (615) 542-8615.

INDEPENDENCE, VA. — Old Time and Bluegrass Fiddler's Convention (since 1959). Last Friday and Saturday. Ball Park.

JUNE
COVE CREEK, N.C. — Old Time Fiddlers Convention. Last Saturday. School Gym. Sponsor: Boone Jaycees. 7:00 p.m.

LINVILLE, N.C. — Singing on the Mountain (since 1925). Last Saturday. MacRae Meadows, Grandfather Mountain. Old-time spiritual music, all day, with TV and radio celebrities. 9:00 a.m.

TERRELL, N.C. — Fiddlers Convention. Last Saturday. Lake Norman Music Hall. Bluegrass music. 7:45 p.m.

BURNSVILLE, N.C. — Music in the Mountains. Last Sunday in June and each Sunday in July. Presbyterian Church and Heritage High School. (Also four weeks of chamber music workshops). Music and ambiance. 3:30 p.m.

UNION GROVE, N.C. — Appalachian Folks Day (since 1975). Last weekend — Friday, Saturday, Sunday. Fiddler's Grove. Music and dance workshops, concerts, hymnal songfest.

JULY AND AUGUST
BOONE, N.C. — Cannon Music Camp Faculty and Student Concerts. I. G. Greer Music Building, ASU. 262-3036.

JULY
INDEPENDENCE, VA. — Country Music and Singing. July 2,3,4. Independence Day Celebration. (See Ch. 52.)

JONESBORO, TENN. — "Jonesborough Days". July 4. Davy Crockett High School. Musical Events. 8:00 p.m.

TERRELL, N.C. — Fiddlers' Convention. First Saturday. Lake Morgan Music Hall, NC 150. Buck Dancing and Clogging. 7:30 p.m.

VOLNEY, VA. — Mount Rogers Music Festival (since 1959). First Saturday. Grayson Highland State Park. Arts and crafts and bluegrass, country, western, old-time and folk music. Noon — 10:00 p.m.

BANNER ELK, N.C. — Anniversary Observance. First Saturday. Concert music. Lees-McRae College.

BANNER ELK, N.C. — Informal Ceilidh. Second Friday. Hayes Auditorium, Lees-McRae College. Scottish dancing, piping, drumming, a preview of Gathering of the Clans on Grandfather Mountain. 8:00 p.m.

BANNER ELK, N.C. — Beech Mountain Folk Festival. Second Saturday. Lees-McRae College, Hayes Auditorium. Dulcimer and banjo concert, dancers, craft show, story teller.

LINVILLE, N.C. — Highland Games and Gathering of Scottish Clans. Second Saturday and Sunday. MacRae Meadows, Grandfather Mountain. Two days of colorful pageantry and music. (See Ch. 54.)

PINEY FLATS, TENN. — Choir Concert. Second Saturday and Sunday. Mary Hughes Jr. High School Auditorium. 8:00 p.m.

LENOIR, N.C. — Black Arts Festival. Third week, Monday — Saturday. Viewmont Recreation Center. Singing, rock music, daily art exhibit. 9:00 a.m.

BANNER ELK, N.C. — Country and Gospel Singing. Third Friday and Saturday. Lees-McRae College, Hayes Auditorium. Sponsor: Banner Elk Volunteer Fire Department. 8:00. — 10:30 p.m.

MARION, VA. — Arts and Crafts Festival. Third weekend, Saturday night and Sunday afternoon. Hungry Mother State Park. Bluegrass concert. (See Ch. 29.)

BLOUNTVILLE, TENN. — Fiddler Convention. Sullivan County Agricultural and Industrial Fair. Fourth Week, two nights. Blountville Junior High School.

BURNSVILLE, N.C. — Music in the Mountains. Last Sunday. Lili Kraus' Benefit Recital. Mountain Heritage High School. 3:30 p.m. 675-4060, 4659 or 5132.

AUGUST
ABINGDON, VA. — Virginia Highlands Festival of the Arts (since 1949). August 1 — 15. Music, square dancing. Saturday. 10:00 a.m. — 4:30 p.m. (See Ch. 54.)

BURNSVILLE, N.C. — Yancey Youth Jamboree (since 1968). First Thursday and Friday. East Yancey High School. Folk music, dancing, singing. 7:00 p.m.

JEFFERSON, N.C. — Bluegrass and Ole Time Fiddlers Convention (since 1971). First Saturday. Ashe County Park Grounds. (In case of rain, Ashe Central High School Gym.) Bands, clogging teams, fiddle, banjo, guitar and mandolin. Camping. Sponsor: Rotary Club. (919) 246-5681.

GALAX, VA. — Old Fiddlers Convention Competition (since 1936). Second weekend, Thursday, Friday, Saturday. Felts Park. 7:30 p.m. Thursday, Friday and Saturday; noon to 6:00 p.m. Saturday. Children under 12 free. Sponsor: Galax Moose Lodge.

SALTVILLE, VA. — Bluegrass Fiddlers Convention. First half. High School.

YADKINVILLE, N.C. — Sunbonnet Festival. Second Saturday and Sunday. Yadkinville school grounds and buildings. Band music, Dixieland, choral and gospel singing. (See Ch. 29.) Sponsor: Yadkin Arts Council.

BLOUNTVILLE, TENN. — **Blountville Country Hoedown.** Mid-August. Main Street between Courthouse and Methodist Church. Bluegrass music and fiddlers.

GALAX, VA. — **Old Time Fiddlers and Bluegrass Convention** (since 1973). Second half, Friday and Saturday. Fries, Sugar Grove Highland Park.

SPRUCE PINE, N.C. — **Western North Carolina Bluegrass Festival.** Fourth Thursday through Sunday. Eighteen miles north on US 19E. Kent Wiseman Memorial Park. Hungry Rock Road. Bluegrass and gospel entertainers, area bands, clogging teams, mountain crafts display, quilting party, apple-butter making.

UNION GROVE, N.C. — **Autumn Square-up.** Fourth weekend.

ELIZABETHTON, TENN. — **Old Timers & Bluegrass Fiddlers Convention.** Last weekend, Thur., Fri., Sat. Slagle's Pasture, Bristol highway, US 19E. (615) 542-8615.

SEPTEMBER
BOONE, N.C. — **Creative Hour for Children** ages 3 — 9. Saturdays. I. G. Greer Building, ASU, Room 224. Music, drama and art. Sponsor: Sigma Alpha Iota. 10:00 a.m. — noon.

PINEY FLATS, TENN. — **Old-Time Fiddlers Convention.** First weekend.

BRISTOL, TENN. — **Bristol Country Music Days.** Labor Day.

MORGANTON, N.C. — **Playmore Beach Fiddlers Convention.** Second weekend, Friday, Saturday, Sunday. More than 50 bands compete for prizes. Banjo, fiddle, mandolin, guitar.

OCTOBER
BRISTOL, TENN.-VA. — **Southeastern Band Festival** (since 1951). First Friday and Saturday. Seventy high school bands from eight states. 9:30. — 11:00 a.m.; 6:45 p.m. Massed band performance.

BANNER ELK, N.C. — **Lees-McRae Talent Show.** Second Saturday. Hayes Auditorium. Lees-McRae College.

VOLNEY, VA. — **Mount Rogers Music Festival.** Second Saturday. Grayson Highland State Park. Noon — 10:00 p.m.

LENOIR, N.C. — **Foothills Fall Bluegrass Festival.** Third Saturday. Lenoir-Burke Speedway, eight miles south, next to Lenoir-Burke Airport. Children under 12 free with adults. Nine hours of Bluegrass music. Sponsor: North Carolina Bluegrass Association.

BOONE, N.C. — **Sunshine Review.** Mid-month, Friday and Saturday. Farthing Auditorium, ASU. Rollicking musical, local talent! Sponsor: Boone Junior Woman's Club.

NOVEMBER
BOONE, N.C. — **Boone Barbershoppers' Annual Show.** First Friday. Whitener Hall, ASU. 8:00 p.m.

TERRELL, N.C. — **Fiddlers Convention and Buck Dance Contest.** Thanksgiving Day. Lake Norman Music Hall. 7:00 p.m.

44. 'all the world's a stage...'

The word "theater" or "play" in any language evokes wonder and excitement, lends color and meaning to life, for all ages. Is it because we want to learn more about ourselves, how to deal with problems of this world, harbor a secret wish to be in the limelight, or are we seeking a complete change of pace from our normal existence? Do we desire to lose our personal sense of self in the performance on stage, or is it merely a feeling of curiosity as to how the actors will enact their roles and what they will bring to the audience that is new and different? Whatever it may be — whether it's a puppet show, an historical outdoor drama of adventure and freedom, or theater-in-the-round featuring Broadway smashes — you'll find a wide, vigorous, provocative variety of histrionics in these culture-happy hills, particularly at colleges, universities and community theaters.

Each summer, for example, more than 75 professional actors and actresses are lured here for a working vacation as performers in the outdoor drama, *Horn in the West*. The play is all about the spirit of adventure, romanticism, and individualism of the pioneers at the time our nation exploded into being. Kermit Hunter's moving spectacle, performed each season since 1952, has romance, gaiety, excitement, moving drama, singing and dancing. It takes place at the Daniel Boone Amphitheatre, the kilometer-high mountain playhouse (highest of its kind east of the Rockies), in the heart of Boone, where the clear, clean, unhurried atmosphere harks back to the days when ole Dan'l himself hunted and camped on the very grounds where the acting now takes place. The play is sponsored by the Southern Appalachian Historical Association, a non-profit organization dedicated to preserving the history and culture of the mountain region. Plan to attend at least one-half hour before curtain time to hear the cast, as troubadors, singing period and folk tunes while strolling up and down the outdoor aisles.

If you're a "late" person who enjoys fine entertainment, take in the 11:00 p.m. performance at the Powderhorn Theater across the parking area from the Daniel Boone Amphitheatre. This intimate little playhouse with room for not more than 100 (thin) persons, stages a variety of theatrical goodies (including original works) such as Gian Carlo Menotti's one-act opera buffa, *The Telephone*, and Neil Simon's hilarious comedy, *The Last of the Red Hot Lovers*. These plays are produced, directed and acted by the *Horn* cast after regular performances at the Amphitheatre on Friday and Saturday nights during July and August.

ASU's Mountaineer Playhouse located at Chapell Wilson Auditorium, presents a series of plays during the summer. This summer theatre group performs five nights weekly, excluding Sundays and Thursdays. Theater-in-the-round season tickets are available to use for one performance, or any combination. They've performed *The Apple Tree*, *Come Blow Your Horn*, and many other popular hits.

ASU's noteworthy Children's Theatre incorporates new and original approaches to children's drama, including audience participation, as part of two special courses given in the Speech Department on directing and producing children's plays. They've performed an adaptation of Kenneth Graham's *Wind in the Willows* entitled *Toad of Toad Hall*, and others. Utilizing some 20 past members, technicians and musicians from the community of students, staff and faculty, the play goes on tour throughout area schools in western North Carolina.

The Pied Piper Players of the Student Theatre Guild of North Carolina have staged a series of four plays for children each summer during July and August at the Watauga High School Auditorium and have returned in the spring for a week of performances. They've offered *Mary Poppins*, *The Pied Piper of Hamlin*, and *The Wizard of Oz*, as well as a musical version of *Heidi*.

For beautifully costumed, moving theatre with authentic, realistic outdoor settings, see *From This Day Forward*, an historical drama of the Waldenses, a group of French-Italian Protestants persecuted in 17th century Europe. The performance is staged in the Old Colony Amphitheatre of Valdese (meaning Valley of our Lord, in Italian). The Waldenses founded the town of Valdese in the foothills of the Blue Ridge back in 1893.

The Amphitheatre with its rustic board walls and ample grounds, is a living outdoor museum of the life and customs of the Waldensians even down to the Boccia court — an Italian version of bowling. Descendants of the original Waldensian colonists are on hand at the theater to greet you and explain their customs and demonstrate the game of Boccia in case you'd like to try your hand at it. There are other things to see such as the well-restored Tron House with authentic artifacts and period pieces, the very first dwelling built by the Waldensians after they arrived in North Carolina. The outdoor stone oven, similar to those used by the Waldensians to bake bread in Italy, is still in use now. And if you'd like to join fellow theater goers in a spaghetti supper before the performance, get to the American Legion Home, one block from the Amphitheatre, sometime from 5:00 to 8:00 p.m.

The Parker Playhouse in Burnsville surrounded by mountain forests and breathtaking views, provides good theater during the months of July and part of August, as well as an exhilarating atmosphere. Such musicals as *1776*, *Oliver*, and other smash hits have established supportive theater audiences of long standing.

Probably the only theater in the world today, where you can still barter a jar of beans, jams, jellies, vegetable produce or a suckling pig for a ticket, is the Barter Theatre of Abingdon, Va. It's probably true, however, that these days, they'd prefer the cash! The Barter has the unique distinction of being the first and only state-subsidized theater in the United States and is known officially as the State Theatre of Virginia. Unique in other ways as well, this jewel of a playhouse, styled in 1830 elegance, has the largest professional company outside of New York operating year-round. Not only does the Barter Theatre present great productions, but also trains promising young people in its school and provides a significant cultural milieu for a large area of the rural South. Many a famous Hollywood star has received early background training at this well-known stage. From April to December, more than 70 actors and actresses spend full days preparing the repertory of plays for the season — from April through October. The Barter Company tours during a 17-week season through hundreds of towns and villages from the Gulf of Mexico to the Atlantic Ocean and west to Mississippi. From plays such as Moliere's *The Imaginary Invalid*, to P.G. Wodehouse's *Candle Light*, the Barter Theatre is a special event throughout the Southeast.

The Barter brings the wide world to children also, with performances from mid-June through August. An original production by the Children's Theatre Company, *Who Am I — Where Do I Come From?* enlisted the aid of the audience in "telling how it all began." The Picadilly Puppets, another goody for the kids, perform too.

This listing of some of the area theaters is for those who agree with Shakespeare that "the play's the thing."

(Phone sponsor or C. of C. to confirm information. If no area code is shown, use 704.)

YEAR-ROUND OR SEASONAL

ABINGDON, VA. — Barter Theatre. April to mid-October. I-81, Exit 8. The State Theatre of Virginia (since 1933). Largest professional company outside of New York City presenting traditional, contemporary and experimental productions. (703) 628-3991. Call free from Bristol, Va.-Tenn., 968-2741; Johnson City, Tenn., 928-4641.

ABINGDON, VA. — The Playhouse — Junior Company. June through August. Children's Theater. Admission: voluntary donation, cash or produce. (703) 628-3991.

BANNER ELK, N.C. — College Productions. School year. Lees-McRae 898-5513.

BANNER ELK, N.C. — Dining and Theater Entertainment. The Hub Pub Club, NC 194. 9:00 and 11:00 p.m. 898-9926 or 297-2895.

BOONE, N.C. — Community Theatre. Sponsor: Blue Ridge Creative Activities Council. 262-1026.

BOONE, N.C. — "Horn in the West" (since 1952). June to Labor Day. Daniel Boone Amphitheatre. 8:15 p.m. daily except Monday. Reserved for special events on Monday. 264-9089.

BOONE, N.C. — Powderhorn Theatre (since 1968). July and August. Across parking lot from Daniel Boone Amphitheatre. 10:45 p.m. Friday and Saturday, following production of *Horn in the West.* 264-9089.

BOONE, N.C. — The Mountaineer Playhouse (since 1971). June to August. Chapell Wilson Auditorium, ASU. Arena Summer Theater. Season Tickets. 262-2221.

BOONE, N.C. — The University Theatre. All year. Farthing Auditorium, Rivers Street. Play series performed and directed by ASU speech students. Musicals presented jointly with Music Department. 262-2221.

BOONE, N.C. — Young People's Theatre (since 1972). Undergraduates of Children's Theatre Class, ASU. Performances at area elementary schools. 262-2221.

BOONE, N.C. — Watauga County Children's Theatre. Sponsor: Blue Ridge Creative Activities Council. 262-1026.

BRISTOL, TENN. — King Players. School year. King College. (615) 968-1187.

BRISTOL, VA. — Little Theatre. School year. Va. Intermont College (703) 669-6101.

BURNSVILLE, N.C. — Parker Playhouse Summer Theatre (since 1947). July and August. Six plays — comedies, musicals, drama. Mountain atmosphere. 682-6151.

EMORY, VA. — Emory and Henry College Play Series. School year. (703) 944-3121.

GALAX, VA. — Galax Little Theatre Guild. All Year. (703) 236-9465.

HICKORY, N.C. — Catawba Valley Technical Inst. Play Series. School year. 327-9124.

HICKORY, N.C. — Hickory Commun. Theatre. All year. City Auditorium, 3rd St., NW.

HICKORY, N.C. — Lenoir-Rhyne College Play Series. School year. 328-1744.

JOHNSON CITY, TENN. — The American Revolutionary Road Company (since 1973). Dramatizes local history. P.O. Box 5278, Johnson City, Tenn. 37601.

JOHNSON CITY, TENN. — Community Theatre (since 1959).All year. (615) 926-2542.

JOHNSON CITY, TENN. — Olde West Dinner Theatre. Year-round. 7:00 — 8:00 p.m. buffet; 8:00 p.m. play. (615) 928-2121.

JOHNSON CITY, TENN. — University Theatre. Year-round. Eastern Tennessee State University. Gilbreth Auditorium and Library Theatre. (615) 929-4241.

JONESBORO, TENN. — Appalachian Theatre Ensemble. Sourwood Regional Art Center. 312 W. Main St. (615) 753-8888.

JONESBORO, TENN. — Jonesboro Repertory Theatre. Year-round. 125½ Main St.

NEWLAND, N.C. — Avery County Summer Children's Theatre. Avery County High School. Sponsor: Mitchell-Avery-Yancey Regional Library, Blue Ridge Creative Arts Council.

SPARTA, N.C. — Alleghany Community Theatre. High school students.

VALDESE, N.C. — "From This Day Forward" (since 1968). July and August. Old Colony Amphitheatre. 8:45 p.m. 874-0176.

W. JEFFERSON, N.C. — Ashe County 4-H Playcrafters. Jefferson School. 7:30 p.m.

W. JEFFERSON, N.C. — Ashe County Little Theatre. Spring, summer and fall. Beaver Creek High School Auditorium. 8:00 p.m (919) 246-9982.

W. JEFFERSON, N.C. — Ashe County 4-H Playcrafters Dinner Theater. BROC Building. 7:00 p.m.

WILKESBORO, N.C. — College Theatre. School year. Dinner Theatre, July and August. Wilkes Community College. Drama Department play series. (919) 667-7136.

YADKINVILLE, N.C. — Yadkin Arts Council Theatre Series. Year-round. Comedy, drama, musical. (919) 879-2941.

ANNUAL EVENTS

APRIL
BRISTOL, TENN. — Dogwood Coronation and Play. Last Friday. King College, Kline Auditorium. 8:00 p.m. (615) 968-1187 Ext. 66 or 72.

APRIL AND MAY
JOHNSON CITY, TENN. — Library Theatre Annual Production. Designed to interest children in good literature and expose them to the value and excitement of the performing arts. Sponsor: Interpreter's Theatre, Dept. of Speech, ETSU. 10:00 a.m. (615) 929-4323.

JUNE
N. WILKESBORO, N.C. — Arts Emphasis Week Play. Wilkes Art Guild. Highway 115 at Armory Road. (See Ch. 28.)

45
the look
of yesterday

A panorama of early Americana, a nostalgic look at yesteryear — homes, mansions, farms, gristmills, historic sites — is being preserved and maintained by historical societies throughout our nation and there's a good representation of them here in this tri-state mountain corner. Sights and sounds of history from frontier and log cabin living to handsome period homes, gracious plantation manors, and sumptuous Victorian structures, invite you to browse indoors as well as outdoors. Some homes may be viewed only from the outside since they are very much occupied and private. Outside viewing is also worthwhile however, particularly when you acquaint yourself with the fascinating historical background which recalls a way of life that will never return.

You'll find a look at yesteryear's astonishing life-styles may serve as inspiration for today as you view the distinctive architecture, native plantings, landscaping, beautiful gardens, interior design and decor, antiques, bric-a-brac, paintings, fireplaces and famous collections.

Jonesboro, Tenn., for example, the first planned community west of the Appalachians, was a major stagecoach center in the 1700's. The stagecoach route ran through the Main Street to points east, west, north, and south. If you like to fantasize about the hustlin', bustlin' colorful times when everyone rode the stagecoach from United States Presidents to outlaws, get the brochure *The Old Great Stage Road* from the Town of Jonesboro, Town Hall, Jonesboro, Tenn. 37659 and follow the route outlined. An official Tennessee Bicentennial Town, Jonesboro is "the place where it all began" for Tennessee. You'll find a variety of architectural styles blending together as well as a combination of two or more styles in a single building, all of which gives this area its own character. These homes mirror the changes in national styles which include Federal, Greek Revival, modified Georgian, Victorian and Italianata Villa. Good examples of the stepped gable are found on many of the brick residences. You'll notice the "frosting on the cake" in the use of ornamental scrollwork for trim and brackets.

Anytime is a good time for a visit to Jonesboro: in summer for the Historic Jonesborough Days; in fall, first part of October for the National Storytelling Festival — two days of storytelling and other festivities with nationally recognized artists; in winter, during the week preceding Christmas, traditional holiday activities; and during late March or early April, a historic potpourri designed for the spring season.

For those who enjoy historic walking tours, three United States designated Historic Districts — Abingdon, Va., Blountville and Jonesboro, Tenn., where America's past is being kept alive — reveal old neighborhoods that live on virtually unchanged. Just follow the outlined routes.

If you'd like more historical information on historical subjects, there's a page listing historical societies. The National Trust for Historic Preservation, Washington, D.C., which is dedicated to helping keep America's past alive through its buildings, issues a monthly paper, *Preservation News* and a quarterly, *Historic Preservation.*

And to introduce you to some examples of absorbing living history and not-to-be-missed homes and gardens, which are certain to add new knowledge and appreciation, here's a listing to get you started.

HISTORIC HOMES & SITES

ABINGDON, VA. — Barter Theatre (Historic District). Main Street. An 1830 structure, second oldest theater building in U.S. (See Ch. 44.)

ABINGDON, VA. — The Cove House Craft Shop (Historic District). Main Street. Old Victorian building operated by Holston Mountain Arts and Crafts Coop. A complete craft shop. (See Ch. 29.)

ABINGDON, VA. — Martha Washington Inn (Historic District). Main Street. An 1830 Colonial mansion, a social and cultural center of the area, original authentic, antique furnishings, still an active Inn with 100 guest rooms. Features a dining room seating 300 plus three private banquet rooms and ballroom (convention hall) accomodating 400. Twelve-acre park, swimming pool, gardens, croquet lawns, shuffleboard and tennis. Excellent meals served buffet and from menu. (703) 628-3161.

ABINGDON, VA. — Brook Hall Antiques. Ten miles east on US 11. A 25-room historic home modeled after "Brook Hall Castle" in Ireland; contains American, French and English furniture, glass, china, silver, bric a-brac, art works, paintings and frames.

BLOUNTVILLE, TENN. — Blountville Historic District (see map and details). 1795 historic courthouse and 18th and 19th century homes.

BLUE RIDGE PARKWAY, N.C. — Brinegar Cabin. Milepost 238.5. Doughton Park. Weaving demonstrations on old loom.

BLUE RIDGE PARKWAY, N.C. — Caudill Cabin. Milepost 241.1. Original mountain cabin. Moonshine still exhibit behind lodge.

BLUE RIDGE PARKWAY, N.C. — Flat Top Manor. Milepost 294. May to October. Moses H. Cone Memorial Park. Gracious 20-room dwelling on Cone estate built at turn of century, overlooking panoramic 3600-acre recreation area of quiet beauty, now housing Parkway Craft Center. (See Ch. 29.) 9:00 a.m. to 5:30 p.m. daily. 295-7938.

BLOWING ROCK, N.C. — Main Street old homes: Guy Hill home, The Hayes House, Lamp Post Antiques, Reeves House. Mayview Section of town built in the 1920's, fine homes, scenic area. Mayview Manor, a favorite resort hotel in process of reopening.

BLUFF CITY, TENN. — Fort Womack (1774). Residence-fort of Capt. Jacob Womack.

BOONE, N.C. — Dan'l Boone Stone Monument. ASU campus on Rivers Street across from Varsity Gym in front of Justice Residence Hall. Placed there by Col. Lewis Bryan, Boone's first Mayor, at his own expense in 1912 to mark site where Boone camped from 1760-1769. Monument is built on stones from the chimney of original cabin.

BOONE, N.C. — William Lewis Bryan House (1895). 124 W. Howard Street. Col. Bryan was Mayor off and on for 25 years. He was a direct descendant of Boone. Outside viewing.

BOONE, N.C. — James Hardin Councill House (1878). 224 Councill Street. Lovely home. Site of Councill's General Store around which town of Boone grew in 1800, near King St. Post Office. It was the focal point of trade and communication. First post office here in 1850. Outside viewing.

BOONE, N.C. — Daniel Boone Inn (1920). Blowing Rock Road and Hardin Street. Built by Dr. Robert Knox Bingham as Watauga County's first hospital. Downstairs contained office and double waiting room; upstairs contained hospital rooms and sunporches. In 1930 a hospital was built and this structure became a rooming house with Dr. Bingham still practicing from his office. In 1960 it was converted to the well-known Inn famous for its country ham biscuits.

BOONE, N.C. — The Judge Green House. 407 Green St. Oldest brick home in county; two-story handmade brick, fourteen-inch thick walls, oak floors. Outside viewing.

BOONE, N.C. — The Hardin House (1821). Trailway Farm, E. King Street. One of oldest in county and now occupied by fifth generation. 75-year-old boxbushes along front sidewalk. Interior woodwork handcarved. Outside viewing.

BOONE, N.C. — Frank Armfield Linny House. Over 100 years old. 209 W. King St. Two-story rock building expanded to 13 rooms; overlooks large terraced lawn. Outside viewing.

BOONE, N.C. — Old Lovill Home. Over 100 years old. Capt. Edward Francis Lovill lived here. North end of Green Street. Two-story frame, now ten rooms, originally three; wide encircling porch. Outside viewing.

BOONE, N.C. — Tatum Cabin. Restored pioneer log cabin. At *Horn in the West* parking lot. Five generations of Tatum family lived here. Contents now on display at Eury Appalachian Center, Belk Library, ASU. Outside viewing.

BOONE, N.C. — Rufus M. Ward Home. Late County Commissioner's home. Watauga Falls section, visible from US 321. Three-story home, unusual architecture. Outside viewing.

BOONE, N.C. — Wilcox Drug Company (since 1900). 123 Howard St. Dealers in herbs, roots, barks, cones, galax, selling to pharmacists around world. Their motto: "When you sell to us, the world is your market."

BRISTOL, TENN. - VA. — Brass Markers equally set in the center of State Street serve as monument of final settlement of 200 years of controversy. In 1903 State of Tennessee ceded to State of Virginia the part of State Street lying north of center of street.

BRISTOL, VA. — Pemberton Oak. An 800-year-old tree under which Col. Pemberton mustered a company of men prior to marching into Revolutionary War Battle of King's Mountain.

BRISTOL, TENN. — Shelby's Fort. Col. Evan Shelby built a stockade and trading post on a hill in 1771. Boone traded pelts for gunpowder here.

CLAREMONT, N.C. — Bunker Hill Covered Bridge. Connor State Park four miles east. One of North Carolina's last remaining covered bridges. Picnicking.

COVE CREEK, N.C. — Dan'l Boone Trail Marker. Cove Creek Road in front of Community Center.

COVE CREEK, N.C. — Wilkinson Cabin (1760). US 421 at N.C. — Tenn. line. Oldest home in Watauga County; two-story. Built of poplar logs 18 inches square; mountain locust used in foundation. Has double chimney of field stones daubed with clay. Was a landmark to early pioneers on their trek westward before the American Revolution. Outside viewing.

ELIZABETHTON, TENN. — Bronze Slab. Marks site, in front of courthouse, of establishment of first independent civil government in America, known as The Watauga Association, 1772.

ELIZABETHTON, TENN. — Covered Bridge (1880). Crosses the Doe River.

ELIZABETHTON, TENN. — Sheltering Rock. On bank of Doe River where the Overmountain Men encamped Sept. 26, 1780, en route from Sycamore Shoals to King's Mountain. The Overmountain Men were victorious; battle was turning point of American Revolution.

ELIZABETHTON, TENN. — Sycamore Shoals Historic Bicentennial Park. Visitor's Center, re-creation of Old Watauga; fort with log cabins surrounded by a log fence.

ELIZABETHTON, TENN. — Sycamore Shoals Monument. Marks area where patriots of Revolution trained and mobilized before fighting Battle of King's Mountain, N.C.

FERGUSON, N.C. — Boone Homesite. Two miles east on NC 268 near mouth of Beaver Creek.

HICKORY, N.C. — Propst Victorian House. Third Avenue and **Sixth** Street NW. Adjacent to Shuford Memorial Gardens. Restored by the Hickory Landmarks Society.

HICKORY, N.C. — Old Wilson Log Home. 100 block of **First** Avenue SE. A replica of first Hickory Tavern, an inn and coach depot after which Hickory is named.

JOHNSON CITY, TENN. — Tipton-Haynes Living Historical Farm. Four eras of Tennessee history dramatized: pre-Revolutionary War, Revolutionary War, Lost State of Franklin, and Civil War. Log buildings, cows, duck pond and other animals. Dan'l Boone camped here on way to Kentucky in 1760; right across Boone's Creek is where he inscribed, "D. Boon cilled a Bar on tree in the yr. 1766."

JONESBORO, TENN. — Tennessee's oldest town. (See Map Jonesborough: A Walking Tour of Historical Sites) Home of Andrew Jackson, a place to "walk" through the pages of history. **Washington County Courthouse. Presbyterian Church** (1848), has original pulpit. **Chester Inn** (1797), in continuous service as inn, hotel, apartment house. Guests included Presidents Andrew Johnson, Polk, Jackson and Gov. John Sevier. (See Ch. 52.)

LAUREL BLOOMERY, TENN. — Dan'l Boone Trail Marker. Tenn 91N, opposite Post Office.

LENOIR, N.C. — Treaty Tree. Monument to peace. Two poplar saplings tied together by Cherokee and Catawba Indians, now huge tree.

MARION, N.C. — The Carson House. May through October. US 70, three miles west. Restored Revolutionary period home. 18th-century furnishings. 1:00 — 5:00 p.m. Wednesday, Saturday, Sunday. 724-4263.

MARION, N.C. — The McDowell House (late 1780's). US 70W. Spacious, ornamental home with original free-standing chimneys.

MOUNTAIN CITY, TENN. — Butler House (1870). Irish manor house, 19th century elegance. 18-inch thick solid brick walls; paneled library floor to ceiling contains some books from original owner. Outside viewing.

MOUNTAIN CITY, TENN. — Old White Oak Tree. Left at sign, "Clinton Chapel Presbyterian Church," for about 500 yards on private dirt road. Near Laurel Creek, Tenn., 91N. 500 years old, largest in Tennessee. Over 30-foot girth. Dan'l Boone and companions passed it in 1769 when it was a mere three hundred years old.

MOUNTAIN CITY, TENN. — Shoun's Log Cabin. Corner Main and Shoun Streets. Appropriately furnished 200-year-old cabin.

N. WILKESBORO, N.C. — Historic Route of Dan'l Boone Wagon Train. See Map.

OLD FORT, N.C. — 15-foot Granite Arrowhead. US 70 near I-40. Marks site of old Indian fort (1756) which was western outpost of United States and North Carolina for twenty years.

PATTERSON, N.C. — Fort Defiance. US 321 near NC 268. Built 1788 — 1792, oldest home in Caldwell County. Home of William Lenoir, Revolutionary leader. Built on site of frontier Fort Defiance.

PINEY FLATS, TENN. — Rocky Mount. April to November 1. Six miles northeast of Johnson City on US 11E. A historical and educational shrine. Only original territorial capital of U.S. still standing. Two-and-a-half story log Cobb-Massengill home; 1770-72 cabin built by Wm. Cobb, best construction of the period; center of frontier life for pioneers. Prepared for Battle of King's Mountain here. At one time this was a post office on stage coach route. Three types of log construction used. Restored kitchen, smokehouse, log barn. Picnicking. Operated by Rocky Mount Historical Association. 10:00 a.m. to 5:00 p.m. Monday through Saturday; 2:00 to 6:00 p.m. Sunday.

VALLE CRUCIS, N.C. — Baird Home. Beautiful old 19th century home.

VALLE CRUCIS, N.C. — St. John's Episcopal Church. Mission established 1842. Bishop's House erected in 1849. Two-room log cabin, one room used for small informal gatherings, second room a sanctuary with altar and two pews from a previous chapel. Near altar stands replica of early 20th century chapel. Now a Conference Center for Continuing Education of clergy and laity.

VALLE CRUCIS, N.C. — Mast Store. Nearly 100-year-old three-story gray clapboard general store, oldest around these parts, includes post office. Over the years has served as a social center for conversation around an old pot-bellied stove. Orderly disarray of wide variety of consumer goods from baby diapers to dynamite. Early Americana bartering still goes on. Old advertisements on walls. Merchandise includes herbs, furs, produce, farm machinery, piece goods, electric equipment, work clothes, ready-to-wear, millinery, men's Chesterfield hats, frozen foods, house furnishings, hardware and lots more!!! Old-time customers know where to find items sometimes better than new owners. 963-4711.

VALLE CRUCIS, N.C. — Joe Mast Farm. 19th century North Carolina mountain farm consisting of ten well-preserved major buildings: 1812 weaving house, main house, latticework gazebo, wash house, spring house, meat house, woodhouse, applehouse, blacksmith shop, great barn; three old family looms and other antiques. Outside viewing.

WILKESBORO, N.C. — Boone Trail Marker. Metal used is from Battleship *Maine.*

WILKESBORO, N.C. — Courthouse Square. North Street near Hill Drive. Tory Oak.

WILKESBORO, N.C. — Rendezvous Mountain. In the Purlear section of Wilkes County where patriots assembled during Revolutionary War and were trained by Col. Ben Cleveland for the Battle of King's Mountain.

ANNUAL EVENTS

(Phone sponsor or C. of C. to confirm information. If no area code is shown, use 704.)

JULY
JONESBORO, TENN. — Historic Home Tours. Independence Day celebration "Jonesborough Days."

AUGUST
ABINGDON, VA. — Tour of Historic Homes and Candlelight Tour. August 1 — 15. Virginia Highlands Festival. (See Ch. 54.)

BLOUNTVILLE, TENN. — Historic Home Tours. Middle of the month. Blountville Country Hoe Downer.

STATE HISTORICAL SOCIETIES

Historical Society of North Carolina, Chapel Hill, N.C.

Tennessee Historical Society, Carnegie Library, Nashville, Tenn.

Association for the Preservation of Tennessee Antiquities. State Headquarters, Belle Meade Mansion, Nashville, Tenn. 37205.

Association for the Preservation of Virginia Antiquities. Richmond, Va.

Virginia Historical Society, 707 E. Franklin St., Richmond, Va.

For more historical information See *Directory, Historical Societies and Agencies in the United States and Canada,* published by the American Association for State and Local History. For more local historical information, contact the local Chamber of Commerce.

HISTORICAL SOCIETIES

ABINGDON, VA. — Historical Society of Washington County.

BLOUNTVILLE, TENN. — Sullivan County Historical Commission.

BOONE, N.C. — Appalachian Consortium, Appalachian State University. Purpose: to preserve and promote appreciation of the culture of the region.

BOONE, N.C. — Southern Appalachian Historical Association. Sponsors *Horn in the West.*

BOONE, N.C. — Western North Carolina Historical Association.

ELIZABETHTON, TENN. — Watauga Historical Association, P. O. Box 951, Elizabethton, Tenn. 37643.

ERWIN, TENN. — Unicoi County Historical Society.

HICKORY, N.C. — Catawba County Historical Association.

INDEPENDENCE, VA. — Grayson County Historical Society.

JOHNSON CITY, TENN. — Tipton-Haynes Historical Association, Buffalo Road, Johnson City, Tenn. 37601.

LENOIR, N.C. — Caldwell County Historical Society.

MARION, VA. — Smyth County Historical Society.

MORGANTON, N.C. — Burke County Historical Society.

N. WILKESBORO, N.C. — Wilkes Historical Society.

PINEY FLATS, TENN. — Rocky Mount Historical Association, Piney Flats, Tenn. 37686.

VALDESE, N.C. — Historic Valdese Foundation, P. O. Box 655, Valdese, N.C. 28690.

*A WALKING TOUR OF HISTORIC BLOUNTVILLE

l. **Captain Deaderick House.** A pre-Civil War brick home which played a part in the Civil War Battle of Blountville in 1863.

2. **The Massengill House.** A three-story frame house of late Victorian architecture, has a cut stone foundation and basement originally used as a kitchen and dining area. Henry Massengill was a county magistrate as well as a Blountville merchant.

3. **The Parrot House** (also known as the Irvin House). Built by the Irvins around 1810,

*Numbers shown refer to location on map.

this early frame home has had many owners including Major Samuel Evans III.

4. The Tipton House. A large log dwelling believed to be the second residence constructed in Blountville, about 1795.

5. First Baptist Church. Organized in 1833, the first church was built west of the present structure which was constructed in the early 1970's.

6. Anderson Hall. An 1802 hand-fired brick home of Federal architecture, is considered a showpiece in Blountville.

7. Miller-Haynes House. A mid-nineteenth century frame house, shows the effects of the Civil War bombardment of Blountville. The west side of the house and the door have cannonball holes.

8. Fain-Taylor House. Built in 1828, this log house with poplar siding is an excellent example of early Blountville style. Formerly occupied by **Lieutenant** Fain of the Union Army and Oliver Taylor, author of *Historic Sullivan*, the only history of Sullivan County in print.

9. Rutledge House. A log house of the late 1700's or early 1800's now covered with white siding; has an early style porch with outside stairs leading to the second floor.

10. The Old Deery Inn. Three buildings built in late 1700's consisting of a two-story frame structure, a three-story stone house, and a two-story log house, all adjacent to one another. The first building was originally a store, post office, tavern and inn; the stone and log buildings were built as homes. The log and frame houses now have poplar siding. Deery was an immigrant peddler who became one of the wealthiest men in Tennessee. On the back lawn of the house are the old slave quarters and kitchen and an old hewn-log barn. Other old buildings rescued by the present owner and moved to her back lawn, include: the King cabin, a lawyer's office, a log spring house and the Granny cabin.

11. Blountville United Methodist Church. This was the first church in Blountville, organized in 1800's, moved to its present site in 1855, and replaced in early 1970's.

12. The Anderson Town House. A two-story hewn-log house built 1792-1795 by the Blountville Town Commissioners to conduct their business. The front wing, with an exposed log exterior and interior finished panelling, is now under restoration by the Sullivan County Historical Commission and Bicentennial Committee. The back wing is also being restored but will be used as offices of the Commission and Committee.

13. First Presbyterian Church. Organized in 1820 at the home of Samuel Rhea. The third church is at the present site.

14. Barr House. A large home built in 1895 as an inn.

15. Sullivan County Courthouse. Built in 1850. Courts were held in private homes until 1792-1795 when Blountville was laid out as the seat of Sullivan County. In 1863 the courthouse was gutted by fires set by the Union Army, but was rebuilt. The old jail on the hill was built around 1870.

16. Kenny House. Sections of this house date back to the first half of the nineteenth century.

17. Joe Rogers House. Dates back to early or mid-1800's.

18. Grist Mill. Only the mill house remains to remind us of the grist mill and saw mill that operated from the early 1870's.

19. Greenberry and Elizabeth Rogers House. Erected before 1867, Greenberry was the local blacksmith who shoed the village horses and fixed tools for the residents.

20. March House. Built around 1848, this house was the parsonage of the Baptist Church and later became the home of James March, a local builder and paperhanger.

21. Blountville Cemetery. Notable citizens and veterans of four wars repose here. The Federal Troops fired on Blountville from Graveyard Hill, the site of the cemetery.

*A WALKING TOUR OF HISTORIC JONESBOROUGH

1. Old Holston Baptist Female Institute. A two-story brick building which has been used as a school for girls, a hospital during the Civil War, a school for boys and a Quaker school for freed slaves.

2. Old Jonesboro Cemetery. Located on a quiet hill, contains graves of town's notables, some dating back to Revolutionary War days.

3. Deadrick-Wood House. Once contained a silversmith shop where the first Great State Seal of Tennessee was designed and engraved. Has well-preserved servants' quarters and carriage house.

4. First Baptist Church. Features outstanding stained glass windows. Built before the Civil War, only minor changes have been made. During the 1890's the original slave gallery was removed.

5. The Gammon-Hoss House. A fine example of the stepped gables found throughout Jonesboro. It is claimed that there are more buildings in Jonesboro with stepped gables than exist in any other town in Tennessee.

6. The Salt House. Salt was rationed to inhabitants during the Civil War.

7. Central Christian Church. Formed when northern sympathizers of the Presbyterian Church left their mother church.

8. The Old Masonic Hall. Formerly was the home of the only lodge in the United States with official documents, including the charter, signed by President Andrew Jackson.

9. The Naff-Baxter House. One of only a few remaining residences in the business area. Blocks for mounting horses may still be seen along the limestone curbs of this historic street.

10. The Old Jacobs House. A rambling frame building, was once occupied by Thomas Emmerson, a member of the Tennessee State Supreme Court.

11. The Shipley-Bledsoe House. Overlooks Jonesboro. Was the home of Dr. William Sevier, nephew of the first governor of Tennessee.

*Numbers shown refer to location on map.

12. The Courthouse. The sixth courthouse to be built here. The first was a small log cabin built in 1779 during Jonesboro's founding. It was here that the "Lost State of Franklin" was created, the nation's first attempt to form a state since the original thirteen. Here Andrew Jackson presided as a judge, and frontiersmen paid their taxes in beaver skins. Picture, if you can, the pillory, stocks, and the whipping post, which once stood on the courthouse lawn.

13. The Chester Inn. The oldest frame building in Jonesboro, if allowed to speak would tell stories of visiting presidents, soldiers and writers, of Andrew Jackson being threatened with a tar and feathering.

14. The Mail Pouch Building. Now houses a saloon. Is noted for its 1900 Mail Pouch Tobacco sign which is in almost perfect shape.

15. The Willett-Stephenson House. Was the home of a West Point soldier who resigned his commission to join the Confederates.

16. The Old First Christian Church. A small brick structure which once housed a lecture hall, a restaurant, a temperance hall and a woodworking shop.

17. The Parsonage. The original one is located behind the church.

18. The Gresham-Keys House. As Reconstruction Governor of Tennessee, William Brownlow published his Whig newspaper here before the Civil War.

19. The Cunningham-Broyles House. Its early occupant was Dr. Samuel Cunningham whose dream was to promote the first railroad through Jonesboro and to have it run in front of his house. Grade requirements resulted in the tracks being laid behind the house instead.

20. The Christopher Taylor House. A two-story, 200-year-old log cabin now restored, where Andrew Jackson boarded for the short time he lived in Jonesboro.

21. The Jonesboro Presbyterian Church. A pre-Civil War building, still has its original pews, pulpit and slave gallery. It is told that the stairway outside the church was enclosed so that the ladies, while climbing the steps, would not be embarrassed by showing their ankles. (A far cry from what you can see nowadays!)

22. The Humpston House. At one time, Jacob Howard's Print Shop was located on the corner of the lawn and during the 1800's America's first periodicals — Elihu Embree's *Manumission Intelligencer* and *Emancipator* dealing exclusively with the abolition of slavery — were published.

23. The Mansion House. A distinctive example of architectural blending, was once a popular inn on the Great Stage Road. Originally built in the Federal style, prevalent during early 1800's, this dwelling added a Victorian style porch with highly decorative woodwork after the Civil War.

24. The Sisters' Row. Consists of three homes in a row. Is Jonesboro's oldest brick structure.

25. The Jonesboro Methodist Church. Of the Greek Revival architectural period.

26. The Griffith-Lyle House. A board-and-batten house. Lived in by the first photographer in Jonesboro in 1847.

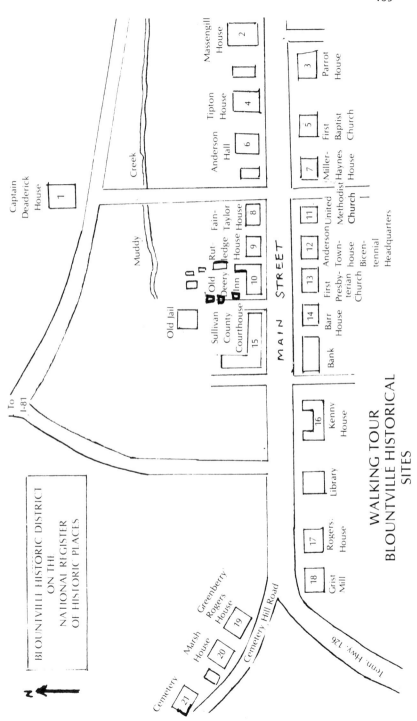

WALKING TOUR
BLOUNTVILLE HISTORICAL
SITES

BLOUNTVILLE HISTORIC DISTRICT
ON THE
NATIONAL REGISTER
OF HISTORIC PLACES

Captain Deaderick House — 1

Massengill House — 2

Parrot House — 3

Tipton House — 4

Anderson Hall — 6

First Baptist Church — 5

Miller-Haynes House — 7

Fain-Taylor House — 8

Rutledge House — 9

Old Deery Inn — 10

Sullivan County Courthouse — 15

Old Jail

United Methodist Church — 11

Anderson Town-house Bicentennial Headquarters — 12

First Presbyterian Church — 13

Barr House — 14

Bank

Kenny House — 16

Library

Rogers House — 17

Grist Mill — 18

Greenberry Rogers House — 19

Marsh House — 20

Cemetery — 21

Cemetery Hill Road

Tenn. Hwy. 126

To I-81

Creek

Muddy

MAIN STREET

N

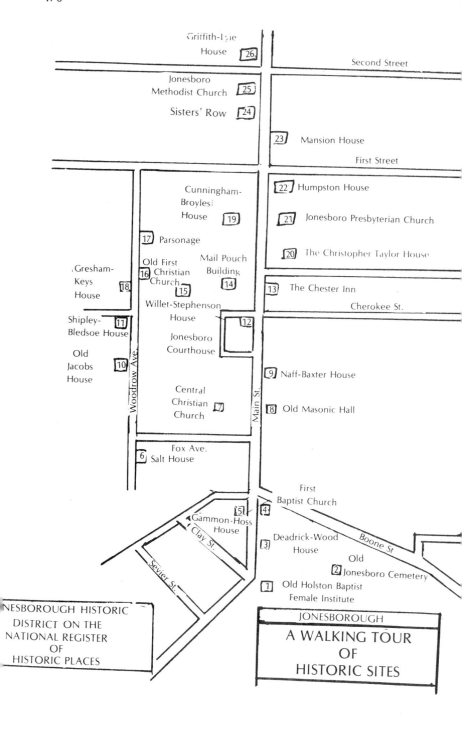

Griffith-Lyle House [26]

Second Street

Jonesboro Methodist Church [25]

Sisters' Row [24]

[23] Mansion House

First Street

[22] Humpston House

Cunningham-Broyles House [19]

[21] Jonesboro Presbyterian Church

[17] Parsonage

[20] The Christopher Taylor House

Old First [16] Christian Church

Mail Pouch Building [14]

[15]

[13] The Chester Inn

Gresham-Keys House [18]

Willet-Stephenson House

Cherokee St.

[12]

Shipley-Bledsoe House [11]

Jonesboro Courthouse

Old Jacobs House [10]

[9] Naff-Baxter House

Central Christian Church [7]

[8] Old Masonic Hall

Woodrow Ave.

Main St.

Fox Ave.

[6] Salt House

First Baptist Church

[5] [4]

Gammon-Hoss House

Clay St.

[3] Deadrick-Wood House

Boone St.

Old [2] Jonesboro Cemetery

Sevier St.

[1] Old Holston Baptist Female Institute

NESBOROUGH HISTORIC DISTRICT ON THE NATIONAL REGISTER OF HISTORIC PLACES

JONESBOROUGH
A WALKING TOUR OF HISTORIC SITES

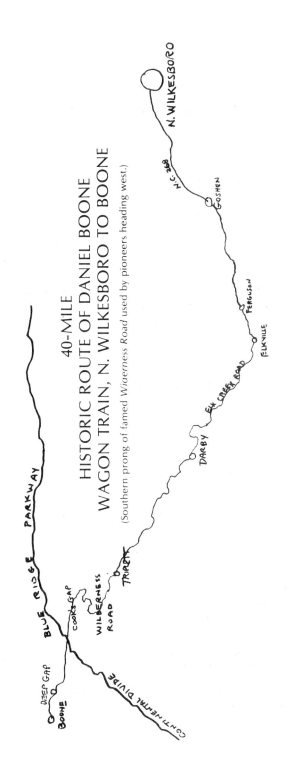

40-MILE
HISTORIC ROUTE OF DANIEL BOONE
WAGON TRAIN, N. WILKESBORO TO BOONE

(Southern prong of famed *Wilderness Road* used by pioneers heading west.)

46   a man's castle . . .

How do other folks live? How do the interior decorating trends of today — color schemes, furnishings, bric-a-brac — compare with those of yesteryear? What's luxury living like? Are there ideas that may be utilized to spruce up my home?

It's a rare opportunity when a group of homeowners will open wide their doors to the public for a home tour. To be invited into the sacrosanct dwelling of a private family to view their prized possessions, and to enjoy their gardens, is really a privilege that money alone cannot pay for, since "A man's home is his castle."

For the homeowner, it's a wonderful way to serve the sponsoring organization for a community cause, and to the "home tourist," it's great fun to visit unusual homes or homes you've perhaps always wanted to see as well as to travel in the company of many kindred spirits.

Listed are a few of the home tours you may take.

ANNUAL EVENTS
(Phone sponsor or C. of C. to confirm information. If no area code is shown, use 704.)

APRIL
WILKESBORO, N.C. — Tour of Homes. Last Sunday. 2:00 — 5:00 p.m. Sponsor: Wilkes Art Guild.

MAY
HICKORY, N.C. — Tour of Homes. 328-6111.

JUNE
N. WILKESBORO, N.C. — Tour of Homes. Arts Emphasis Week.

JULY
JONESBORO, TENN. — Historic "Jonesborough Days" Home Tour. July 3 — 6. Historic homes of distinct character. (615) 753-3311.

BLOWING ROCK, N.C. — Tour of Homes (since 1960). Third Friday. Bazaar, raffle and lunch at Parish House, St Mary's of the Hills Episcopal Church. Sponsor: the Women of St. Mary's of the Hills. 11:00 a.m. to 4:00 p.m.

AUGUST
ABINGDON, VA. — Virginia Highlands Festival Tour of Historic Homes. August 1 — 15. Sponsor: Historical Society of Washington County. 10:00 a.m. — 4:30 p.m. Saturday.

BLOWING ROCK, N.C. — Hound Ears Tour of Homes. Sponsor: Greater Grandfather Arts Guild of the Blue Ridge Activities Council. 10:00 a.m. — 3:00 p.m.

47
industry
shows off

Ever wonder how hosiery is woven, porcelain is fabricated, how a bakery operates behind the scenes, how furniture is built, what makes a newspaper tick, how a mudpie is transformed into an extraordinary dinner plate?

See the inner workings of factories, take advantage of free, conducted tours. It's not only informative but fun for the family as well. One never knows what will pique the interest of the small fry in a future career. Exposure to all kinds of experiences provides young people with choices to help them reach right decisions.

Many of the companies listed below run tours at set hours; others are by special appointment and arrangements. Because of the nature of the work, in some plants children are not allowed.

For adults, it's a great opportunity to purchase off-beat items. Before you get in your car, however, call the company you plan to visit to verify time and day of tour.

Following, is a schedule of plant tours in the nearby areas.

Also, for other tours, call any place you'd like to visit, be it TV or radio station or business; if they have no tours, they may make suggestions. Please note that all furniture companies are closed to the public during the months of April and October, so that furniture buyers may attend the Southern Furniture Market.

There's nothin' else like it! Thought you'd like to know.

ABINGDON, VA. — Cumbow China Decorating Company, 436 Main St. World-famous hand-decorated china displays. (703) 628-2471.

BLOWING ROCK, N.C. — The Goodwin Guild Weavers. Cornish Road, off US 321 Bypass. Visit loom room, hemming and "adding fringe" rooms. Articles include afghans, napkins, place mats, potholders, tablecloths and others. 295-3577.

BOONE, N.C. — Blue Ridge Shoe Company, Greenway Road. Shoe factory. 264-2489.

BOONE, N.C. — Shadowline, Inc. Shadowline Road. Lingerie plant (panties, pyjamas, nighties). 264-8828.

BOONE, N.C. — TRW/IRC, Greenway Rd. Resistors for radio, TV, radar. 264-8861.

HICKORY, N.C. — APCO Chemical Coating, Inc., 908 Lenoir Rd. N.W. Furniture finishes. 322-4937.

HICKORY, N.C. — Crest Hosiery Mill, Inc. 245 12th Ave. N.E. 324-4719.

HICKORY, N.C. — Hickory Chair Company, 37 Ninth St. Place S.E. 328-1801.

HICKORY, N.C. — Hickory Fry Furniture Co., Inc. Conover Road. 328-2341.

HICKORY, N.C. — Hickory Manufacturing Company, 890 7th Ave. S.E. Bedroom, living-room, dining-room furniture. 322-8624.

HICKORY, N.C. — Kayser Roth Hosiery, 70 8th St. Place S.E. Men, women, children's hosiery. 328-5351.

HICKORY, N.C. — Ryalyn Cosco, Inc., 585 11th St. N.W. Pottery and porcelain products. 322-6413.

HICKORY, N.C. — Southern Desk Company. 1720 1st Ave. SW. 327-3282.

HICKORY, N.C. — Southern Elastic Corp., 343 23rd St. S.W. Elastic yarn. 322-8510.

HICKORY, N.C. — Stevens Hosiery, 3000 2nd Ave. N.W. Ladies' hosiery. 328-2491.

HICKORY, N.C. — Superior Continental Corp., 1928 Main Ave. S.E. Wire and cable for communications. 328-2171.

LAUREL BLOOMERY, TENN. — iron mountain Stoneware Pottery. Well-known for its original craftsmanship. (615) 898-4414.

MAIDEN, N.C. — Carolina Mills, Inc., 618 Carolina Ave. Yarn manufacture. 464-2457.

MARION, VA. — Rosemont. Canopies, coverlets, fringes and rugs. (703) 783-4663.

MONTEZUMA, N.C. — Patterson's Flowers. Cut flowers and potted plants. 733-2363.

NEWLAND, N.C. — Avery County Farm Extension Agent. Arranges tours of ornamental shrubbery, greenhouses. 733-2415.

NEWTON, N.C. — Lenoir Chair Company #2, 2309 N. College Ave. Bedroom furniture. 464-0211.

PINEOLA, N.C. — Vaughn Blue Ridge Nursery. Carnations, mums, roses, snaps, cut flowers. 733-4323.

TERRELL, N.C. — Duke Power Company, Marshall Steam Station. Steam-electric generating station. 478-2121.

E. VALDESE, N.C. — Waldensian Bakeries, Main Street. Bakery tour. 874-2136.

VALDESE, N.C. — Valdese Manufacturing Company, Columbo St. W. Crestline, industrial yarn. 874-2156.

WILKESBORO, N.C. — Holly Farms Poultry Industries, Inc., River Street and South. Chicken plant. (919) 838-2171.

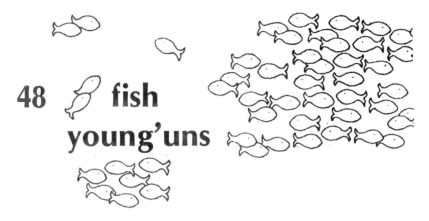

48 🐟 fish young'uns

Want to see a remarkable sight? Ever wonder about the birth of fish? Any questions about their life cycle? Have an encounter at a fish hatchery, especially if there are youngsters along. It's a pleasurable way to add to your fund of knowledge on a subject that's good enough to eat!

Take your choice of the following:

(If no area code is shown, use 704.)

BURNSVILLE, N.C. — Hersel W. Higgins, dealer. Route 6. 682-3360.

ELIZABETHTON, TENN. — Watson Trout Farms, dealer, near 19E and NC 321, Route 8. Brook, brown and rainbow trout. (615) 543-3223.

ERWIN, TENN. — National Fish Hatchery, US 23 between Erwin and Unicoi. Rainbow trout. (615) 743-4712.

ERWIN, TENN. — State Fish Hatchery, US 23 S. (615) 743-4842.

MARION, N.C. — Armstrong State Fish Hatchery, 9.5 miles north on NC 226, left for two miles on NC 226A, left to dirt road SR 1443 for four miles. Trout. 756-4179.

MARION, N.C. — Marion State Fish Hatchery, Route 6, six-tenths mile north, US 221, right on Hankins Road, SR 1501 for 2.5 miles, left on SR 1553 to end of road. Trout, muskelunge, striped bass, largemouth bass. 652-4040.

MARION, VA. — Buller Fish Hatchery, six miles south on Va. 672, Jefferson National Forest. Bass. (703) 783-4172.

MARION, VA. — Marion Fish Hatchery, south on Va. 16 for 3.5 miles.

MORGANTON, N.C. — Table Rock Fish Hatchery, Route 5. Ten miles northwest on NC 181, left three miles on SR 1240, to SR 1260, right on SR 1260 to end of road. (Warm water). 437-3977.

ROARING GAP, N.C. — Roaring Gap State Fish Hatchery. Signs will point the way on US 21. Trout. (919) 363-2305.

RUTHERWOOD (BOONE), N.C. — Fred Greer Fish Hatchery (private). Site of old state fish hatchery. Rainbow, brook and brown trout raised year-round.

49   grist for the mill

This may be your last chance — if you pass up visiting an old grist mill — to watch an enormous wheel in operation, turned by buckets filled with water from a creek, which in turn, turns shafts which move the grinding stones to grind the cornmeal, whole wheat flour, and buckwheat flour. This enterprise, you may not recall, was indispensable to life when our nation was in swaddling clothes — grinding meal at the mill for baking bread.

The social center of the day where oftentimes folks had to spend the night because of inclement weather or while waiting for their flour, it was a great place to debate the political issues of the times, as well as to swap tales.

The kids are sure to get a big kick out of this activity, especially when they compare it to the simple shopping for flour at the supermarket of today.

Here are a few mills to visit:

ABINGDON, VA. — White's Mill. Five miles northeast. More than 150 years old, still grinding cornmeal and bolted (finely sifted) flour. Monday to Saturday, Sunday afternoon.

BOONE, N.C. — Winebarger's Grist Mill. Nine miles west at Meat Camp, two miles from junction US 321 and 421. Founded about a century ago by present owner's grandfather. Still operating. Water-powered. Grinds corn, buckwheat and other grains.

NEWTON, N.C. — Murray Flour Mill (inoperative). East on Sherrills Ford Road.

ROAN MOUNTAIN STATE PARK, TENN. — Grist Mill.

50

smoke puffs for rail buffs

Can you remember how long it's been since you took a train ride and heard the tracks talk to the train and the train talk to the tracks: clickety-clack ... clickety-clack? For many, riding over the terrain by train is no longer a way of life. But even though train travel opportunities are dwindling, in this corner of lofty mountains and scenic splendor, rambling, rhythmical, romantic reminders of a bygone heyday — fabled steam locomotives — are alive and well.

Watch the cobwebs of your mind blow away as you settle down for an old-fashioned "iron horse" ride in a reclining seat coach, lounge or parlor observation car and let your heart be at peace and still on a day's excursion over fields and valleys, hills and dales. And by the end of the journey, when it's time to debark, your world will have fallen back into its proper place and you will feel part of the whole scene, more whole than before, and discover that you hadn't left your world at all.

For the kids, there are very special rides, so EVERYBODY: A-L-L A-B-O-O-O-O-A-R-D!

(If no area code is shown, use 704.)

BOONE, N.C. — Tweetsie Railroad. An action-packed 30-minute ride through the mountains for three miles on a narrow-guage, full-size steam locomotive running on three-foot-wide tracks. From the early 1900's to the early 1940's the train made regular freight and passenger runs from Boone to Johnson City, Tenn. The folks who lived along the original railroad route named the train *Tweetsie* because of the whistle sound, and this nickname was adopted in 1956 for this special attraction park. Trains leave every half hour from 9:00 a.m. to 6:00 p.m. June through August and on a reduced schedule from Labor Day through October. The "1890 Western Town" includes a sheriff's office and jail, *Tweetsie* Palace saloon with can-can girls, post office and general store. Loads of fun for the small fry! 264-8630.

BRISTOL, TENN. — Steele Creek Park. Just a sample — a one-half mile ride on *The Old General,* a colorful locomotive, one of the many attractions in the park besides swimming, fishing, golf, wilderness area and naturalist programs. (615) 764-4023.

BURNSVILLE, N.C. — Yancey Railroad Color Excursion on "South Toe Rambler." Saturdays in October. From Burnsville to Kona. Picnic at Kona Island where North and South Toe Rivers meet. Photo stops along the way. Other trips, too. Sponsor: Spruce Pine Junior Women's Club, P. O. Box 444, Spruce Pine, N.C. 28777. Time 1:30 to 6:00 p.m. 765-7242.

BURNSVILLE, N.C. — Weekend Mountain Excursions. Passenger charters only. Yancey Railroad Company. 682-2311.

ERWIN, TENN. — The Clinchfield Railroad. Excursions throughout the spring, summer and fall. Claimed to be the most scenic ride east of the Rockies, *The Clinchfield No. 1,* built in 1882, the oldest steam locomotive still running in the United States, pulls an open platform Parlor Car and a Club-Lounge Car from Spartanburg, S.C. to Erwin and back through the picturesque Blue Ridge Mountains and the fantastic Nolichucky Gorge. This exciting trip includes 18 rocky tunnels in 13 miles (try counting 'em) with many reverse loops, steel bridges and passes over the Eastern Continental Divide. Six stops just for photographs of the spectacular scenery and "The Gorge." The train leaves Spartanburg at 8:30 a.m., arrives at Erwin at 1:15 p.m., leaves Erwin at 2:00 p.m. and returns to Spartanburg at 7:00 p.m. after a carefree day of steaming through the mountains. Other round trips run between Erwin and St. Paul, Va., and a 184-mile all-day round trip from Marion to Erwin. Trip schedules are available from Office of the Superintendent, Clinchfield Railroad Company. When you get your copy, you'll notice that most trips are sponsored by clubs and organizations, so write to the organization in whose trip you're interested for reservations.

HAMPTON, TENN. — Doe River Gorge Railroad. Hillbilly World's Amusement Park. The *Little Whistler,* a narrow-guage train, runs the longest ride (nine miles) in the Smokies, through a breathtaking mountain gorge, three tunnels and across two river bridges. (615) 725-2051.

HILTONS, VA. — Southwest Virginia Scenic Railroad. A 1926 steam locomotive makes the 22-mile round trip to Mendota weekends—Saturday, Sunday and holidays—April through November at 2:00 p.m. and 4:30 p.m. For pickin', singin', and picnickin' catch early train to picnic area near Mendota and late train back to Hiltons. Historic and scenic. Southwest Virginia Scenic Railroad, P. O. Box 31, Hiltons, Va. 24258.

W. JEFFERSON, N.C. — Autumn Leaf Train Excursion. Around October 15. It chugs over the mountains of Ashe County, N.C., and Grayson County, Va., during the height of the Fall Foliage Season. The train goes to Abingdon, Va., for the Barter Theatre play and returns the same day. Because of its popularity, reservations should be made well in advance. Sponsor: W. Jefferson Women's Club. (919) 246-4121.

Any train buffs out there? For information about joining a train buff organization, write: E. Tennessee Rail Fan Association, Inc., 129 Rosefield Dr., Kingsport, Tenn. 37660. (615) 246-8998.

51

star trek

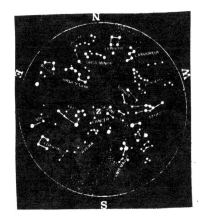

Where does the darkness come from? Where does it go when light appears? Are there little green people on Mars? Why does the moon change its shape? For answers to these and other questions about some of the mysteries of outer space, and for beholding the wonder of the sky, visit the local university or college observatory.

Viewing phenomena "of the starry skies above" through a high-powered telescope and introducing youngsters to the heavenly domains, is a "being-in-touch" experience you and they are not likely to forget. For the youngsters whose space awareness today is extraordinary, such exposure may awaken a budding astronaut or astronomer or maybe an astrophotographer of the future. Why not a poet, for "The Heavens declare the Glory of God...."

And here's a goody for you, astronomy lectures at a variety of levels can be arranged by calling the Physics Department of ASU. Open House for groups who wish to visit mornings or evenings, may also be arranged. This "show of shows," this virtuoso performance, is yours to see just about every two weeks through the school year at Appalachian State University in Boone. Be a witness to such heavenly spectacles and special astronomical events as the Andromeda Galaxy, Aquarids, Perseids and Capricornids Meteor Showers, the waning and waxing moon, the globular star cluster and double stars Alcor and Mizar. Call for details or write for the quarterly programs.

But always remember, although you may believe that the stars may tell — they do not compel!!!!

Schools with telescopes which hold Open House on a scheduled basis include:

BOONE, N.C. — Appalachian State University. Has a unitron telescope with an 8-inch refractor. 262-3090.

BRISTOL, TENN. — King College. Observatory, Cedar Street. (615) 968-2411.

EMORY, VA. — Emory and Henry College. (703) 944-3121.

HICKORY, N.C. — Lenoir-Rhyne College. Minges Science Building. 328-1741.

JOHNSON CITY, TENN. — Eastern Tennessee State University. Planetarium, Home Economics Building, Room 207. (615) 929-4306.

52   independence day!

What will make you feel more at home when you're away from home than a good old-fashioned Fourth of July celebration with fireworks and all the trimmings? The Fourth is always a family fun day all day and evening in each community. So, just wear a pair of comfortable walking shoes 'cause you'll be on your feet a lot as you celebrate our country's birth!

Special events for participants (visitors are welcome to participate too) with prizes awarded and a barrel of laughs for onlookers, make it a favorite day for area residents, especially for the small fry who look forward to making this annual festival the most fun of the year!

Just to give you a random sampling of gala events and activities over the Fourth, let's start with the annual "JONESBOROUGH DAYS" shindig, in Tennessee, where for four lively days, starting on the third and ending the evening of the sixth, you'll be kept "hopping" by the busy schedule sponsored by the Town of Jonesboro and Jonesboro Civic Trust. "Jonesborough" or "Jonesboro," the oldest town in the state (1780), was home to President Andrew Jackson, and his historical cabin is the oldest building in the entire state. A remarkable restoration of the town is taking place which will help preserve some of the historical roots of our country. Several parks are planned and the streets of the historic district will be an antique brown paved surface with brick sidewalks, among other restorations, including Andrew Jackson's log cabin. The town winds up and

180

makes a national splash during the rip-roarin' Independence Day celebration, and no wonder. . . ! There are games, sports, old-fashioned family picnics, old-time church services, guided historic homes tour and walking tour, flea market and antique show, craft demonstrations, Blue Grass music, Horse Show, "Best Old-Fashioned Costume" contest, and Miss Historic Jonesborough Days Pageant. Each year this Tennessee highlight grows in popularity.

At Blowing Rock, a typical Fourth starts with a synchronized swim show at the Outdoor Pool followed by a clown show and all-day fun activities at the Town Park: there's a greased pig contest — if you think this is easy, come and watch the squeals and delight of kids, grownups, and pig when this show takes place. Then, there's a shinnying up a greased pole contest, another "impossible" that somehow is achieved, followed by sack races, apple bobbing and horseshoe contests, finishing with dancing on the tennis courts to Blue Grass music. For those who prefer indoor activity as a change, visit the Annual Rummage Sale and Flea market, two separate events, sponsored by the local Garden Clubs. And then you can rest a while in the Park on the comfortable wooden lounge chairs facing Main Street, watching the world go by.

The Country Fair at *Tweetsie* goes on all day with kiddie rides, craft shows, live music and entertainment and the exciting rides to the top of Mouse Mountain and on the *Tweetsie Railroad,* winding up with a bang at 9:00 p.m. to a Giant Fireworks Extravaganza!

Boone, blessed with the Watauga Swimmming Pool Complex, provides a family fun-packed day of action: a "Greased Watermelon Contest," a Diving Contest, a "Little Miss Bikini" Contest and a "Little Mr. America" Contest, and swimming races including a long-distance, underwater swim in the Olympic-size pool. All the neighborhood parks hold special events for the entire family, too.

And, as you can imagine, Independence Day at Independence, Va., is always an exciting affair where you're asked to "Relax now — and enjoy three days of Independence, Independence style!" The day generally starts with a mile-long parade of bands, old cars, horses, wagons and mountaineers. You'll get to be an animal lover if you aren't already as you witness the Annual Horse Show on the high school grounds with trophy and ribbon awards. The Beef and Dairy Show includes judging of Angus, Hereford, Charolais and Shorthorn under Beef Classes; and Brown, Guernsey, Holstein, Jersey and Swiss under Dairy Classes; and all breeds of lamb. There'll be taste thrills galore at the food booths, lots of native arts and crafts, young people's accomplishments, and rollicking country music, square dancing and 'teen dancing. You may even be lucky enough to walk off with a coveted door prize.

Away from home on the Fourth provides you with a special opportunity for fellowship with your fellow countrymen of the mountains (especially at a club or church supper) you shouldn't miss!!!

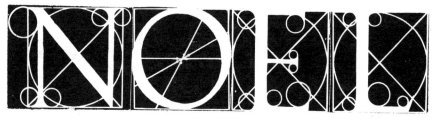

53 christmas

Christmas is many things to many people. For some it's a time for laughter and gaiety, joy and sparkle; for others it's a time for reflection and inner solitude, a time to renew bonds of spiritual brotherhood and universal love which know no season.

In this area, in the land of white-mantled, mountain-clad communities, there's a time to enjoy an old-fashioned Christmas, and time for inner communion — to be alone with one's thoughts, away from the hustle and bustle of Christmas in a big city.

There's no better place to listen to the sounds of an old-timey Christmas surrounded by nostalgic picture-postcard scenery envisioned the world over — clear, brisk nights under diamond-studded deep, blue skies . . . plunging through the powdery, silent snow. . . glimpsing a shy deer in the woodlands . . bushes of holly and mistletoe supporting black-capped chickadees, juncoes, nuthatches, Christmas-red cardinals. . . red berries festooning the shrubbery . . . majestic, soaring evergreens laden down with glistening, shimmering icicles. . .strings of bright, twinkling lights and little angels. . .the sound of happy carolers . . .Santa and his reindeer decorating housetops. . . chimes of joyous Christmas bells ringing loud and clear. . . doors trimmed with holly wreaths. . .a Child in a Manger. . .blazing logs in the fireplace with chestnuts roasting in the fire. . . cookies baking in the oven. . . gaily wrapped packages. . . .

Spirits are higher and hearts become light as a feather as Christmas approaches, and here, to help you celebrate this greatest of all celebrations, are a number of holiday activities and events to choose from. And you'll find, too, a place of rest, to help release the magic of the Christmas spirit, "to become as a little child" and to join in the benediction: "PEACE ON EARTH, GOODWILL TOWARD MAN."

(Phone sponsor or C. of C. to confirm information. If no area code is shown, use 704.)

OCTOBER
BOONE, N.C. — Christmas Fair (since 1973). Fourth Thursday and Friday. County Courthouse Lobby. Exhibits, demonstrations, handmade articles. Sponsor: The Extension Homemakers Council.

NOVEMBER

BANNER ELK, N.C. — Christmas Bazaar. Third Saturday. Fireman's Hall. Sponsor: Banner Elk Garden Club.

N. WILKESBORO, N.C. — Christmas Bazaar. Third Saturday. N. Wilkesboro Armory. Knitted, crocheted and embroidered handwork, dried flowers and arrangements, Potted plants, beaded flowers, woodcrafts, Christmas decorations, food, baked goods, toys. Sponsor: N. Wilkesboro Junior Woman's Club.

DECEMBER

BOONE, N.C. — Christmas Craft Festival. Plemmons Student Union, ASU. Special week of Christmas events, crafts, demonstrations, displays, caroling tour, Christmas Ball.

MILLIGAN COLLEGE, TENN. — Madrigal Dinner Festival. First week. Milligan College. Week-long Festival of Christmas music and carols in a 16th century atmosphere. Sponsor: Music Department.

BLOWING ROCK, N.C. — Christmas Parade. Santa Claus and floats depicting winter fun in the mountains. 11:00 a.m.

BOONE, N.C. — Christmas Bazaar. First Saturday. Worthwhile Women's Club Clubhouse, Cherry Drive. Handmade ornamentals, wreaths, table arrangements, unusual one-of-a-kind gift items, baked goods. Sponsor: Worthwhile Women's Club.

BOONE, N.C. — Community Carol Service and Visit from Santa (since 1971). First Sunday. Post Office. Sponsor: Junior Woman's Club. 3:00 p.m.

GALAX, VA. — Community Christmas Concert. First Sunday. Sponsor: Galax Music Club.

SPARTA, N.C. — Christmas Parade. Second week. Colorful floats.

NEWLAND, N.C. — Christmas Parade and Floats. Second Friday.

BANNER ELK, N.C. — Christmas Bazaar. Second Saturday. Banner Elk Elementary School. Handmade articles by art class children, baked goodies, unique gifts. Sponsor: the Greater Grandfather Arts Guild. 10:00 a.m. to 4:00 p.m.

CROSSNORE, N.C. — "The Christmas Carnival of Crafts." Second Sunday. Annual Open House. Crossnore School campus, Skills Center. Handmade items by students and staff: Christmas wreaths, ceramics, candles, centerpieces, plant and sand terrariums, dried flower polydomes, seed flower arrangements and art work. Demonstrations and exhibits of the crafts program at school. Bake sale; live entertainment. 2:00 — 5:00 p.m.

BOONE, N.C. — Choral Society Christmas Concert (since 1975). Second Sunday. ASU.

BOONE, N.C. — Open House. Third Saturday. Watauga County Public Library. Entertainment and refreshments.

JONESBORO, TENN. — Old-Fashioned Christmas. The week before Christmas.

BLOWING ROCK, N.C. — Christmas in the Park. Christmas Eve. Bonfire, caroling, Santa, refreshments in Town Hall Conference Room. Sponsor: Blowing Rock Recreation Commission.

Hugh Morton

54 other mountain doin's

Although the chapters of this book are chock full of special events, and the local newspapers and radio announcements will clue you in on many others, below is an additional listing of timely and choice activities which do not fall under any of the other chapter headings. They range from a riotous donkey basketball game to antique car parades, from a karate championship to agricultural, industrial and other fairs, from rhododendron festivals to a Blue Ridge Wagon Train Parade.

It's all happening each month of the year in this "neck of the woods," as wide a range of sports and recreational events to be found anywhere!

And only here will you witness the Gathering of the Scottish Clans and their colorful, exciting, dramatic Highland Games. You don't have to be Scottish to either participate or to be a spectator joining the thousands who come up each July to MacRae Meadows on the slope of Grandfather Mountain in Linville. The wailing of the Bagpipe Bands and whirling of the plaid kilts will stir your "innards" and keep your toes tapping. Pageantry and competition vie with each other during the Parade of Tartans and the dancing, drumming and piping competitions. Athletic prowess reigns supreme as the standard Amateur Athletic Union events take place alongside of native, typical Old Scottish contests.

So. . . take advantage of what's available — it may be a one-time opportunity. It won't be our fault if you don't find some activity or special event to satisfy your whim or fancy!

(Phone sponsor or C. of C. to confirm information. If no area code is shown, use 704.)

YEAR-ROUND
FOSCOE, N.C. — Foscoe Fire Department Shooting Match. Friday. 7:30 p.m.

JANUARY
BOONE, N.C. — ASU Indoor Invitational Track Meet (since 1973). Last Friday. Varsity Gym. Field and running events.

FEBRUARY
BANNER ELK, N.C. — Winter Carnival Festivities. Second Week. Winter Carnival Fashion Show. Hayes Auditorium, Lees-McRae College. 898-5513 Ext. 27.

VALDESE, N.C. — Independence Day for Waldensians. Third Monday. 879-8451.

BETHEL, N.C. — Watauga County Foxhound Show (since 1974). Last Saturday. Ten miles west of Boone. Bethel Gymnasium. Hornblowing contest precedes show.

BOONE, N.C. — Heart Ball (since 1968). Last Saturday. Dinner Dance. Sponsor: Watauga County Heart Association. 7:00 p.m. — 1:00 a.m.

MARCH — SEPTEMBER
ALL OVER — World of Spring and Summer colors. A Spectacular! (See Ch. 32.)

MARCH, APRIL, MAY
BOONE, N.C. — Great Decisions Discussion Group (since 1967). Foreign policy topics. Sponsor: League of Women Voters of Watauga. 264-4576 or 5715.

MARCH
BLOWING ROCK, N.C. — Heart Fund Fashion Show. First Saturday. Hound Ears Lodge. 2:00 p.m.

BOONE, N.C. — Chancellor Wey Kite Flying Contest. First Saturday. ASU Baseball Field. Stunt flying, altitude contest, novelty and artistic competition, and a kite battle. 10:30 a.m.

BOONE, N.C. — Donkey Basketball Game. Third Tuesday. Boone Optimist Club members vs. Watauga High School male faculty members. Watauga High School Gym. The funniest basketball game of the year! Sponsor: WHS Athletic Association and Boone Optimist Club. 264-2407.

BOONE, N.C. — Black Expo Week. Third Sunday through Thursday. ASU. 262-3030.

SPRUCE PINE, N.C. — Spring Clothing Festival. Last Tuesday. First Baptist Church. Dressmaker techniques and demonstrations. Sponsor: Mitchell, Avery and Yancey Counties Extension Service and Extension Homemaker Clubs. 682-2113.

APRIL

BOONE, N.C. — Industry Appreciation Week in Watauga County. From first Sunday to second Sunday. Once every two years. Locally-made products displayed in shop windows of Boone stores. Climax on Thursday, 6:30 to 9:30 p.m., Boone Area Industrial Fair at National Guard Armory; exhibits on process and end products by local industries — educational and entertaining. Sponsor: Boone Area Chamber of Commerce, Industrial Affairs Division.

JONESBORO, TENN. — Historic Potpourri. A variety of spring season activities.

COVE CREEK, N.C. — High School Oldtimers Basketball Game (since 1973). Saturday before Easter.

BOONE, N.C. — Easter Sunday Sunrise Services. Daniel Boone Amphitheatre. Sponsor: Area churches.

BANNER ELK, N.C. — Appalachian Culture Day. Second Saturday. Lees-McRae College. Exhibits of mountain crafts, art, herbs, food sampling, dulcimer music, video tapes and slide shows. Mountain culture in brief.

BOONE, N.C. — Language Arts Festival (since 1974). Second or third week. Appalachian State University. North Carolina high school foreign language students present skits, plays, dances. Foreign meals served; open to the public. Display booths sell foods, perfume and other very interesting items. Sponsor: ASU Language Clubs. 262-3095.

BOONE, N.C. — Language Arts Festival. Third weekend, Friday and Saturday. Appalachian State University. For elementary school teachers, librarians in North Carolina and for elementary education majors at ASU. Famous celebrities and personalities on programs. Sponsor: Elementary Education Department. 262-2225.

BOONE, N.C. — Bike-a-thon (since 1973). Fourth Sunday. Pickup point at Old US 421. Fifteen miles along Meat Gap Road to Camp Broadstone. Sponsor: Watauga Association for Exceptional Children. 264-7700.

MAY

BURNSVILLE, N.C. — Jaycee's Ramp Festival. Early in month. Since ramp is a wild leek reminiscent of garlic — a little goes a long way. The North Carolina Society for the Friends of the Ramp, Inc., meets annually. If you don't like garlic, be cautious. Sponsor: Yancey Jaycees.

WILKESBORO, N.C. — Spring Fun Festival. First Friday. Wilkes Community College. Live entertainment, games, auctions, flea markets, rummage sales.

BANNER ELK, N.C. — Spring Festival. First weekend, Friday, Saturday, Sunday. Sports and other recreational events: golf tourneys at Seven Devils, Beech and Sugar Mountains; tennis tournaments for men and women; fishing contest; bicycle races; cloggin', pickin' and singin', dancin' and barbecuein' and scenic wildflower tours. Sponsor: Banner Elk Area Resort Ass'n (BEARA).

BOONE, N.C. — Appalachian Karate Championships (since 1973). First Saturday. Watauga High School. Largest Karate tournament in North Carolina. 11:30 a.m. to 5:30 p.m. eliminations; 7:30 to 9:00 p.m. finals. Sponsors: Appalachian Karate Academy and Watauga County Rescue Squad.

BOONE, N.C. — Watauga County Spring Festival (since 1974). First Saturday. ASU Varsity and Broome-Kirk gymnasiums. Watauga's "Rite of Spring." Numerous display booths and demonstrations of creative activities by all age groups. Foods reflecting cultural heritage as well as heritages of other countries for sale. Folk dancing, singing, cloggers, bands, dance teams, performing groups — great entertainment! 10:00 a.m. — 9:00 p.m.

FOSCOE, N.C. — Foscoe Fun Day. Fourth Saturday. Foscoe Village Campgrounds. 10:00 a.m. to 4:00 p.m. Auction sale. Miss Foscoe Fire Department Contest, entertainment and fun games. Sponsor: Foscoe Volunteer Fire Department.

ABINGDON, VA. — Spring Sampler (since 1972). Fourth weekend, Friday — Monday. (703) 628-3966.

BOONE, N.C. — Boone Jaycee Junior Champ Day (since 1956). Fourth Sunday. ASU Conrad Stadium. Track events for elementary school children. 2:00 p.m.

JUNE

ELIZABETHTON, TENN. — Country Music Days in Elizabethton. Third week. Doe River Bridge. Fiddle playin', dancin', beard contest, parade, good family entertainment, "down home" music, wood choppin' contest, "fun" auction, and jes' plain grinnin and pickin'.

BAKERSVILLE, N.C. — Rhododendron Festival and Crowning of Queen (since 1947). Third or fourth week. Gala activities each night include pageant of crowning Junior and Senior Miss Rhododendron, square dancing, tours to top of Roan Mountain, golf tourneys. Saturday night finale with judging and crowning of Queen at Bowman High School. Sponsor: Bakersville Lions Club. 688-3113.

ELIZABETHTON, TENN. — Roan Mountain Rhododendron Festival (since 1947). Third or fourth week. Miss Rhododendron, Tennessee Contest and Rhododendron Parade.

Nationally recognized as one of the outstanding festivals in the United States. Tennessee and North Carolina hold separate festivals one week apart alternating for earliest weekend every other year and each state chooses a Queen. Miss Rhododendron Tennessee becomes eligible for Miss Tennessee Pageant. Sponsor: Roan Mountain, Tennessee Citizens' Club. (615) 543-2122.

NEWTON, N.C. — Jamboree. Third Saturday. Courthouse Square. Sidewalk art show, baby contest, bike parade, horticulture exhibit, bluegrass music.

JULY

W. JEFFERSON, N.C. — Blue Ridge Wagon Train Parade (since 1964). July 1 — 4. More than 100 covered wagons and 500 horseback riders. From N. Wilkesboro northwestward up the mountains. Overnight at Parsonville and again at Idlewood, finishing with parade at 10:00 a.m. in W. Jefferson.

BOONE, N.C. — Inner Tube Race down the Watauga River. First Tuesday. Appalachian State University. 5:00 p.m. 262-2090.

SPEEDWELL, VA. — Wagon Train. First Tuesday and Wednesday.

BOONE, N,C, — Watauga County Horseshoe Pitching Tournament. *Horn in the West* grounds. First Saturday. Watermelon-eating Contest, Cracker and Whistle Race, Three-legged Race. 1:00 p.m.

BANNER ELK, N.C. — Anniversary Celebration (since 1900). Lees-McRae College.

LENOIR, N.C. — Gamewell Invitational Slow Pitch Softball Tournament (since 1975). First and second weeks, six days. Gamewell-Collettsville High School field. Sponsor: Gamewell Ruritan Club.

MORGANTON, N.C. — North Carolina Angus Field Day. Second Friday. Windy Hill Farm. 11:30 a.m. registration; 1:30 p.m. judging contest; 4:30 p.m. herd walk.

LINVILLE, N.C. — Highland Games and Gathering of Scottish Clans (since 1956). Second weekend, Saturday and Sunday. MacRae Meadows, Grandfather Mountain. Two-day unfolding pageantry includes:Highland dancing and bagpiping competition, track and field events, Highland shoot archery competition, fencing exhibition; also, Old Scottish athletic contests — cabar toss, sheaf toss, weight tossing and throwing, standing broad jump,Highland wrestling,sheep herding by trained sheep dogs, tug-o-war. Colorful Parade of Tartans. Loads of Scottish and other foods and souvenirs.

LINVILLE, N.C. — 27.2-mile Mountain Marathon. Second Saturday. Part of the Highland Games activities. Starts on King Street, Boone, continues south on the Blowing Rock Road to Blowing Rock, then west to Grandfather Mountain finishing at MacRae Meadows. Some 50 competitors of varying ages participate.

PINEY FLATS, TENN. — Community Day (since 1972). Second weekend. Mary Hughes, Jr. High School auditorium. Games, entertainment, concert.

BANNER ELK, N.C. — Beech Mountain Folk Festival. Third Saturday. Lees-McRae College. Craft show, dulcimer and banjo playing, storyteller of tall tales.

BOONE, N.C. — Horseshoe Tournament (since 1971). Third Saturday. Doubles playing. Sponsor: Watauga County Parks and Recreation Dept. Noon. 264-9511.

BLOUNTVILLE, TENN. — Sullivan County Agricultural and Industrial Fair. Fourth week, Monday — Saturday. Fiddlers convention, exhibits, entertainment. 4:00 — 10:00 p.m. Monday — Friday, 10:00 a.m. Saturday.

HUDSON, N.C. — Golden Age Antique Car Parade. Fourth Tuesday. From Baptist Church to Main Street through Farnum Shopping Center and back to Church for buffet lunch. Colonial costumes worn. Sponsor: Hudson Com. Development Assn.

BLOWING ROCK, N.C. — Blowing Rock Charity Horse Show. End of July, Wednesday — Sunday. The Green Park Hotel. 11:00 a.m. to 2:00 p.m. Traditional Horse Show Breakfast; 9:00 pm. Horse Show Buffet Dinner-Dance. (See Ch. 22.)

SPRUCE PINE, N.C. — Mitchell County Homemakers Handmade Crafts. July 31 — August 1. Deyton Elementary School. Exhibits and sale. Sponsor: Roan Valley Extension Homemakers.

AUGUST
ABINGDON, VA. — Virginia Highlands Festival. Aug. 1 — 15. Main Street mainly. Mime, dance and music youth workshops, Barter Theatre Festival schedule including Children's Theatre productions, fashion show, annual benefit party, historic home tours. Continuous fascinating craft demonstrations at Cave House Craft Shop. Festival information booth on lawn of Martha Washington Inn. Sponsor: Historical Society of Washington County.

BURNSVILLE, N.C. — Yancev Youth Jamboree (since 1968). First Thursday and Friday. E. Yancey High School. Folk Music, singing, dancing. Sponsor: Yancey Chamber of Commerce. 682-2512.

JONESBORO, TENN. — Washington County 4-H Pullet Show and Sale. Second Friday Courthouse Square, Stephenson parking lot. 9:00 a.m.

BOONE, N.C. — Children's Festival. Third Friday. Boone Playground. Games of skill, prizes. Sponsor: Watauga County Parks and Rec. Dept.

HILDEBRAN, N.C. — Hildebran Karate Contest. Second Saturday. Hildebran Recreation Center, five miles west of Hickory. Breaking of blocks, boards and bricks with hands, heads and feet. Sponsor: Martial Arts Association. 12:30 — 6:30 p.m.

BOONE, N.C. — Mid-Summer Horseshoe Tourney (Singles). Second Saturday. Watauga County Recreation Complex. Hunting Lane. 264-9511.

BOONE, N.C. — Antique Car and Gun Show (since 1970). Second Saturday and Sunday. Watauga High School. Sponsor: Boone Jaycees. 10:00 a.m. — 10:00 p.m. Saturday; 10:00 a.m. — 4:00 p.m. Sunday.

LINVILLE, N.C. — Grandfather Mountain Camera Clinic. Second half. Saturday and Sunday. Skyscraper Room at Visitor Center. Open to all professional and amateur photographers. Outstanding lecturers, winning photos exhibited. Sponsor: Carolinas Press Photographers Assn.

BOONE, N.C. — Meet the Mountaineers and The Pioneers Football Teams. Late in month. ASU Varsity Gym. 7:30 p.m. 262-2038.

BLOUNTVILLE, TENN. — Blountville Country Hoe Down. Third Friday. Main Street between Courthouse and Methodist Church. Bluegrass music, fiddlers, clogging, street dancing, square dancing, historic home tours, Chuck Wagon supper. Sponsor: Sullivan County Bicentennial Committee. 5:30 — 10:00 p.m.

JOHNSON CITY, TENN. — Appalachian District Fair (since 1927). Third week, Monday — Saturday. Gray Fair Grounds, six miles northwest. Beauty pageant, arts and crafts show, ceramics display, photography, floral work, needle work, daily spectaculars.

N. WILKESBORO, N.C. — Senior Citizens Fair (since 1970). Fourth Friday. Smoot Park. Loads of crafts, baked goods and produce. 11:00 a.m.

BOONE, N.C. — Autumn Corvette Show (since 1975). Last Sunday. Mack Brown Chevrolet-Olds. Class competition in stock, semi-custom, custom and race-prepared.

SEPTEMBER

N. WILKESBORO, N.C. — Northwestern North Carolina Agricultural Fair. First week, Monday through Saturday. N. Wilkesboro Speedway, Old Highway US 421E. Horticultural products, field crops, general exhibits, dairy, poultry and cattle judging. Sponsor: Rotary Club. 10:00 p.m. Monday, fireworks.

GALAX, VA. — Lord's Acre Harvest Sale. Second Saturday.

BOONE, N.C. — Fall Fashion Show. Third Wednesday. Holiday Inn Convention Center. Sponsor: The Boone Worthwhile Women's Club, Inc. 7:00 p.m.

CHILHOWIE, VA. — Chilhowie Apple Festival.

LENOIR, N.C. — Caldwell County Fair (since 1947). Last week.

HICKORY, N.C. — Catawba County Fair.

MORGANTON, N.C. — Fall Festival. Old Burke County Courthouse Square.

OCTOBER THROUGH MAY

W. JEFFERSON, N.C. — Blue Ridge Beagle Club Field Trials. Third Saturday. Blue Ridge Beagle Club Grounds. Varied classes of events.

OCTOBER

BOONE, N.C. — Fall Horseshoe Roundup. First Saturday. Watauga County Recreation Complex. 264-9511.

JONESBORO, TENN. — National Storytelling Festival. Early in month for two days. Nationally-known artists featured.

ALL OVER — Foliage at its Peak Autumn Display. Oct. 5 — 25. (See Ch. 4)

BOONE, N.C. — Farmers' Harvest Festival. First Sat. All day. Watauga County Farmers' Market, *Horn in the West* grounds. Sports events, auctions, crafts, flea market, baked goods; Harvest Queen crowning.

BOONE, N.C. — Watauga Hereford Association Sale (since 1943). Second Saturday.

ABINGDON, VA. — Burley Tobacco Festival and Farm Show (since 1950). Second weekend, Saturday, Sunday, Monday. Southwest Tobacco Warehouse, US 19. Beef and dairy cattle, sheep and crops judging; farm products, livestock, home economics and commercial displays; Nashville entertainment nightly. Saturday 10:00 a.m. Parade and square dance at night.

BOONE, N.C. — Fall Festival. Third Friday. Bethel Elementary School. Country store, bakery, crafts, white elephant sale, bargains galore, auction, games, prizes; talent show. Sponsor: Bethel Elementary PTA. 6:00 — 10:00 p.m.

BOONE, N.C. — ASU Homecoming (since 1900). Last weekend. Open House in many departments including Art Gallery; crowning of Homecoming Queen; annual "Alumni Luncheon." Southern Conference football game.

BOONE, N.C. — Hallowe'en Carnival. Oct. 30. ASU Broome-Kirk Gym. Sponsor: Appalachian Physical Education Academy. 7:00 — 10:00 p.m.

SPARTA, N.C. — Harvest Days Parade. Old-fashioned costumes and old-fashioned bargains in shops and stores.

VALLE CRUCIS, N.C. — 'Lasses Bilin' Time on the Farm. Dutch Creek Road, Townsend Farms. Time-honored tradition for country folk. It's work from early mornin' until 10, 11 or later at night with lots of waitin' 'round. It's a farm process and a homespun social gatherin' — watchin' the sugar cane being ground, boiled, skim removed and strained. The pigs are part of the act, feasting on the green skim off the top of the bilin' 'lasses. Lasts about ten days. It used to be a time for "swappin' pocket knives, dogs and pistols."

FLEETWOOD, N.C. — Harvest Festival. Last Saturday. Fleetwood Elementary School. Turkey supper from 5 to 8 p.m. Old-fashioned country fair: crafts, baked goodies; variety of games and fun, entertainment. Sponsor: Fleetwood PTA. (919) 877-3387.

NOVEMBER
NEWLAND, N.C. — Fashion Show (since 1973). First Thursday. Mountain Glen Clubhouse. Entertainment, door prizes, refreshments. Sponsor: Avery Jaycee Auxiliary.

when
55 the sun
goes down

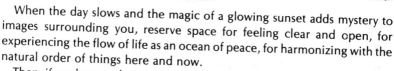

When the day slows and the magic of a glowing sunset adds mystery to images surrounding you, reserve space for feeling clear and open, for experiencing the flow of life as an ocean of peace, for harmonizing with the natural order of things here and now.

Then, if you're wondering what's doin' at night in these hills and hollers, wondering perhaps whether the sidewalks are "pulled in" because you may be "out in the Boone docks," have a look at the INDEX for the goin's-on listed below. Take a gander at what nighttime fun is like from watching the enigmatic Brown Mountain Lights to making and playing a dulcimer:

Art Exhibits
Auctions
Baseball
Basketball
Beauty Pageants
Birdlore
Bowling
Bridge
Brown Mountain Lights
Club Suppers
Craft Shows
Dancing: Ballet, Ballroom, Buck, Clogging, Folk, Lessons, Scottish, Square, Street
Dinner Theatre
F irs
Festivals
Fishing
Flowers
Football
Golf Driving Ranges
Gymnastics
Historical Dramas
Hobby Courses
Horse Shows
Ice Skating
Karate

Kiddie Entertainment
Lectures
Libraries
Miniature Golf
Mountain Speshuls
Movies
Museums
Music: Bagpipe, Band, Barbershop, Blue Grass, Choral, Classical, Country Western, Fiddlers, Folk, Gospel, Instrumental, Recordings, Sweet Adelines
Musicals
Naturalist Programs
Other Mountain Doin's
Plays
Roller Skating
Shooting Matches
Skiing
Stargazing
Stock Car Racing
Storytelling
Swimming
Tennis
Track
Volleyball
Wrestling

And don't overlook the excitement of just ordinary window shopping, planning your purchases for the days ahead!

Index

(By chapter numbers)

193

(By chapter numbers)

JOY IN THE MOUNTAINS
P.O. Box 2532, Boca Raton, FL 33432

Name _____
        (please print)

Street _____Apt #_____

City _____ State_____Zip_____

Please send_____copies of JOY IN THE MOUNTAINS @ $3.95 each plus 65¢
mailing and handling charges per copy.
Enclosed is check ☐ or money order ☐ payable to JOY IN THE MOUNTAINS
for $_____. Florida residents add sales tax.

JOY IN THE MOUNTAINS
P.O. Box 2532, Boca Raton, FL 33432

Name _____
        (please print)

Street _____Apt #_____

City _____ State_____Zip_____

Please send_____copies of JOY IN THE MOUNTAINS @ $3.95 each plus 65¢
mailing and handling charges per copy.
Enclosed is check ☐ or money order ☐ payable to JOY IN THE MOUNTAINS
for $_____. Florida residents add sales tax.